LEAPS

COMMENTARY

"This is an extraordinary book. Well-examined details in the treatment of severely dysfunctional patients permit the reader to gain insight into the mind of a gifted therapist. The principles of psychoanalytic theory and technique are here combined with empathy and appreciation of the way a therapist's responses may either move forward or retard the delicate balances of a treatment process." —Anna Ornstein, M.D.

"Freud once quoted the poet Rückert: 'What one cannot reach flying, one must reach limping. It is no sin to limp.' In his new book, Mendelsohn suggests that what one cannot reach, as one helps patients through conventional therapeutic approaches, one may reach leaping. Have patients changed since the days of Freud? Can we learn through Mendelsohn's excellent contribution to enrich our technical armamentarium and thus learn to leap—though carefully, as he suggests—not into empty space, but within an established therapeutic alliance?"
—Rudolf Ekstein, Ph.D.

"In this book, Dr. Roy Mendelsohn, a physician and psychoanalyst fiercely dedicated to truth and to his patients, introduces the concept of leaps. Leaps are deviations from basic psychoanalytic principles of treatment, most usually with severely disturbed patients, when the traumas and developmental arrests occur at a preverbal level and the patient has no way of symbolizing. By engaging in carefully thought-out actions with the patient, the therapist may find a new bridge to the unconscious preverbal material.

"But you must read this book to grasp the full meaning of a leap. The clinical examples are excellent and challenge us to rethink our work with difficult patients. It is a different and well-reasoned approach to the use of countertransference. A leap may prevent the failure of some treatments."
—Stuart Averill, M.D.

LEAPS

Facing Risks in
Offering a Constructive
Therapeutic Response When
Unusual Measures
Are Necessary

Roy M. Mendelsohn, M.D.

JASON ARONSON INC.
Northvale, New Jersey
London

Production Editor: *Adelle Krauser*
Editorial Director: *Muriel Jorgensen*

This book was set in 10 point Times Roman by Alpha Graphics of Pittsfield, New Hampshire. It was printed and bound by Haddon Craftsmen of Scranton, Pennsylvania.

Copyright © 1991 by Jason Aronson Inc.

10 9 8 7 6 5 4 3 2 1

All rights reserved. Printed in the United States of America. No part of this book may be used or reproduced in any manner whatsoever without written permission from Jason Aronson Inc. except in the case of brief quotations in reviews for inclusion in a magazine, newspaper, or broadcast.

Library of Congress Cataloging-in-Publication Data

Mendelsohn, Roy M.
    Leaps : facing risks in offering a constructive therapeutic response when unusual measures are necessary / Roy M. Mendelsohn.
      p. cm.
    Includes bibliographical references and index.
    ISBN 0-87668-566-1
    1. Psychotherapy. 2. Psychotherapist and patient. I. Title.
RC480.5.M39 1991
616.89'14—dc20   90-22584

Manufactured in the United States of America. Jason Aronson Inc. offers books and cassettes. For information and catalog write to Jason Aronson Inc., 230 Livingston Street, Northvale, New Jersey 07647.

*This book
is dedicated
to those who believe
what they know*

CONTENTS

Introduction ix

Chapter 1
Leaps: The Response to a Therapeutic Dilemma 1

Chapter 2
*Abandoning the Sound Principles
of Psychoanalytic Treatment* 59

Chapter 3
Leaps and Empathic Responsiveness 91

Chapter 4
Leaps and Countertransference 117

Chapter 5
Leaps and Acting Out 151

Chapter 6
Leaps and Reenacting Preverbal Traumas 179

Chapter 7
Leaps and Errors of Commission 211

Chapter 8
Leaps and Errors of Omission 237

Chapter 9
Out of the Darkness into the Light 261

References 285

Index 291

INTRODUCTION

Many therapies that turn out to be less than successful contain noteworthy moments that stand out because they have suggested that the therapist veer off from the standard course of sound psychotherapeutic procedures and methods. These moments may be identified from subtle hints given by a patient that were then ignored, overlooked, or considered to be unimportant. At times they may involve specific demands that are not followed because they seem to lead in a direction considered to be detrimental at best and destructive at worst. The tendency is to use familiar techniques that protect against unknown or unseen dangers and problems. It is easy to do so and be supported in adopting such a stance. In most instances a therapist's entire period of training has been devoted to stressing the validity of such an approach, and in large part there is justification for this attitude. It is easy to be led astray in the field of intense infantile emotions with which we work. If we are to find new ways to enlarge the frontier of therapeutic influence, we must be both willing and prepared to face risks not blindly and impulsively, but with knowledge, stability, integrity, compassion, and respect for the complexity and diversity of human experience. This book represents an attempt to explore that frontier, while at the same time offering some meaningful guidelines in doing so. Mistakes are inevitable in our therapeutic endeavors, and their impact is increased when we abandon known principles. However, the alternative of clinging to these concepts without question closes the door to discovering new inroads; it is a stance that can be equally as hurtful.

There is general agreement among clinicians, even those who advocate a strict adherence to the formal conditions of psychoanalytic treatment, that with certain patients—usually those exhibiting extreme ego distortions—there are moments when modifications are absolutely necessary. The need for this kind of flexibility is clearly identified. However, the times when it is deemed appropriate are those designated as life-threatening emergencies, or when there are extreme disruptions in the relationship that indicate some changes have to take place if the treatment is to continue. These considerations are often presented as an afterthought, implying that they do not really occur very often, and their specific nature may then only be alluded to with the tacit assumption of their being well known to everyone. This is a book about these exceptions, which from my personal experience appear to arise much more than the idea of their being unusual would imply.

Throughout this book I have tried to demonstrate the need for changes in technique, along with legitimate concerns about the advisability of doing so—if the treatment requirements of a shrinking field of difficult-to-reach or impossible-to-treat patients are to be met. Chapter 1 defines the concept of "leaps," the establishment of the groundwork for a constructive therapeutic response when unusual measures are called for, and a description of a secure psychoanalytic treatment framework and the prerequisites that have to be in evidence before any alterations can be considered. Chapter 2 covers the detrimental effects of unnecessary modifications. In Chapters 3 and 4, the concepts of empathy and countertransference are explored, since a therapist's subjective responses are so crucial. Chapters 5 and 6 discuss the concepts of acting out and reenacting infantile and preverbal traumas. These chapters show how the distinctions between empathy, countertransference, acting out, and reenacting infantile and preverbal traumas can be made, placing emphasis upon their respective roles in determining when a leap is indicated and when it is counterproductive. Chapter 7 describes the consequences of errors caused by acting inappropriately, while Chapter 8 describes the consequences of errors caused when an action is required but is withheld. The final chapter gives an overview of the problem and summarizes the guidelines that are available for entering new and unexplored psychological territory.

I would like to express my deep appreciation to those patients who have been able to live through my mistakes and expand my vision, and my heartfelt apologies to those who have suffered unnecessarily from my efforts to grow and learn.

1

Leaps: The Response to a Therapeutic Dilemma

Leaps: A Definition

The term *leap* refers to a therapeutic dilemma in which some special and unique measures are called for in order to further intrapsychic growth and give impetus to therapeutic progress. It is an attempt to delineate those situations that encompass a therapist's willingness to be led into unseen areas. A form of active participation may be required, which results in a new experience that is essential before the effects of early trauma can be represented. The ensuing interaction may appear unorthodox, or on the surface seem to go against existing therapeutic guidelines. However, a critical factor is that of being directed by spontaneously emerging unconscious perceptions in both patient and therapist, which reflect what is needed to facilitate growth, while at the same time offering safe ground rules and boundaries. The therapist is thereby presenting actual concrete behaviors and experiences that have heretofore been unavailable to a patient, providing the only accessible pathway for infantile and preverbal traumas to surface into the realm of mental representation. The task is to apply sound psychoanalytic principles, but they must be in accordance with the patient's level of psychic structuralization. Ultimately, it eventuates in a new intrapsychic solution to an impossible infantile dilemma, bridging a gap that had previously prevented developmental progression.

I first became acquainted with this dilemma, without identifying it as such, in my early years of psychotherapeutic work with children. At the time I was learning how to blend my sensitivity, intuition, and empathic responsiveness with therapeutic principles that were somewhat foreign. My efforts to apply them were awkward and stilted. However, with the first children I saw, my efforts appeared to me to be remarkably effective. I noticed, particularly with younger children, that pressure was exerted upon me to engage in various games and fantasy play activities. The games were very revealing of the children's psychic reality, and showed me how they experienced the external world in general and their relationship with me in particular. My role in the games was most frequently that of narrator of interpreter, which seemed useful in eliciting material that lent itself to my efforts to express verbally the unconscious meaning of the play or fantasy.

I also noticed that the demand for me to be a more active participant escalated at moments of anxiety, as resistance or defensiveness heightened. When I complied, however, it had a negative effect on bringing forth new material. In its place the stories and games reflected themes of distressed exploitation, or of others imposing obstacles to attaining a desired goal. It gradually became apparent that I was participating in avoiding the emergence of regressive transference experiences in the patient, and not confronting aspects of myself that were hidden and uncomfortable. My recognition was helpful and made it possible for me to maintain a more objective listening posture. After interpreting the defensive meaning of the demand for my participation, I was rewarded with a deepening of the transference relationship. Concomitantly, previously inaccessible instinctual wishes and prohibitions were expressed that could now be exposed to integrative therapeutic work. It made me aware of the defense-reenforcing influence of a form of interaction that I had justified as being necessary for children. My treatment approach was readily nestled within the concept of play therapy and easily rationalized, since a child's primary mode of communication focused around play activities. There were a number of children who benefited from my widening view of their use of play as a defensive operation, and surprisingly, they exhibited a remarkable ability to enter into therapeutic dialogue, retreating into play only at moments of inordinate conflict.

Clinical Example

In the midst of this change in my professional development I began my first contact with a severely disturbed child, who immediately showed me that whenever I maintained an objective stance, it had a debilitating effect. He was an 8-year-old boy, just admitted to a residential treatment center. I had been designated as his therapist and we came together to initiate a relationship. He spent all of his waking hours in a sitting position, rocking back and forth and incessantly humming. He would be brought to his daily sessions where he continued this unending, repetitive pattern, seemingly unmoved by any of my efforts to understand his internal world or to make sense out of his behavior. Over a period of several months I became increasingly frustrated, anguished, and discouraged about the possibility of ever reaching this extremely troubled child. My early interpretations were largely based upon a variety of concepts concerning schizophrenic and autistic pathology that I had gleaned from the literature. But they slowly gave way to more personal expressions of my reactions to being unable to establish contact with him, probably colored by an internal sense of narcissistic injury. I was totally helpless in penetrating what seemed to be a wall of unresponsiveness, though I also felt compassion for the exquisite pain and loneliness I imagined him experiencing somewhere in his internal world. After many months he finally spoke directly to me, explaining that his behavior was dictated by a compulsive need to drown out a vicious attacking voice from the little man on his shoulder who unendingly assailed him. On the morning that he first communicated this to me the voice had spoken in a different manner than ever before. To my amazement he described the voice reflecting back the many words I had been uttering, and especially those expressing my personal feelings.

From this point on our therapeutic sessions became lively and animated. They were filled with his very frightening fantasies, his deep sense of inadequacy as an effective human being, his wishes to participate in the world of relationships, and his tremendous fear of annihilation. Concurrently, he slowly became more involved in activities and relationships outside of his treatment. Looking back, the conceptual model that seemed to be serving as my guide was more of a topographical, structural view of intrapsychic functioning—a model in which I consciously viewed my task as one of facilitating the emergence of unconscious fantasies and of strengthening what appeared to be a shattered ego. I paid little direct attention to the actualities of the interaction itself, although this was the primary preconscious and unconscious stimulus for my choice of interventions. I did notice that whenever I adopted my version of a therapeutic stance of objectivity, only dimly aware of the defensiveness embodied in such a position, it resulted in the return of his destructive voice and a profound withdrawal in the relationship. Slowly, I realized that this powerful voice was taking on the characteristics of a caricatured mirror of my defensive attitude toward regressive experiences, and giving me a picture of how my stilted therapeutic words sounded to him. My acknowledgment of this recognition was almost always followed by a willingness to engage in the interaction, and to communicate more fully the nature of his internal experiences. The need for my active, personal involvement was increasingly apparent, as was the importance of my maintaining clearly defined ground rules and boundaries. Only then would the flow of narrative associations be forthcoming.

At this point an incident arose that faced me with taking a leap of faith in the trustable qualities of the relationship. I was asked to participate in an experience that on the surface appeared to violate the principles of sound therapeutic management and conduct I was following. It carried with it ingredients that could readily be perceived as (1) gratifying to unconscious fantasies; (2) potentially resulting in a blurring of therapeutic boundaries; and (3) possibly counterproductive to constructive growth. Although in some ways it was a relatively small matter, the issues it raised were large in scope. For the first time I was confronted with the dilemma of whether to act upon an intuitive affective response that had countertransference implications. It triggered many doubts as to its advisability, for I was afraid to foster a form of acting out and obstruct therapeutic progress. However, I also had the impression that I was being given an important opportunity to provide a much needed experience. It seemed to me that if I were to adopt a safer, seemingly more orthodox stance it would be an error of omission. In that case it could rupture the thin thread of trust that had been established and work against any ongoing movement.

The situation came about immediately after a difficult period during which he expressed extremely powerful cannibalistic fantasies. He was an obese child, and as he was talking about the distortions in his body image he revealed a strong belief that he had totally swallowed up his thin and frail mother. He was convinced that she existed inside him and was the source of his fatness. I had begun to interpret his fear of an overpowering dependency, but did not realize how much I was reacting to the strength of his oral cravings, and that I did so from an emotionally distant position. This therapeutic posture had instigated a profound withdrawal, which was not alleviated until I was able to see and acknowledge my defensiveness and address the patient's concern as to whether I could tolerate his regressive needs.

He entered the next session with a frantic appeal for me to attend a band concert at his school in which he was to play the cymbals. He was terrified that under the impact of the watchful, probing eyes of strangers he would totally crumble and be immobilized. His only hope was to have me in the audience so that eye contact could be established, which he felt would give him a sense of inner strength, enabling him to feel pride in his accomplishment. Without this source of support he felt at the mercy of uncontrollable forces that would tear him apart. My immediate internal response was to imagine myself simply stating that I would love to be there, with a feeling that this would solidify the bond of connectedness that had so recently been strained. However, in place of expressing this reaction, I became filled with doubts about its countertransference implications.

I was concerned that my feeling reflected some continuing difficulty that made me reluctant to interpret the unconscious significance of his request; perhaps I did not want to meet the primitive aggression or withdrawal I anticipated. In addition, I questioned the meaning and appropriateness of leaving the confines of the therapeutic environment, thereby blurring the boundaries of the relationship. My hesitation, rather than eliciting a withdrawal from the patient, precipitated tears of disappointment. When I then indicated a willingness to consider acting upon his request, after there was an opportunity to explore its internal meaning, he brightened up and spoke at length. His thoughts conveyed the life-giving qualities accompanying a feeling of sharing in a relationship. He remembered brief moments of shared contact with an uncle, rare but meaningful play activities with an older brother, and the vitality he experienced in joking with a favored child-care worker. I commented that it sounded as though my coming would be an important aid to our work together.

The experience of attending the concert was a deeply moving one for both the patient and me. Eye contact was made in the course of the performance, and a strong connection was felt by both of us, which was expressed in a mutual smile. His performance was a source of pride that he frequently remembered afterward. This incident is mentioned in some detail because it illustrated the effect of strengthening the bond of trust in the therapeutic relationship, which enabled this child to more fully develop a capacity for useful internal exploration, bridging a gap in his intrapsychic functioning. It is also mentioned because it was a prelude to a much more extreme and dramatic event having an opposite effect, most likely due to its not being attended to in a similar fashion.

Approximately one year later, during which there had been considerable therapeutic progress, I discovered that it would be necessary to move to a distant city. Long before I planned to tell anyone of this impending move, it seemed as though the patient sensed it, for he began each session with questions reflecting his concern about my leaving. When it was finally acknowledged, the questions changed from asking where or when I was going to could he come with me. In a way more powerful than in the previous incident, I once again had the internal impression that it would be in the patient's best interest to simply state that I would see what could be possible in trying to arrange such a move. On this occasion, however, the stakes were much higher, and the level of responsibility for the patient's care and well-being much more all encompassing. Therefore, the action was much more extensive and committed, and the likelihood of its representing a countertransference-based response seemed more relevant.

The impression was strong enough that I sought supervisory, consultative, and therapeutic help. I was trying to sort out and distinguish how much the temptation to act upon this request was an expression of: (1) unresolved countertransference issues; (2) an intuitive response including preconscious and unconscious components; and (3) an unconsciously empathic response to the actual needs of the patient, emanating from the nature of the treatment over a period of three years. All outside parties giving input in these deliberations seemed to agree that it involved aspects of unresolved narcissism, fantasies of rescue coming from early childhood experiences, and unresolved conflicts around separation. I accepted this input as relevant to my internal motivations, and felt relieved of the responsibility of dealing with the multiplicity of extremely complex issues that would arise were I to act upon the patient's wish to accompany me. My attention was then largely focused upon the patient's feelings of abandonment and loss due to the impending separation. At the same time I had a persistent and nagging internal sense that although the situation was more extreme, and the external difficulties would be imposing, in principle it was no different than the earlier circumstance that had seemingly been essential for furthering the patient's psychological growth. The sensation was that were I solely motivated in the patient's interest I would have acted upon his request, if just to explore the possibility. Each time the temptation arose it was pushed aside and identified as a countertransference-based obstacle that would be destructive to the patient's well-being—then I would experience the same feeling of relief.

The move was made and I was advised to discontinue any contact with the patient because it would interfere with his ability to engage in another therapeutic encounter. The nagging sensation persisted. I frequently asked for permission to communicate with him, but was dissuaded with the statement that it would be disruptive to any new relationship. Five years later I was informed that it was now all right to visit, because the patient had been considered to be unreachable and was being transferred to a state hospital. I made arrangements to meet with him, and a now 16-year-old young man entered the room with a blank and distant expression on his face. He proceeded to pace restlessly back and forth and mumble in an incoherent fashion, as I spoke of my reasons for coming. I expressed my concern upon hearing about his unreachability, and of my continuing interest to see if there was some spark of life.

He continued to pace giving no indication of having registered my words. There was a long period of silence during which I was filled with memories of the earlier contact, and noted the striking changes that were now observable in this uncommunicative young man. After an extended passage of time he stopped abruptly and in a coldly, emphatic voice stated, "I know who you are." He then went on to talk in a dispassionate tone of how totally betrayed he had felt when I left, not just because of the leaving, but because he knew it had been important to discuss the possibility of his going too. He also knew I was aware of it, and in refusing to either act or consider it openly with him, he had felt abandoned and cast adrift. He was no longer willing to enter into a world where such experiences could occur. He had decided at that time to remain in his own world and would continue to do so. He returned to his pacing, his eyes became vacant, and he then left the room.

The impact upon me was enormous, and it brought back in full force my earlier internal struggle. It demonstrated the difficulty and importance of determining the fine line within a therapist between a countertransference-based motive and an empathic, intuitive response. On the patient's part it illustrated the equally fine line between a form of acting out, designed to deny the disruptive effect of an important separation—thereby avoiding the early memories and experiences it evoked—and a reenactment of early traumatic experiences that required a new solution in a current relationship. The incident has remained ingrained in my mind to stand as a beacon light calling attention to the need for making a penetrating exploration of these distinctions with each new patient. It showed how an error of omission, justified by seemingly sound therapeutic principles, can be as devastating as an error of commission—an error that either reenforces a pathological defense or re-creates an infantile trauma through engaging in an inappropriate action.

In order to adequately ascertain the relevance or appropriateness of introducing a leap, a number of factors must be taken into account. These include a careful assessment of the therapist's internal motivations, the structural organization of the patient's personality, the specific composition of pathological defenses and the way they are manifested in an interaction, and the status of the therapeutic alliance. It is then possible to delineate those situations in which a therapist must participate in an actual, concrete experience before an underlying infantile or preverbal trauma can be represented, or to enable sufficient structure to develop for processes of symbolization to become functional. These steps may have to be taken first if a process of internal exploration, based exclusively upon a verbal interchange with interpretive interventions, is to be effective. The interaction itself is the arena in which this difficult distinction is made, and the patient's unconscious perceptions of the growth-promoting or destructive properties of the relationship are a vital source of information.

The Dangerous Opportunities Associated with Engaging in a Leap

In considering the introduction of interventions that go beyond the province of accepted therapeutic procedures, a therapist is in essence treading upon uncharted psychological territory, guided by the unknown and sometimes unknowable. However, to take this degree of responsibility for a patient's welfare expresses a total commitment to the treatment, which may establish a bond of trust that leads to the development of a previously unformed capacity to symbolize. Light may then be shed upon the particular elements in the interaction that are constructive in addition to those that are harmful or detrimental. Therefore, a leap must be a carefully considered step, undertaken only when every other possibility has been exhausted and there appears to be no other alternative. At such a juncture it can be vital to be led into the darkness by whatever means a patient has available to indicate a direction, even though validation may not be immediately forthcoming. There will always be a background of concern as to the potential for re-creating an infantile trauma, or for blurring necessary therapeutic boundaries, and it may seemingly go against well-established therapeutic principles. Each moment must be as carefully monitored as possible in order to identify errors at their inception, not only to correct them and interpret their effects, but also to achieve greater clarity in establishing a growth-promoting experience.

Clinical Example

The perils and rewards of traversing this difficult journey were illustrated in the treatment of a 15-year-old girl who was initially referred when her therapist felt overwhelmed by her constantly recurring self-destructive tendencies and a seeming total inability to respond to the therapeutic properties of the relationship. My treatment of her spanned a ten-year period of time, and confronted me with a series of difficult and anguishing dilemmas. Interventions that had previously been unimaginable were considered and introduced, which seemingly violated important principles governing effective therapeutic functioning. They led both parties into dangerous and risky situations, yet the alterations in technique appeared to lead toward constructive growth. They also included errors, which were perpetuated beyond their period of timeliness and had to be rectified. The treatment ultimately achieved a successful outcome.

Over the course of therapeutic contact there were periods of clearly defined changes in the nature and conduct of the interaction, which could be categorized within the context of five distinct phases. The first phase lasted several months, during which she gave lengthy descriptions of the important people in her life, punctuated by elaborate psychological explanations of their effect upon her. She factually presented what she considered to be the important circumstances in her personal history, and outlined the events leading up to her seeking therapeutic help. She spoke of a dominant father exercising control over everyone in his environment, distorting the meaning of any communication to fit his own self-interests. Upon his insistence, the entire family had to give allegiance to his aging and psychotic mother. The patient's mother was visualized as outwardly passive and submissive, particularly to the father's dominance, but possessing a silent core of subtly controlling behavior. She described being especially close to the mother in a way that was ill defined and difficult for her to articulate. There was an explosive older sister, who had terrorized the patient in her early childhood. She had become extremely adept at provoking this sister's aggressiveness, to the point of getting her in trouble with others. A younger brother was portrayed as being sensitive, helpless, and vulnerable, and as seeking the patient's protection. A much younger sister was viewed as being babied by the entire family.

She gave a lifeless account of her early history, focusing on a series of interests and activities that were never carried to completion. She described a deepening depression upon entering her teenage years; she was then given a battery of psychological tests and referred for psychotherapy. She had seen a therapist for almost a year, thought it helped somewhat, but was told she needed a psychiatrist. Interspersed throughout were her statements about an oedipal attachment to her father, jealousy and sibling rivalry, and a concern that the relationship with her mother would be seen as sick. This phase of the treatment dramatically shifted after a session in which she demanded to know my opinion of what was wrong. I had simply stated that I did not know, adding that throughout the time of our meeting I had no clear view of what the events and situations she had talked about meant to her. I was in fact confused and uncertain about what was wrong. After many accusations that I was keeping my true feelings hidden by avoiding an answer, and I really knew but was afraid to say, she stormed out of the office.

The following session introduced the second phase with a striking change in her entire attitude. She had thought a great deal about what I had said, realized the sincerity with which it was spoken, and had decided to reveal what was wrong. She had anticipated getting a response that imposed my meaning upon her, and tested me by withholding anything possessing internal significance to see if that would occur. With that she told me about the cockroaches she felt invading every body orifice; about looking in the mirror only to see an unrecognizable image; about her constant turmoil in battling with powerful infantile yearnings. These hungers for an extremely dependent attachment aroused panic whenever they pushed for expression. She knew these longings had to be experienced in a relationship, and in a way that could allow them to be present without the threat of total destruction.

She subsequently tried desperately to reveal to me the conditions she knew were necessary to reach this position, but the very act of doing so aroused anxiety of traumatic proportions, and an uncontrollable effort to distort my understanding. Interpretive interventions were not only of no value, but they triggered her attempts to create distance or defensiveness in me through a very cold analytical probing of my weak spots. It gradually became apparent that the depth of the regression required to gain contact with her split-off and infantile world could not be safely contained within a relationship alone; this is because such regression unleashed powerful forces motivating self-destructive behavior designed to curb the regression. We both recognized that while this was taking place she would need to be surrounded by the soft protective walls of a total hospital environment.

Seeing the need for this type of care is not equivalent to locating a proper facility, and though a hospital was found it proved to be inadequate. The demands upon the environment for providing a receptive attitude to the profound regression the patient was undergoing, went counter to the hospital staff's entire orientation. Thus the patient was constantly met with contempt, disapproval, and openly expressed pressure for her to "function more appropriately." She responded by becoming increasingly defensive, thus making it impossible for her to be open and vulnerable. After a period of two months, in great despair, the patient left.

She continued to be engaged in the therapeutic relationship, but was blocked by the extent of her underlying panic. In one particular session, during which the inaccessibility of her infantile world was especially distressing, she reacted to the ineffectiveness of my interpretive words with a deep sense of hopelessness. She had heard about hypnosis and began to plead with me to be offered the experience. Any attempt to interpret the underlying meaning of her demand, or the frantic way in which she presented it, met a cold wall of hostility. She had the feeling of needing to be "under your control" in order to find the dimension of safety she had been seeking, and sensed my uneasiness about such a venture. She also felt my interpretive comments were only reflecting self-protective reactions, an observation that contained a large element of truth.

I acknowledged the accuracy of her perception, but in trying to explain the reasons I thought hypnosis would be contraindicated, I was met with strong opposition. Ideas of it being potentially exploitative, overly manipulative, and reenforcing her pathological defenses were always countered with what seemed like plausible arguments that these were the very reasons she wanted it. This was the only way she could think of to face these obstructive forces and gain some access to their source. She worked hard to eliminate my objections. For example, when I raised my concern about the submissive attitude that hypnosis would require from her, along with an abandonment of autonomy, she expressed her feeling that this was exactly what she had to experience in a relationship. She felt sufficient trust in me to know that it would only be used to enable her to retrieve her autonomy in a fuller manner. Explanations having to do with the bypassing of defenses were equally seen as reasons rather than obstacles, in that this was precisely the source of her great despair. After a difficult session in which she felt she had brought everything possible to convince me of the importance of at least trying, she left feeling totally defeated. She had angrily and sadly commented upon how it seemed that other people's defensiveness appeared to be a never-ending wall she met, preventing her from attaining something she needed. I then spent considerable energy in exploring my internal motives. I recognized that whatever was relevant about my reservations was being fed by deeper anxieties, possibly in response to the potential depth of the regression I sensed would ensue, and I agreed to introduce hypnosis into the treatment.

Initially, the results were extremely promising. She felt contained within a hypnotic state, which enabled traumatic infantile memories to enter the realm of communicable psychic content without the disruptive effects previously in evidence. She was also capable of inducing an hypnotic trance outside of the office at moments of panic, or at times when she was threatened with losing contact with the external world. The traumatic memories that surfaced involved sexual abuse at the hands of an overcontrolling and destructive grandmother. These were linked to the thoughts that had plagued her of cockroaches invading every orifice. However, she still was constantly filled with the overwhelming terror of being at the mercy of an overpowering, annihilating, impinging object, which reflected the impact of a pathological symbiosis. While she maintained a trusting connection to me, it was much too dangerous to feel helplessly dependent.

These beginnings gave an indication of therapeutic progress, though regressive infantile yearnings continued to dominate her internal world and mobilize dangerous, life-threatening behaviors when she was away from the sessions. She felt she was in an increasingly tenuous and unstable position. In an effort to find relief she was drawn to using various mood-altering drugs. Any interpretation of this behavior as acting-out transference feelings that were aroused in the treatment, and related to her response to being hypnotized, was met with extreme panic. She felt totally misunderstood and was terrified that I would discontinue what she was experiencing as helpful, or worse that I would so disapprove of her actions that I would withdraw or abandon her. She was convinced she was on the right track toward healing the gaps in her internal life, and was searching for something to contain her in a more complete fashion without interrupting the regression that was unfolding.

In the process of experimenting with different drugs, she took heroin, which amazingly provided the internal sense of safety she had been seeking. It not only allowed her infantile hungers to become more alive, but also markedly diminished the powerful distorting influence of an internal saboteur that had constantly lurked in the background waiting to destroy any movement toward an attachment. She often marveled at how frequently she was in what appeared to be dangerous circumstances in her external world, in order to achieve safety in her internal world. What she could only allow to a minimal degree in a relationship, she was able to find in this addictive substance. She could feel a need so compelling that she couldn't exist without fulfilling it, and then regardless of the consequences somehow managed to meet it. At the same time she felt her infantile strivings in the background starting to become more alive without the accompanying panic.

I was faced with an enormous dilemma, in that she was finding the necessary experience of containment through illicit drugs, obtained under dangerous and potentially destructive circumstances. She was becoming dependent upon an altered state of mind rather than an ongoing relationship, and assumed total responsibility herself for this action. I did not think she was in a position where she was capable of exercising reliable judgment. It dawned upon me that I was slowly yielding my part in taking responsibility for the management of the treatment, and in doing so was insidiously weakening the therapeutic alliance. If ancillary measures, such as drugs, were required to further her growth, it seemed vital that I be the one to designate the importance.

I was confronted with whether I truly believed her movement in this direction was useful, in which case it might be critical for the prescription to come from me, thereby concretely underscoring my support. However, at least on the surface, it possessed all the features of a destructive form of acting out. If this was true I would be encouraging a process antithetical to constructive growth that ultimately would work to the detriment of the patient and jeopardize the therapeutic properties of the relationship. Thus I began a long period of soul-searching. I felt extreme anxiety at the prospect of prescribing such a powerful, potentially destructive drug, as well as having to come up against many unspecified internal and external hazards. The temptation to visualize it as the patient's responsibility, with my role being one of interpreting the destructiveness of the acting out, was accompanied by a feeling of relief.

Meanwhile the patient was unyielding in her conviction of the drug's helpfulness, and in fact it did appear this way. I vacillated back and forth, trying to get my bearings. Were it to represent a form of acting out, I knew I had to be involved in some fashion, although how was not clear. Conversely, were it to represent a peculiar pathway toward enacting a preverbal experience, I knew I would eventually have to participate or it would not be included within the relationship. The patient then became preoccupied with stories about people who were fearful of taking risks in order to protect their own self-interests, at the expense of being helpful to others. These were quite relevant to my internal attitude, and I thought more deeply about the two alternatives.

If the direction the patient had chosen was one heading toward constructive growth, the fact that she was traversing it on her own would work against integration, and something that had growth-producing potential would thereby be undermined. On the other hand, if what was happening was destructive, and my interpretive efforts were in no way altering the course of her behavior, my ineffectiveness only emphasized how the patient was being abandoned by my unwillingness, inability, or refusal to follow her lead. The only direction being offered seemed to emanate from within the patient, and all other options had already, to some extent, been explored. With this in mind I finally decided to follow her guideline, and to begin taking responsibility by supporting it. So I stated that I thought it was important for the drug she was taking to be a part of the treatment. The decision as to what amounts should be prescribed and when could then be made on the basis of what was needed to progress.

Once again there was a striking change in the character of the interaction. The patient felt deeply understood, and became more open in expressing infantile longings in the relationship. Many dreams were reported in which new areas were being explored, sometimes with great trepidation, or in which bridges were constructed to cross a raging river or bottomless chasm. Simultaneously, her addiction to the drug was quite pronounced, which was experienced as an extension of her dependency upon me. She expressed many fantasies of being manipulated, controlled, and otherwise used for my narcissistic needs, as the price for having her own needs met. She was now displaying increasing evidence of an internal capacity to represent traumatic experiences, to engage in a transference relationship that was amenable to interpretive interventions, and of the emergence of conflicted instinctual wishes.

It became apparent that the experiences she needed to recover through a benign regression were now available to her. The intrapsychic capacity to function within an interpretive framework was becoming viable, and the time was approaching when the addictive medication had outlived its therapeutic usefulness. This was further verified by her dream of being in a hospital receiving intravenous medication. A firm, kind nurse entered to announce that the medicine was no longer necessary. However, the patient's physiological and psychological addiction was at its zenith, and she exerted every conceivable means to confuse and distort my understanding that it was time to stop. Her insistence that it was premature—that she had to be on more solid ground, and that more infantile traumas needed to be uncovered—made me waver. My inability to maintain a firm stance in discontinuing the medication was now perpetuating a dependence that was being used defensively.

It had clearly become time to work with the disturbing and frightening feelings associated with being a more separate and autonomously functioning individual, and in hesitating I was colluding with a pathologically defensive attitude. In some ways I was behaving like an enveloping mother, fearful of allowing a child to move independently. This realization was coming to the forefront of my mind when she altered a prescription, making it abundantly clear that it needed to be terminated. It was a form of acting out that called attention to my failure, rather than a reenactment of a preverbal trauma. After acknowledging the part I played and interpreting its resonance with destructive interactions from her past, she came to know the extent and depth of her pathological defenses.

Disengaging from her addiction was accompanied by a giving up of the search for pathological attachments, and the nature of the therapeutic interaction shifted once again. Instinctual wishes that mobilized conflict and defense were expressed, as more stable neurotic transferences emerged. The mental representation of the therapeutic interaction had served to fill in the gaps of her psychic functioning, enabling previously inaccessible traumatic experiences to be incorporated within a unity of self experience. The process of symbolization became actively viable, as interpretive interventions could be received, internalized, and their effects rise to the forefront of her attention. An exclusively verbal communicative modality was used to gain insight through self-exploration.

The nature of this patient's disturbance vividly illustrated how my initial efforts to provide unconscious understanding through verbal interpretations were not only ineffective, but also had no meaning. In the depths of her regression the only available psychic contents were the consequence of the impact of infantile traumata, which elicited primitive, archaic, symbolic activity, and the internal imprint of unmet needs created gaps in mental structure formation.[1]

It was necessary for me to overcome my anxieties about deviating from a verbal interpretive modality. On the surface, my interventions appeared to be supporting what might be considered as acting out or as a destructive pathological means of attaining gratification. However, it turned out to be a pathway toward constructive growth, bringing insight into the source of her trouble. Eventually, meaningful psychological change could evolve. The patient had the experience of my willingness to be guided by her, in spite of my obvious discomfort. She could not articulate what could not be mentally represented, yet it continued to exert a powerful influence upon her. The subsequent relationship offered the new experience she had to represent before continuity could be established within her personality. When this had been accomplished, with all of the attending risks it entailed, the patient could function usefully within the context of what is generally considered to be a psychoanalytically derived therapeutic interaction. In the course of this venture I did get caught up in reenforcing a pathological defense, and it was essential that it be identified, rectified, and its effects interpreted before any further progress could be made.[2]

---

[1]. McDougall (1979) noticed the difficulty in detecting what psychic contents are missing from a patient, especially since their ejection has left no unconscious trace. Therefore the patient's problem in thinking must be captured through the effect it has on the therapist's experiences, in order to eventually recover these failed representations and stifled affects. They may be rendered into archaic fantasy, capable of being expressed verbally, and the associated feelings can be then contained and explored within the therapeutic relationship. The durability of this relationship functions as a guarantee that powerful affect may be safely experienced without damage to either patient or therapist.

Stolorow and Lachman (1980) referred to the task of analytic treatment with structurally deficient, developmentally arrested patients. The therapist strives not so much for the realignment of existing pathological structures, but rather for the maturation of representational structure that is missing or deficient as a consequence of developmental interference.

[2]. Langs (1975b) introduced the concept of misalliances, which arise out of pathological unresolved intrapsychic conflict and prior disturbed object relations experienced by the patient and therapist. These can lead either one to seek inappropriate gratification and defensive reenforcements in the therapeutic relationship. When a complementary response occurs in the other party a misalliance is effected. Because misalliances interfere with the patient's ongoing and incorporative identifications with the therapist, the development of an analyzable transference, and the effectiveness of interpretations, their resolution takes precedence in the analytic work.

This treatment process emphasizes the carefulness required when embarking on such a therapeutic journey. Rather than giving free rein to inappropriate gratifications or destructive ruptures of a contained treatment framework, it underscores the importance of consistently paying attention to the emergence of the slightest indication of some pathological input by the therapist. At these moments of profound regression the patient's vulnerability to its destructive influence is even more pronounced.

The Importance of Action and Behavior in Furthering Therapeutic Progress

A patient's need for open, concrete evidence of a therapist's genuine interest, concern, and caring may at times be vital before a bond of trust can develop that is sufficiently strong to support an internally directed process of self-exploration. These expressions of feeling are generally a silent accompaniment of any therapeutic endeavor, but there are individuals whose need is so extreme it can only be perceived through action and behavior.[3]

Even though such a need may be recognized by a therapist it cannot be introduced artificially, because that would be an imposition. Such an attempt would involve a lack of appreciation of the patient's difficulty in managing the give and take of a human interaction, and would ignore the associated fear of a blurring of interpersonal boundaries. Were it to occur in this fashion it would also suggest some impatience, impulsivity, or lack of containment on the part of the therapist. It might reflect an unhelpful and inappropriate regressive identification with the patient's internal plight, and eventually elicit defense in place of facilitating the unfolding of a benign regression.

---

3. Little (1981) viewed a therapist's ability to express feelings as critical, particularly with more primitive patients. She felt that real feelings for the patient, along with the desire to help, had to be expressed clearly and explicitly when they occurred spontaneously, sincerely, and were appropriate. Very disturbed patients cannot make accurate deductions, so even talking about them is meaningless. There has to be some actual direct expression, as and when, but not whenever, they occur. Reacting is different, although there are times when a reaction of quite a primitive type is not only not bad but is helpful.

The impetus for a therapist to openly express feelings, or offer behavioral interventions that are empathic with unconscious communications, must emanate from the therapeutic needs of the patient. In most instances the need arises out of a realm of extremely primitive psychic activity that has no other route for expression. The patient is then an active agent in eliciting a constructive response to vital developmentally unmet needs, which are essential for continuing progression. When these opportunities are presented and met with reluctance, unwillingness, or some other hesitant response, it is often perceived by a patient as having some kind of malicious intent. At best it is seen as evidence of a lack of understanding, or of the therapist not realizing the seriousness of the disturbance.

The demand and subsequent opportunity usually arises spontaneously, and under circumstances that may not allow the luxury of extended contemplation. The availability of a therapist's intuitive responses, and the willingness to take risks with a sense of confidence that mistakes can be repaired, are frequently being tested. A therapist's holding back—or actually refusing to openly react—can be most disruptive, since it not only serves to repeat the unseen, unarticulated infantile trauma but also leaves it untouched by any positive therapeutic influence. The destructive impact then continues with the therapist blind to the core difficulty of the patient. If a patient's surface attitude is compliant and submissive it can eventuate in a treatment devoted exclusively to strengthening pathological defenses at the expense of any hope for structural change. The task of facilitating the expression of inarticulable traumatic or preverbal experiences may be complicated further when their effects emerge relatively early in the course of a therapeutic encounter, before the therapist has had the chance to gain enough of an in-depth understanding of the patient's overall personality organization and before a therapeutic alliance has been well grounded.

Clinical Example

This was shown in the treatment of a 14-year-old boy whose initial contact took place under very intense and dramatic circumstances. I had received a telephone call from his parents and the police asking if I was available to see the patient immediately. He had barricaded himself in the basement of his house with a shotgun, threatening to shoot anyone who came close, but agreed to come out if he could talk to a psychiatrist.

He was then brought to my office by the police and sat sullenly in a corner, giving no outward indication of any willingness to communicate. I could tell that trying to encourage him to talk would only deepen the extent of his silent withdrawal, so I decided to describe my reaction to his situation. I talked about imagining what it would be like to feel trapped in a dangerous position unable to trust anyone or anything, and of being paralyzed; having no sense of where to move or what to do. While I spoke he visibly relaxed and began to look around the room. I went on to comment that it seemed at this point more important for me to be known, before it would be possible to learn about him. His response was to ask many questions in a clipped and guarded fashion. The questions at first concerned my credentials, which I answered factually after remarking on how little these external facts about my education and training had to do with what was really significant about my credibility. He smiled briefly, but sarcastically added that he couldn't imagine how he would ever know that. I stated that that would be my job rather than his, and the first thing I thought of was the need to find a safe place for him to be. After some mild protest, accompanied by noticeable signs of relief, he agreed to be hospitalized for a long enough period of time to determine whether we could work together and whether his home environment would be a safe enough place.

He was hospitalized for two weeks during which there were frequent sessions limited to talking about his experiences within that setting. He had explicitly declared there was nothing else he either could or would discuss. He then went into lengthy descriptions of the other patients, stressing their peculiarities, and displaying a sense of humor that centered around the irony of his being the youngest and sanest of the people there. When I reflected upon this capturing the position he felt in his family, he laughingly nodded and then said he felt ready to return. He challenged my willingness to be guided by this direction by defiantly stating he knew I was uneasy about such a move, but unless I allowed him to return home I might just as well not come back for any additional sessions. I simply commented upon the ultimatum, which seemed to imply he was most worried about my unwillingness to risk a mistake. It seemed to me that if he found he couldn't be at home we could both learn something from it. The next day he left the hospital and a short time later I received a telephone call in the middle of the night. The patient did not identify himself but tersely stated, "Doc, come over here right away," and then hung up.

I had immediately recognized his voice and did not experience even the slightest hesitation about responding to his urgent request. The situation, however, stirred many questions as to the appropriateness of extending the boundaries of the therapeutic relationship. The patient had issued a discrete, unambiguous invitation for me to participate in an action, apparently on his behalf, suggesting that at least in some measure I was perceived as a source of help. Although it hinted that a bond of trust had been slowly developing, there was no clear indication as to whether he was seeking support of a pathological defense or whether some hidden, split-off, or unrepresentable sector of psychic activity required this concrete experience for growth to become viable. Furthermore, there were no derivatives available to help me in determining the unconscious significance of his call, nor any other means to guide and validate my decision. I was left in the dark, confronted with a demand for an immediate intuitive response.

The way in which the urgency was delivered gave me plenty of room to either rationalize or justify not acting, since the patient neither identified himself nor gave any direct explanation of where he was located. I could conceivably confess ignorance, yet in a silent but powerful way I could tell that he knew I had recognized his voice even from the brief moment of telephone contact. It would certainly have been possible to explain my not acting on the basis of being bound by therapeutic principles, making it important to protect the existence of clearly defined boundaries and ground rules. Any effort to modify them would need to be identified, understood, and interpreted, rather than translated into behavior. However, to treat therapeutic principles as rules is to replace their flexibility with rigidity, just as to treat the principles as license is to replace their containing function with chaos and disorganization. My task was to determine whether the patient was acting out an unconscious fantasy, in which case my action would be supporting his avoidance of remembering and understanding; or whether he was reenacting some inarticulable transference experience based upon an unmet need, in which case my participation would be required to enable the experience to be represented and communicated.

The absence of a chance to attain validation made it mandatory for me to depend upon the events having transpired in the treatment up to that point. It would communicate to the patient the nature of my understanding of him. He would have firsthand knowledge of my vulnerability to countertransference-based reactions leading to disruptive modifications in necessary therapeutic boundaries on the one hand, or on the other hand to what extent I was open to following his lead into new and uncharted territory based upon intuitive and empathic responsiveness. There was an element of risk involved, which would show how concerned I was with protecting my self-interests. Any inclination to withdraw when faced with an unknown and potentially anxiety-arousing situation could be identified, as well as noting whether I was subject to entering blindly when caution might be more appropriate.

Nevertheless, the urgency required an immediate response, though I did have an opportunity to explore my internal reactions. In this sense the circumstances were unusual, in that these kinds of demands generally arise within a setting that does not grant the time and space for internal exploration. There is then little room to do more than come forward with a spontaneous response depending largely upon intuition. The advantage of having a chance to examine the meaning of the patient's request, without ongoing pressure, was offset by the disadvantage of not having the patient's input to obtain validating material. I had no indication of conflicted countertransference feelings, but I did wonder if some unseen regressive identifications or narcissistically determined rescue fantasies might be at work. I considered the meaning of his call within the context of the overall sequence of material already available, and decided on a course of action after careful deliberation. There had been little glimmers of the patient perceiving me as a helpful figure in previous sessions, but they were always tempered by his guardedness and paranoid expectation of being attacked or abandoned. This was the first open expression of an appeal for assistance, and as such if he was failed it might conceivably be irretrievable. The earlier sessions suggested that errors of omission could be much more devastating in their effects than errors of commission. Therefore, I decided to act upon his request, keeping in mind that there was a potential for reenforcing a pathological defense or encouraging some form of acting out. The action itself could very well be a means of extending the treatment framework beyond the confines of the office without sacrificing its containing properties, although this could not be known until the patient's responses could be received.

With this in mind I went to the patient's house, knocked on the door, and was invited into a foyer by the patient's mother. From there I saw the patient's father slumped in a chair surrounded by four unfamiliar men. Unbeknownst to me, the patient was stationed in a darkened hallway, having direct view of my entry, from which point he silently watched. Much later he revealed that his motive for calling was based upon his need to see me react to the scene in front of me before any words of explanation were given. Without knowing what had occurred I had an image of a wounded animal surrounded by vultures, and the accompanying sensation of horror apparently showed on my face. At this point the patient emerged from out of the shadows, asking me to tell the others to leave and requesting that I meet with his family. The men left, and the events of the evening were then described by the patient. His father had been drinking and erupted in a violent rage directed at his mother. She became frightened and called a number of his friends and co-workers to help in subduing his aggressive behavior. The patient in turn had become infuriated and called the therapist. He appeared to be extremely protective of his father, while acting sullenly hostile toward his mother. By this time his father was extremely contrite and guilt-ridden, whereas his mother was coldly aloof. I spoke of their need for help as a family, and made a referral to someone else for this purpose. The patient was visibly relieved and smiling when I stressed the importance of protecting and safeguarding the contained space of our own therapeutic relationship.

This incident marked a turning point, for in the ensuing sessions the patient displayed a striking change in his entire attitude. He became eager to explore his internal reactions, and exposed his innermost thoughts and feelings on a background of trust. Whenever he noticed his defensive posture or seemed internally guarded, he exhibited a readiness to search for its source. In the process he recognized how sensitive he was to even the slightest lapse in my empathic connection to him. These moments could be traced to early traumatic situations, and he became increasingly aware of the disturbing fantasies that existed behind what appeared outwardly as a paranoid attitude. He recalled vivid episodes of extreme parental violence, usually instigated by his mother's paranoid anxieties and bitingly hostile attacks upon his father. The patient was left as a frightened and silent observer, who also felt enraged and helpless.

It was in this context that he talked about my visit to his home. He had noted the look on my face, which made him feel I would understand the position he was in. Everyone around him saw his father as the source of the family difficulty, with his mother as the helpless victim. The father was a chief executive in a large corporation, and the people surrounding him were all individuals the patient felt were eager to see the father fall from grace. There they were acting as the mother's agents. This scene revived early memories of his feeling in a similar position. He anticipated that the father, like himself, would be totally misunderstood. The image of a need-supplying object's distance and hostility made him feel helplessly enraged. Any emotional distance he encountered with me was a silent and inarticulable reminder of these early events. He needed the experience of my active involvement with him in order to see that the emotional distance periodically surfacing in the therapeutic relationship was eliciting this unverbalized response.

The significance of his request to alter the therapeutic framework could now be seen more clearly, and it enabled him to be more fully engaged in the relationship. It did not escalate into an unending spiral of attempts to modify the secure features of the therapeutic environment, nor did it precipitate previously frequent periods of sullen withdrawal. Instead it operated as a source of material for further interpretive work. The actual experience appeared to have been internalized, bridging the gap that was created by powerful mechanisms of splitting whenever he was confronted with emotional distance or defensiveness.

The Construction of a Treatment Boundary and the Evolution of a Therapeutic Alliance

A treatment boundary refers to the nature and quality of the interaction between patient and therapist, with the therapist taking total responsibility for determining the conditions and conduct of the treatment relationship. Managing the therapeutic properties of the environment is carried out by gaining a sensitive and accurate reading of a patient's unconscious perception of what is required from a relationship to promote constructive growth, while continuously communicating what can be offered and expected. A therapist is devoted to identifying the specific factors that will facilitate progress in this direction, and is alert to those working in opposition—whether they emanate from the patient, the therapist, or both. Those aspects that can be ascertained are provided in order to expand self-knowledge and self-awareness, or to heal developmental deficits, defects, and arrests. All of this occurs within the limitations imposed by psychological discourse, the particular structural organization of a patient's personality, and the unique skills and abilities of a therapist.

A therapeutic relationship is initiated in a state of imbalance. The individual seeking help is in a vulnerable position, affected by powerful intrapsychic forces that have an infantile, regressive character; the tendency will be to look at a helping figure as one who possesses the necessary attributes to alleviate whatever distress is experienced. A therapist in turn is there to provide assistance but possesses the additional perspective, unavailable to a patient, of the many complex determinants that must be unraveled so that the help being sought can ensue. The imbalance is skewed further by a patient's projection of unwarranted authority onto a therapist, and all of the internal reactions that this elicits in both parties. However, an optimal level of imbalance is essential to foster the unfolding of a benign regression, and to enable the expression of transferential experiences. This necessary imbalance is based upon the patient's revealing as much as possible, whereas the therapist reveals only what is required to illuminate the meaning of the therapeutic interaction. Within this boundary a patient's characteristic mode of adaptation, the defensive constellations in the forefront, the effects of unconscious fantasy activity, the exposure of deficits and their source, and the identification of pathways toward achieving healing and integration are discovered.[4]

The responsibility for sustaining the proper imbalance in the relationship rests entirely with the therapist. In order to operate effectively in supporting a benign therapeutic regression, the therapist must have a broader perspective on what is taking place. Any emerging signs of a malignant regression are in most instances indicative of a lapse in a therapist's empathic responsiveness: either some omission in introducing the conditions needed to

---

4. Milner (1952) compared the temporal, spatial frame that marks off the special kind of reality of a psychoanalytic session to the frame of a picture marking off the differences of reality within it and outside of it. In psychoanalysis it is the existence of this frame that makes possible the full development of the creative illusion we call transference.

Stone (1961) stressed the significance of maintaining respect for the patient's vulnerable position, pointing out that a nuance of a therapist's attitude can determine the difference between a lonely vacuum and a controlled but warm human situation. It does indeed offer the gratification of security, support, and tolerance along with its undoubted rigors.

Giovacchini (1974) noted that the psychoanalytic process aims at preserving and promoting autonomy, and thus many patients—regardless of how seriously disturbed—adapt well. It is designed not to impose values, nor manipulate and manage one's life, but is dedicated to release a patient's developmental potentials.

establish an effective therapeutic alliance, or a failure to maintain an optimal imbalance in the management of the interaction.[5]

A benign regression is associated with the emergence of new material, the undoing of repressive defenses that results in the appearance of previously unavailable childhood memories; the exposure of developmental deficits, defects, and arrests on a background of safety and containment; and the surfacing and expression of infantile yearnings and hungers, which add richness and depth to the understanding of a patient's internal world. A benign regression is furthered by a therapist's unconsciously empathic interpretive attitude. When projective identifications are relatively mature, so that self and object are clearly differentiated, all that is required are well-timed interpretations, appropriate silences, and sound, careful management of the treatment framework. In such situations any other input would be impinging, overstimulating, or infantilizing, and thereby would interfere with the full unfolding of the transference.

A malignant regression is associated with a demand for (1) the reenforcement of pathological defenses; (2) an escalation of regressive cravings pushing for action; (3) the relative absence of new material; and (4) abundant evidence of a lack of regulation, control, and containment occurring on a background of distrust with high levels of fragmentation anxiety. A malignant regression is suggestive of an unempathic environment, an improper imbalance in the therapeutic interaction, the sudden eruption of primitive projective identifications with little differentiation of self and object, and/or a psychic disturbance too extensive or based upon internal damage beyond the capabilities of psychological treatment. A great deal is then required of a therapist in order to reestablish the appropriate balance in the relationship. First and

---

5. Balint (1968) referred to regression as not only an intrapsychic phenomenon but also an interpersonal one, making it important to distinguish between benign and malignant forms. A benign regression is manifested in the wish for tacit consent to use the external world in a way that allows the experience of internal problems to reach and gain recognition, and requires the consent, participation, and involvement by the therapist, though not necessarily with action. It is a special relationship needed for a true beginning. By contrast, in a malignant regression the patient's primary aim is to achieve gratification, and this is manifested in the patient's seeking an external event and action.

foremost is a search for any signs of unnoticed, or inadvertently disruptive, modifications in a secure framework, followed by an exploration for the presence of an empathic lapse. Finally, an assessment can be made of what has to be offered to strengthen the therapeutic alliance, which may take the form of a now more accurate interpretation, more effective management of the boundaries, ground rules, and conditions of the treatment, or most likely a combination of both.

Establishing Flexible Therapeutic Boundaries

Generally, a therapeutic boundary is established by the use of interpretations and appropriate silences. Only if these interventions are attuned to what is needed to enable the expression of psychic contents in the deeper layers of a patient's personality, will a boundary reflect the therapist's separateness, rather than a defensive wall. However, when a therapist is confronted with gaps in a patient's psychic functioning, it becomes vital to ascertain whether concrete behaviors must be introduced so as to bridge the gap without impinging upon or overstimulating the patient, and to determine whether silence is depriving rather than enabling. To lose sight of the fact that a given patient at a given moment may be literally unable to grasp the meaning or intent of an interpretation—created either by the effects of primitive splitting mechanisms or by absences and deficiencies in mental structuralization—can lead to serious errors of omission. The legitimate concern for maintaining a clearly defined therapeutic boundary must not result in a rigid adherence to communicating exclusively in a verbally interpretive mode. It is in this realm that a therapist's willingness to at least struggle with clarifying or illuminating the difficulty will give expression to the degree of commitment he has toward sustaining the therapeutic properties of the relationship.[6]

---

6. Fairbairn (1957, 1958) indicated how it was impossible to separate the interpretation from the personal influence of the therapist, and stressed the importance of the relationship between patient and therapist. The role of the therapist is not simply to be the screen onto which the patient projects fantasies, because his personality and motives make a significant contribution to the therapeutic process.

A therapist's commitment is embodied in the attempt to discover and provide whatever operates in the service of expanding a patient's autonomy, independence, self-awareness, and self-knowledge. This requires not only a commitment, but also a deep grasp of the responsibility that must be assumed for discerning what is genuine, undistorted, straightforward, and honest in human communication. Truth and honesty are therefore the domain of a therapist, which is exemplified in a constant process of self-examination to search for any evidence of countertransference-based "blind spots," defensive withdrawals, or regressive identifications that are an inevitable accompaniment of therapeutic functioning. It is also expressed in a therapist's interpretations and management of the framework, which are designed to bring out the presence or absence of distortions in a patient's communications. With more primitively organized patients this can be a difficult and confusing undertaking, since so much of the patient's efforts are devoted to destroying understanding when it arises. In addition, the impact of primitive projective identifications can be hard to absorb and process without their eliciting, at least to some extent, residual or latent narcissistic needs.

An appropriate therapeutic boundary is strengthened by a therapist's appreciation of the role of feeling responses in furthering the growth-promoting properties of the relationshp. Along with it there must be an openness to, and respect for, the patient's contribution toward identifying lapses in empathy and in calling attention to the presence of both warranted and unwarranted authority. The derivatives of a patient's unconscious perceptions aid a therapist in gaining an accurate reading of what is required to advance therapeutic progress, and in the process give a clearer definition of how the boundary is operating between both parties. The therapist emphasizes separateness—respect for the patient's autonomy—and brings a positive differentiating influence to the interaction. This involves making a commitment to the overall welfare of the patient, identifying the presence or absence of undistorted or truthful communication, expressing affect that is empathically responsive to a patient's unconscious experience, and being open to receiving the patient's unconscious perceptions to help in the conduct of the treatment.

When a patient assumes responsibility for a clearly defined boundary in the relationship it is usually indicative of: (1) a heightened level of defensive resistance to allowing a regression; (2) anxiety over the potential for a blurring of interpersonal boundaries; or (3) the expression of an unconscious perception of the therapist's inability to perform this essential function. When the circumstances of the treatment are unconsciously empathic there is no necessity for a patient to invoke defensive responses to external impingements or noxious stimuli, and all available psychic content can be directed into the relationship without regard for the existence of a boundary. The makeup and composition of a patient's self-boundary, and the manner in which it is manifested in an interaction, then emerge with more clarity. Disturbances in this vital psychic function can be delineated; and when the source is revealed, integration becomes possible. This perspective underscores the primacy of the interaction as the arena in which therapeutic influence is effected. Whenever a patient manifests difficulty in establishing a self-boundary, attention must first be focused upon the therapist's role before intrapsychic factors can be addressed. Nothing else is either expected or called for from the patient than to engage in the interaction in whatever manner is demanded by the structural composition of the underlying personality. The imbalance necessary for facilitating a free flow of projective identifications to fuel the transference is ensured by the nature of the therapist's participation, which gives a patient the opportunity to present workable derivatives of both unconscious fantasy and unconscious perceptions.

A patient's characteristic style of adapting to a new situation, in conjunction with the mobilization of defensive constellations that are elicited by the unique circumstances of psychoanalytic treatment, will more than likely include efforts to subtly or explicitly alter the imbalance. This is particularly the case when the defensive opposition to intrapsychic stimuli becomes a significant factor before the therapist has enough information to offer a useful interpretation. However, it does provide the material required for an increasingly in-depth view of the patient's personality makeup, and for determining the uniquely optimal level of imbalance at which a given patient is capable of accomplishing the integrative work of treatment. To the extent that the patient is successful in altering the imbalance in the direction of a friendly interchange, the necessary emotional distance for effective therapeutic influence is narrowed; the potential for a blurring of boundaries is increased, especially with more primitive personalities; pathological defenses will tend to be reenforced; the opportunity for achieving structural change is diminished; and a pathway for the emergence of regressive transference experiences is compromised.

Conversely, if the patient's efforts to alter the imbalance are unsuccessful due to a rigid authoritative stance on the part of the therapist, the emotional closeness necessary for attaining an optimal interchange will not develop, and unnecesary defensive opposition to the lack of empathy will have to be invoked. Moreover, the conditions of safety required for supporting a benign regression will not be forthcoming, the therapist will be experienced at too great an emotional distance to allow unimpeded projective identifications, there will be obstacles in the way of internalizing interpretations, and an adversarial climate will be introduced.

The degree to which concrete actions, behavior, or expressions of emotion are necessary to produce the optimal distance in a therapeutic relationship is generally proportional to the level of psychic structuralization operating within the patient. The more primitively organized the personality, the more imperative it is for the wide imbalance in the relationship to be redressed—not so much by personal revelations but by personal involvement. The more advanced the structuralization of the patient's personality the more the therapist's personal involvement is expressed symbolically, primarily through sensitive encouragement of the use of latent internal resources. The primitively organized patient who manifests unstable narcissistic transferences is least effective at establishing a well-defined self-boundary. Consequently, maintaining differentiation is more precarious. It is precisely this kind of individual for whom increased interpersonal contact is necessary, but also for whom a self boundary can readily be invaded in a detrimental fashion. The manner in which the conditions of the treatment are introduced evolves from a therapist's listening attitude. The conditions will then incorporate a therapist's best understanding of their unconscious significance and also contain those elements a therapist requires to sustain ideal therapeutic functioning. It is important for a therapist to possess an internal readiness to make appropriate adaptations when the conditions of treatment are beyond a patient's capacities. A therapeutic relationship is launched with the therapist's manner of participation providing an immediate experience of how the treatment will be conducted.

The Formation of a Contained Framework, an Effective Therapeutic Alliance, and the Introduction of a Leap

The following example illustrates how the construction of a therapeutic framework evolves, and highlights the various facets pertaining to the establishment of the ground rules and their role in defining an appropriate therapeutic boundary. It shows how paying close attention to the effect of the therapeutic situation upon unconscious mental activity is especially relevant, and how the necessary conditions for carrying out the treatment can be gradually integrated into a contained relationship. With each step the therapist's grasp of what specific features were required to construct a secure framework was deepened, until the foundation upon which the therapeutic interaction was built became strong and safe enough for a benign regression to unfold. Within this context a strong alliance developed between the patient's unconscious perception of what was growth-promoting in the relationship and the therapist's unconsciously empathic responsiveness. Eventually, a point was reached where the patient's request for the therapist to engage in a leap could be examined, and derivative material was available for considering its advisability.

Clinical Example

The patient was an airline pilot in his late thirties. In his initial telephone call he stated that he had reached a friendly parting of the ways with another therapist and now felt desperately in need of help. The first meeting immediately addressed the question of a therapeutic boundary, as the patient approached this new relationship with a broad, friendly smile while extending his hand in greeting. Although on the surface this might be viewed as a relatively innocuous social gesture, the intensity with which it was presented carried with it an aura of it being the conveyor of a powerful implied and unconscious communication. I had no idea what it meant and was reluctant to respond in kind. Of course, it was impossible to have any knowledge of its unconscious meaning, and a relationship had not yet been formed that could be devoted to such an exploration. I knew my refusal to respond could readily be received as a rejection. Most importantly it gave me an opportunity to acquaint the patient with my manner of discovering the unknown.

Without at first directly acknowledging his gesture, I simply invited him to enter the office and noted the brief look of dismay that crossed his face. He immediately began to talk about the referral from another therapist, whom he had seen for approximately one year. He had liked him a lot. He was friendly and down-to-earth, and seemed absolutely correct in advising the patient to leave the very destructive love relationship in which he was currently enmeshed. The patient had left the treatment because he was totally unable to follow the advice and extricate himself from the relationship. Although he knew the therapist was right, he was drawn to the relationship like a moth to a flame. He and the former therapist had gone around in circles getting nowhere in trying to help the patient understand the source and meaning of this attraction. He spent some time emphasizing his chagrin at having left this therapist, since he had liked and trusted him; that experience caused him to worry about the prospect of receiving any help through talking and understanding.

I then remarked that he must have been particularly upset when his handshake was not reciprocated. It looked as though it aroused some concern as to what he would find in this new relationship. He paused, commented on a momentary feeling of having been cast aside when I did not return his handshake, but quickly added that it was of no particular importance since he assumed it was a product of my professional style. He went on to describe his first attempt to obtain professional help. He had become increasingly distraught about his personal life, and to soften his anguish he had gotten overly dependent upon marijuana, which he felt was interfering with his performance in a very responsible job. He had worked as an airline pilot for a number of years, and it was a responsibility he took very seriously; he was concerned that his internal state was going to jeopardize his passengers' safety. Although he was aware that it might be a detriment to his career, he nevertheless—with great trepidation—notified those in charge. He was then referred for evaluation and treatment.

He was seen by a very authoritarian psychiatrist, who communicated an aura of assuming control over the patient's life and told him that he was seriously depressed and needed to be hospitalized. The patient was aware of the depth of his depression. He had tried hard to not hold back any information, so as to give an accurate picture of his internal state, but he could not tolerate the inroads on his highly valued autonomy. He thought his strengths had been ignored, and he felt completely misunderstood. In spite of his concern about the consequences in relation to his job, he refused the recommendation and left. He wondered if he had made a mistake in seeking help, or whether it was poor judgment to put out what he was feeling without holding back. He felt the doctor did not appreciate the strength of his desire to understand the dark, depressive experiences he had revealed, or the resources he thought would enable him to understand them. He was insulted by an offer of medication and the instruction that he needed to be in a hospital.

I commented that he seemed to be making it clear that friendly advice in a trusting relationship was of no use, that authoritarian attitudes were untrustable and destructive, and that he needed to explore his innermost thoughts and feelings in an environment where he could be understood rather than imposed upon. His handshake appeared to be a very good way of reaching out to try and determine what he could find here. He smiled broadly and referred to how much he had used this forthright approach of warmth and friendliness in his external life. Underneath it all he felt extremely alone, depressed, and aching for a warmth and closeness that seemed unattainable. He then spoke with great anguish of an intense love relationship with an untrustable, unpredictable, extremely promiscuous woman, who alternately clung to him and abandoned him. She made him feel very inadequate and jealous, yet he suffered from an inexorable need to hold onto that relationship. He wanted desperately to understand the source of these powerful yearnings, for they were also behind his turning to marijuana and had precipitated his search for help.

In this initial interchange I was beginning to construct a therapeutic framework, which would eventually be designed to meet the patient's unique treatment needs. His friendly smile and handshake had the potential for expressing an unconscious message, and though I had no immediate way of decoding it I did have a chance to try and create the proper imbalance in the relationship. This was accomplished by offering a receptive, listening attitude, but not directly responding to the open invitation to join him in his action. The unconscious meaning of his behavior was unknown, and my position was to encourage him to bring material that could lend itself to an exploration of its significance. At the same time, I was indicating the importance of my not participating blindly. I continued to build up the framework by giving a tentative interpretation concerning the patient's reaction to his handshake not being returned. His response unveiled a deeper level of meaning to this surface behavior. He was able to recognize that his seemingly polite, friendly facade was both covering over a more painful, depressive inner core of experience, and testing the nature of the new relationship he was entering. Thus the gesture of friendship could also be seen as an effort to alter the imbalance in the relationship, so as to diminish the threat of an emerging regression. He implicitly indicated that although it temporarily alleviated an internal danger, it prevented him from reaching the conflicted internal experiences for which he sought help. His associations reflected a deep concern about being imposed upon or controlled, suggesting that this had been an important part of the developmental experiences shaping his mental representational world.

Right from the outset my mode of participation was introducing the basic psychoanalytic principles, which would be guiding the conduct of the treatment. At the same time, I was beginning to establish a therapeutic boundary and starting to find the ground rules that would be in the patient's best interests for promoting constructive growth. The patient had already pointed to the presence of a serious psychic disturbance, had given evidence of a search to be unconsciously understood, and had indicated how vital it would be to maintain firm boundaries in order to provide the containing influence he needed to facilitate a benign regression. In turn I had tacitly underscored the value of his input for determining the proper conditions, and within this context had focused upon understanding his unconscious communications. The patient's handshake, my response, and his reaction to it operated as a nodal point for presenting a skeletal outline of what would evolve into a more clearly defined framework.

The patient then spent the bulk of the session detailing his anguish at constantly clinging to a hopelessly destructive love relationship, which confronted him with unending rejection and depreciation. He emphasized how he knew that it was linked to his early relationship with his mother, but that did little to alleviate his suffering. He went on to explain how incomprehensible it was to him that he would seek to re-create an attachment that at least in his conscious mind was abhorrent. His mother had been an alcoholic who worked as a prostitute, bringing many men within his surroundings in undisguised and ugly sexual encounters. Although he was now involved in providing for her financial care he felt no other connection to her whatsoever. Toward the end of the session I commented on his acute awareness of the internal nature of his suffering, and of his need for broadening and deepening his self-awareness. However, he seemed to have many doubts about the efficacy of psychotherapy as a solution for his difficulty. I wondered how he felt about continuing to meet to explore the possibility of working together, and discussing what conditions would be necessary to facilitate the work. He was eager to continue meeting, expressing a sense of urgency lest he cover over the feelings he was coming in touch with as he talked. An appointment was scheduled two days later.

The spacing and frequency of the sessions was then determined in a similar fashion as the relationship progressed, until it became a specified part of the framework. Alternate days were identified as what he needed to sustain the unfolding regression, rather than being imposed as a condition of the treatment. This was of special significance with this patient, who had already given strong hints that impositions resonated with some as yet unseen infantile traumas. If this schedule was presented as part of the ground rules it could then continually operate to obstruct the evolution of an effective therapeutic alliance.

The patient began the next session wanting to discuss the fee. He did not see it as a problem, and offhandedly mentioned the use of his insurance. After a slight pause he commented on how preoccupied he had been with the return of memories of his mother, placing emphasis on the destructiveness of the various people she brought into their home. These were most often men who were drunk, violent, and frightening to the patient. He had constantly struggled with the inroads on his attempts to achieve some privacy or to escape from this threatening and overstimulating external world. He went on to recall a period of time when his mother had remarried, remembering his stepfather as extremely passive and totally ineffectual in protecting either himself or the patient from these invasions by others. I noted how he had thought about third parties intruding upon and interfering with his growth right after he mentioned the insurance, which would also bring a third party into the treatment relationship. His reaction was striking, in that he first looked startled and fell silent for a moment, and then described having a feeling in the back of his mind of grave concern about involving the insurance company. He fantasied that they would use the information obtained from me against him in some vague and indefinable way, but as he talked he was amazed at how he visualized me being allied with the insurance company. He was surprised at this revelation, for he thought he trusted me. It made him wonder if something similar happened in every relationship, and he could see how including the insurance company might put an obstacle in the way of his progress. Although it meant an additional financial burden, he decided to manage payment himself. He felt relieved that this was brought out into the open, for he had automatically assumed I would accept his insurance without question. After pausing briefly he realized there was another matter he felt very anxious about but hesitated to bring up. It concerned the federal government's demand for detailed information about his treatment. Unless it was forthcoming he could not return to his job.

The next several weeks were spent focusing on what this meant to him. He elaborated upon the importance of his occupation and the role it played in giving him a strong sense of personal identity. He felt terribly threatened at the prospect of having it taken away from him by a powerful agency over which he had no control. He vacillated between wanting to resist their demand for information and feeling he had to submit or all would be lost. He also alternated between angrily putting intense pressure on me to simply comply with what they wanted, and feeling relieved when I did not act; I either interpreted his anxiety or silently listened for more derivative material. His perceptions of me shifted back and forth from that of a powerful figure controlling his destiny to that of a strong ally offering him the courage to face his internal reactions. These images were accompanied by some poorly focused passive homosexual longings.

Centered around this issue the framework of the treatment was more solidly established. There was a clearer definition of a therapeutic boundary as the transference became more consolidated. It slowly became apparent to him that he was completely in charge of any information released from me. At the same time that a more discriminating view of the confidentiality of the relationship became available to him, he realized that he was reacting as though he was harboring a prohibited internal secret that was in danger of being revealed. Shortly therefter a traumatic early memory erupted into consciousness, accompanied by intense affect that contained a mixture of sadness, a deep sense of loss, anxiety, and almost uncontrollable rage. He had returned home from school one day to find his mother standing by the side of the bathtub having just drowned his baby sister. He was stunned and overwhelmed. The police came and took her first to jail and then to a mental hospital, while he was placed in a boys' home where he lived for several years. It was in this setting that he first began to develop a sense of direction and purpose in his life, and learned to use the friendly, polite facade that had served him well. He managed to keep the traumatic events of his early life in the background and eventually forgot them himself.

It now was possible for both of us to compose a short note to the federal agency. It simply stated that the patient was in treatment and progressing, which turned out to be enough for him to return to work. In discussing the way in which he had built up his characterological facade, he also noted how much of his energy was invested in obtaining clues from my facial expressions as to what was expected from him, and how effectively this operated to reenforce his defenses. He could see what a barrier this posed, and the question of using the couch arose. He felt anxious about the internal sense of being submissive in this position, but along with it had a desire to confront the source of his discomfort. With the use of the couch regressive transference experiences became more intense, homosexual fantasies emerged, and their function in defending against positive oedipal wishes could be seen.

The conditions of a firm psychoanalytically conducted treatment framework were now well in place. Their containing influence operated as a silent background presence, allowing the residuals of early trauma and its effect on psychic structuralization to enter the picture. Early episodes of contact with a very frightening maternal figure that aroused rage, primitive anxiety, and experiences of instinctual overstimulation were buried deep within his personality, feeding the more accessible genital oedipal dangers. He was able to gain a fuller grasp of the meaning of his powerful attraction to a destructive love relationship, as he noted how its onset coincided with the feelings and fantasies evolving in the transference relationship. The love relationship had begun after he had a serious motorcycle accident and was hospitalized for several months. This woman had given him her full attention with nurturing loving care while he was totally immobilized and helpless, feeling much as he did when using the couch. He was vulnerable, injured, and filled with regressive yearnings to be loved that were reminiscent of his early developmental years. With his recovery she lost interest in him, turning her attention in a promiscuous fashion to a multitude of others, again repeating the traumas of his past. The resultant feeling he had was parallel with his present concern in the treatment that as he achieved more effective levels of functioning he would be abandoned, and I would turn my interest to others.

It was abundantly evident with this patient that the ground rules and boundaries of the treatment had powerful unconscious transference meaning, and had they been presented to him as a set of conditions to which he must adapt, his reactions would have been extreme. The resonance of infantile traumas with the actual circumstances of the treatment would in all likelihood have made effective therapeutic work relatively impossible. It was equally clear that the containing influence offered by a well-managed psychoanalytic treatment framework was absolutely essential to enable a benign regression. Only then was it possible to reach his infantile traumas, unconscious instinctual conflicts, and the residuals of some early deficits in psychic structuralization. The fee, time, frequency, and position all played their part in creating the proper imbalance in the relationship necessary for a free flow of projective identifications to fuel the transference. The way these fixed elements of the framework were decided upon was guided by the basic psychoanalytic principles, demonstrating how the treatment would be conducted. The resulting therapeutic boundary offered enough safety for a benign regression to unfold, with interpretations being the primary mode of communication.

Within this context the patient was able to achieve significant progress in the resolution of intrapsychic conflict, and also some measure of healing of the residuals of deficits in psychic structuralization. The latter were probably a consequence of constructive positive identifications. These changes were reflected in the patient's disengagement from the pathological relationship that had led to his entering treatment, and in his forming a new and healthy attachment. Therapeutic progress continued to be manifested, along with improvements in his external life. One facet of this resulted in his being offered an important promotion in his job, confronting him with the prospect of moving to a distant location. He struggled a great deal with its meaning for his treatment, and was reluctant to stop prematurely since he had come so far. At the same time, he did not want to pass up what appeared to be a golden opportunity for advancement in his career.

As the time for a final decision approached he felt the strength of his desire to accept the promotion. He recognized that his conflict emanated from a feeling of anxiety associated with the separation, and wondered if he could continue his treatment with another therapist and face this internal difficulty in that setting. However, his reluctance to do so made him feel that his old tendency to go on with his life while ignoring internal trouble might again surface. He recalled earlier therapeutic contacts, contrasting them with the importance his current treatment now held. He had developed a sense of trust, no longer had to be inordinately alert as to how his productions were being received, and knew he needed my input even though he might continue the process of self-exploration on his own. He then raised the question of arranging telephone appointments, which seemed to him like a good solution.

At first I was concerned about participating in a way that had all the earmarks of avoiding his separation anxiety. However, his associations centered more around the idea of solidifying a bond of trust based upon a mutual devotion to finding the truth. I finally agreed to begin in this fashion, with the common recognition that it might not work—due either to my inability to function well under those conditions, or to the fact that the unconscious meaning to him might make it inadvisable. We both felt that if a problem arose it could be addressed at the time. I was thus asked to join in altering what had proven to be an effective therapeutic framework. Although it was brought up and colored by reality considerations it also was accompanied by anxiety that was emanating from an internal disturbance. At best it could represent an extension of the therapeutic framework facilitating ongoing self expansion; at worst it could be a modification working against maintaining the proper conditions for the transference to flourish. I accepted the idea because of both the underlying strength of the therapeutic alliance, and the potential opportunity for furthering the constructive identifications that were filling in the early deficits at the foundation of his separation anxiety.

Early developmental experiences of severe trauma in response to his attempts at individuating, autonomous movements had left some gaps in the patient's psychic functioning, and my refusal to consider the request could very well exaggerate their effects. In this sense the step involved taking a leap into somewhat unknown territory, but with an acute awareness of the potential risks and upon the solid foundation of an effective alliance. I felt that if this leap were counterproductive it would soon become evident, and in that event it could be rectified and its effects interpreted. Thus it did not seem to jeopardize the therapeutic properties of the relationship. More importantly, even in a treatment situation with an essentially neurotically structured individual, the need for engaging in such a venture had relevance.

The move took place with regularly scheduled appointments arranged by telephone on a biweekly basis. He placed himself in a reclining position in an isolated sector of the house when making his call, and as the session progressed the emotional distance narrowed. My image in the patient's mind and the patient's image in my mind became more alive, and the interchange took place as though the physical distance had dissolved. Regressive transference experiences served as a magnet for the return of childhood memories, while dream material reflected the increasing integration of unconscious instinctual wishes. The derivatives of his unconscious perceptions gave validity to the decision to conduct the treatment in this fashion. Interspersed with the phone calls were periodic trips to see me in person, and after a period of a year his treatment was successfully completed.

The motive for instituting this modification in the therapeutic framework seemed to have arisen from a desire to gain support for autonomous, independent strivings. Later, his overall therapeutic progress, in conjunction with the derivatives of his unconscious perception of the growth-promoting effect of the change, added validation to the assessment of its advisability. In addition, there was much to suggest that to interpret the move and the request for telephone appointments solely as an expression of his separation anxiety, although this was partially correct, would be experienced as an error of omission. Overlooking the growth that was also embodied in his decision would tend to resonate with the infantile traumas created by a similar failure during his developmental years, when efforts to achieve autonomy were seriously invaded and undermined.

My refusal to consider altering the framework, on the basis of assuming it was an unwarranted collusion with the patient's defensive structures, would have communicated an authoritative attitude. It most likely would have indicated either an unwillingness or inability to be affected by the patient's input. However, were it to have been refused on the basis of an inability to function effectively over the telephone, it would have had an entirely different significance. The patient would then be freer to choose what had most priority for him, without it evoking a transference repetition. It illustrated the importance of being open to the exploration, not just to examine the patient's unconscious fantasies but also to give credence to the possibility of becoming an active participant in actualizing the experience. Within this atmosphere it was possible for the patient to distinguish and integrate the infantile anxieties associated with movements toward separateness, without the added dimension of having the healthy aspects of the move and his request go unrecognized. In this patient primitive anxieties and preverbal experiences were linked to more advanced psychic structures, giving time and space for an exploration of the meaning of his request and room to correct any mistakes. With the primitively organized personality a similar dilemma may be presented, but it is usually in a more urgent and extreme form.

The Introduction of a Leap Expressing the Extent of the Therapist's Responsibility and Commitment

Whenever a therapist is considering the possibility of modifying therapeutic boundaries and ground rules created by sound psychoanalytic principles, or of engaging in action in place of an exclusively verbal interpretive mode of communication, the question as to whether there is at least some component of a counterproductive acting out in the transference–countertransference sphere is ever present. Even in those situations where a positive, progressive movement does result, a question still remains as to whether it could not have been accomplished another way. A therapist always has to wonder to what extent a hidden sector of an unconscious collusion between both parties may continue to exist. It may very well be that a given therapist with a given patient may have only this recourse available. The nature and intensity of the resistance in the patient, the therapist, or both, may be such that a direct pathway to the unfolding of unconscious forces is prevented, and therefore the detour has been made necessary.

Clinical Example

This problem was consistently present in the treatment of a 17-year-old girl, during which I engaged in an escalating sequence of "leaps" that seemed necessary to enable a constructive treatment process to take place. I introduced extreme measures in the process of giving concrete expression to taking responsibility for her well-being, and to my commitment toward sustaining the treatment situation. My personal feelings and reactions became a crucial feature of the interaction, which eventually resulted in a successful outcome with remarkable structural changes. However, there were areas in which conflicted unconscious wishes continued to operate. She was also able to shed light upon the reasons why these extreme measures were necessary, making it possible to delineate how departing from the therapeutic framework was called for, and how it interfered with her attaining a more adequate resolution of her remaining intrapsychic difficulties.

The initial contact was made when a consultation was sought at the behest of a relative who was concerned about her. The patient had been visiting from a distant city to get away from her family, shortly after having run an automobile into a tree in a self-destructive act. It had been instigated by an upsurge of infantile longings in a relationship, and was the harbinger of the explosiveness that would show itself in the transference. The strength of her motivation for attaining the help she needed was reflected in her response, in the first session, to feeling that I understood her. Even though she worked very hard to present herself as a competent, capable, bright young woman having a temporary episode of difficulty, the psychotic process operating within was almost immediately apparent to me. This was received by her with a combination of relief, excitement, and anxiety. She then proceeded to uproot her entire life, moving to a new and strange environment, and began treatment.

The early months were spent gaining a clearer picture of her internal world. She indicated how much she needed to feel contained, as she was constantly threatened by overpowering self-destructive impulses. A great deal of attention was directed to a search for the conditions of safety she required for the fragmented regressive experiences held deep within her personality to be expressed in the relationship. It soon became evident that her psychic functioning was dominated by a basic schizophrenic process, and that the regressive movement toward a therapeutic symbiosis was escalating in intensity. Along with it a powerful defensive and destructive force was mobilized, which distorted and interfered with all links of attachment. When she felt understood the regression continued, activating insatiable infantile hungers that were accompanied by a fear of annihilation. At the same time an uncontrollable tendency to engage in self-destructive acts, to halt the intolerable anxiety, jeopardized any sense of safety or containment. The containing influence of the therapeutic interaction was simply too limited and could not be sustained.

When I failed to understand her, or was in some way defensively distant, she experienced feelings of anger, distress, and despair. At these moments, however, she felt in less danger of self-destruction. She knew that a regressive merging of a world of infantile experience with a world of more advanced psychic functioning had to occur, in order for her to attain the integration required for psychological growth. She was frequently caught up in a maelstrom of destructive forces, or became lost in vivid fantasies, resulting in a disconnection from perceptual contact with the external world. She also became increasingly convinced that the soft containing walls of a hospital would be necessary in order to extend into all corners of her life the safety she experienced in the sessions. Increasing the frequency of sessions, although in the right direction, was woefully inadequate.

Interpretations were only periodically effective in creating an aura of safety; telephone calls at moments of extreme internal danger served as a stopgap measure, but a sense of containment could not be sustained beyond the confines of the session. In this phase of the treatment her experience of me shifted and fluctuated rapidly. I was perceived as coldly depriving, impervious to her hunger and pain, and defensive and frightened of the depth of her regression. She also saw me as the powerful bearer of much-needed supplies, waiting to envelop and annihilate her, and encouraging her dependencies in order to invade her very being while robbing her of autonomy and individuality. These shifting attitudes reflected the instability of the transference, and revealed the various facets of her infantile experiences. When they were interpreted, the result was a less fragmented narrative of her developmental past through the revival of childhood memories, side by side with a deepening of the attachment. However, the emergence of infantile longings then had to be warded off at all costs. She was gradually moving toward establishing a therapeutic symbiosis, leaving her increasingly nonfunctional in adapting to the circumstances of her external world. It was abundantly apparent that there was insufficient psychic structuralization to contain the necessary regression, and that ancillary measures would have to be introduced.

The extension of therapeutic boundaries to include the use of the telephone had some limited value, though it only emphasized that the relationship in and of itself was insufficient. I recognized it was essential to delegate the responsibility of some elements of her care to trustable others, since therapeutic progress was being manifested, but I was reluctant to do so because of my knowledge of existing hospitals in the area. I did not think they were capable of creating the total treatment environment the patient needed. This phase of the treatment came to a head when I received a phone call from her in the middle of the night, informing me that she had totally destroyed her apartment and was on the highway driving toward self-destruction. I listened, stated simply that I thought she should return to the apartment, clean it as best she could, call back, and at that time I would make a decision about meeting. The patient immediately became calm and agreed to do so. Several hours later she called feeling safer and able to think clearly. She went on to refer to some important realizations that she had to discuss before they faded away. A session was held during which she vividly described her acute awareness that her inner feelings needed to be given full rein in order to be expressed and known, but in order to allow it she had to feel protected. It was simply not available in her current environment. I in turn shared my recognition of the validity of her observations, but was doubtful about the hospitals I knew. We agreed to search for a hospital together, with the patient feeling she could sense a hospital's potential to offer her the world of protection and care she so desperately needed.

During the next few weeks the patient was admitted to a hospital for short periods of time until she finally found a setting that appeared to be trustable. I met with the hospital administrators, who agreed to grant me the authority to meet with the staff and arrange a total therapeutic environment. In this experience I was discovering that my stepping out of the physical confines of the treatment, while looking for a proper hospital, was having the effect of making a therapeutic boundary more clearly defined within the patient. This was a striking revelation, for she frequently experienced a blurring of that boundary. It usually happened when some quality of the interaction was resonant with traumas of the past, or when I inadvertently colluded with a powerful unconscious fantasy of fusion and merger. At these moments she felt completely entrapped, hopelessly paralyzed with no connection to a sense of autonomy, and totally in despair. Thus my behavior, in becoming more actively involved in these external aspects of the patient's life, appeared to be providing a new experience of attachment. It was beginning to establish a link to split-off psychic contents buried deep within her personality and unavailable to the more advanced functions in contact with the external world. In addition, the therapeutic alliance appeared to be strengthened by this concrete evidence of my commitment to finding a way to help her attain a means of realizing constructive psychological growth.

My decision came from the sense of responsibility I felt for the proper management of the treatment, and this form of participation appeared to be headed in the right direction. Continuing to maintain a solely interpretive posture, although eliciting the impact of infantile traumas and regressive experiences, did not offer enough containment for these split-off psychic contents to be integrated. Words were certainly evocative to the patient's internal world, but they aroused inarticulable experiences that were unable to gain access to preconscious representation. They seemed to call for her to use functions that were as yet unavailable. Hence at profoundly regressive moments the exclusive use of words only served to intensify her feeling of despair, since she was incapable of symbolizing what could only push her into self-destructive acts. It looked as though she needed to have the concrete experience of another's active involvement with her in order to build a pathway through which symbolization and understanding could include split-off preverbal experiences. The pressure she was exerting for me to be engaged in actual behavior with her seemed designed to foster her growth, rather than her participation in a collusion meant to reenforce a pathological defense.

It is always essential for the framework of the treatment to be in accordance with the psychic organization of a patient's personality. Within this context the relationship must be guided by the basic psychoanalytic principles so as to create an interpersonal environment resonant with the patient's unconscious perceptions of what is required to promote growth. The framework of the treatment can then operate as a silent background of containment, allowing the benign regression, which is essential for integrating previously inaccessible psychic content. Whenever anything arises that would modify the composition of the framework, it requires an in-depth exploration of its meaning to both parties. The patient's attempts to extend, rupture, or alter any of its components may represent a need to test its solidity and firmness, or it may reflect a reaction to an intolerable rigidity or to projected impositions. Modifying the framework may represent a therapist's defensive, countertransference-based response to the fear of an emerging regression, an unconsciously motivated attempt to be perceived as a good parental object, or a means of gratifying residual narcissistic needs. Conversely, a therapist's inordinate need to maintain a firm but rigid framework may reflect some overconcern about moving into unknown territory. The range of experiences a patient may require to enable the full revelation of primitive, action-oriented transference repetitions may thereby be unduly limited.

Although there may be some disagreement as to what specific conditions are encompassed in a firm psychoanalytic framework, most clinicians would agree that any alterations or modifications are generally undesirable, and should be undertaken with great care, under special circumstances. There would also be agreement that, should life-threatening emergencies arise, changes in the framework might be necessary.[7] When crises demanding some

---

7. Strachey (1934) brought a substantive formulation for the importance of maintaining a firm therapeutic framework, within which an interpretive posture should be sustained. He pointed out that the analytic situation constantly threatened to degenerate into a "real" situation, meaning the opposite of what it appeared to mean. It described the tendency to turn the real object of the therapist into an archaic one, making the therapist like anyone else—a fantasy object. This was the fundamental reason why the analyst must avoid any real behavior, for it was likely to confirm the patient's view of him as a bad or good fantasy object. Such behavior diminished the therapist's power to function as an auxiliary superego and lessened the patient's tendency to become aware of id impulses.

To balance this point of view, and as a product of working with primitively organized patients, Weigert (1954) regarded the technique of psychoanalysis as

LEAPS: THE RESPONSE TO A THERAPEUTIC DILEMMA 47

modification in the conditions of the treatment arise, a question always remains as to whether they are a product of a failure in empathy or whether they are an inevitable consequence of the severity of the particular pathology. Implicit in this dilemma is the area of uncertainty concerning the manifestations of an unmet therapeutic need, as opposed to the effects of a powerful unconscious fantasy.

In this situation being described the patient appeared desperate in her efforts to show me, in a dramatic fashion, the existence of an unmet need. It placed her in the intrapsychic position of being incapable of containing the self-destructive internal battle against an inexorable regressive pull. Her whole manner of relating suggested that what she required to make an interpretive mode of communication effective had not as yet been provided. She was convinced it could be acquired only in a totally safe external environment that offered restraint and protection. Her visible signs of relief in response to my agreement to join in the search for a hospital, along with her sensitive and careful observations of her internal reactions to the environment selected, tended to verify the validity of her need for total care. Her participation in the decision-

---

being built on a set of rules that could not cover the infinite variety of therapeutic situations. The main reasons for flexibility in technique include the personality of the therapist and the importance of spontaneity, which should not be muffled by rigidity, the need to suit the technique to the unique type of illness being treated, and the scientific discoveries providing insight calling for shifts in technique.

Similarly, Maenchen (1970) saw technique as dictated not by the symptomatology alone, or the developmental stage, but by the actual and particular state of the ego functioning and its connection with psychopathology. She thought that standard technique was not applicable in patients who had early defects, since it interfered with the adaptation to reality and with the development of synthetic functions. Technique must be determined by the functioning of the ego as it is found, on whatever level the fixation or regression.

Langs (1975a), however, continued to assert that the present ground rules and boundaries of the therapeutic relationship offered an optimal hold and setting for the patient. A therapist's appropriate and definitive management, and ability to offer correct and well-timed interpretations, are among the most significant expressions of the therapist's humanness and concern. Langs did leave room in these formulations for exceptions, but felt that deviations should be limited to clear-cut emergencies, and to those relatively rare situations in which a thorough analysis of a patient's ego dysfunctions and the unconscious fantasies that maintain them have failed to produce change. A therapist's careful scrutiny of countertransference and full consideration of other disturbing factors is a prerequisite.

making process was a significant feature, for it stood in bold contrast to her lifelong experience of being a slave to the wishes and expectations of need-supplying objects. It represented a small beginning toward preparing the way for regressively moving into the undifferentiated state she was constantly drawn to, in order to discover the necessary ingredients for healing self splits and attaining integration.

Within the hospital she immediately became engaged in intense interactions with a variety of personnel. She was allowing herself to experience the ways in which they responded to her—specifically, to her most advanced levels of functioning based upon a submissive, rigid, brittle representational world bearing all the attributes of a "false" self; also to her most provocative, manipulative, distorting mode of functioning, based upon the defensive organization of an internal saboteur designed to maintain the split in self experience; and finally, only momentarily to her most regressive mode of functioning, based upon a split-off world of infantile longings that were reflective of her "true" self. These powerful infantile experiences were extremely brief, and always accompanied by an overwhelming annihilation anxiety. They mobilized seemingly uncontrollable self-destructive behavior, requiring restraint for safety and protection, and triggered extremely disruptive outbursts of rage. She was testing the environment's ability to bring containment without control, restraint without punishment or attack, and empathic understanding of her infantile hungers without enveloping or undermining her autonomy.

Daily sessions were strikingly productive. Childhood memories of engulfment and abandonment surfaced along with the accompanying rage; instinctual activity became available accompanied by extremely archaic prohibitions. Affective expressions could hardly be contained, often erupting into violent actions during which her entire body trembled. It was important for me to delegate responsibility to carefully selected individuals in the management of her overall care, and with the patient's help "yes," "no," and "maybe" people were identified. "Yes" people were sensitive to regressive infantile strivings and capable of firmly limiting manipulative, destructive behavior without making her feel bad, and they possessed a firm sense of their own limitations and capacities. "No" people were either extremely frightened of regressive experiences or defensively guarded; they made subtle or overt demands for behavioral conformity, and were closed to new learning. "Maybe" people tended to vacillate from one position to another, but were flexible enough to learn. It was vital in her overall care for people to be able to make independent decisions, which had to be made immediately without opportunity for consultation. "Yes" people were given this authority. "No" people were strictly prohibited from entering her carefully constructed treatment orbit. "Maybe" people could participate in interactions not involved with her infantile needs.

The patient then made an intense infantile attachment to a very warm, sensitive, but firm and unyielding woman, who was designated as a "yes" person and was responsible for her care in the evenings. The attachment possessed all of the characteristics of the transference incorporated in a therapeutic symbiosis, fostered by the actuality of the physical ministrations of good nursing care for a very regressed individual. Her previously split-off infantile experiences came to life in that relationship, and the patient was representing body ego experiences of an attachment to an object that facilitated her capacity for symbolization. This newfound ability was manifested in the therapeutic relationship. She became increasingly capable of engaging in a process of internal exploration, particularly of archaic internal imagos, and of examining the significance of early memories and current experiences. Fantasy elaborations abounded. For the first time she could feel a convergence of her previously disparate worlds.

I had some concern about this development. First, because it seemed to be splitting the totality of the transference relationship—focusing upon the nurse as a maternal imago and the therapist as a paternal imago; and second, because I was entrusting another individual with some of the responsibility for her therapeutic care. There was the still unknown aspect of whether the duality in the transference relationship would ultimately serve to prevent full integration, since splitting mechanisms were such a predominant feature of her pathology. In addition I was uneasy about having the full force of her infantile regressive strivings directed into a relationship with an individual who, though sensitive and well motivated, might not be able to tolerate the patient's demands and hence defensively withdraw at crucial moments outside of therapeutic control. However, the regression was extremely productive for the patient. The distorting influence of her internal saboteur was losing its destructive effects, and her advanced functions were gradually being relinquished.

I thus took another step into the unknown by encouraging the symbiotic attachment, while continuing my interpretive activities. This facet of the treatment was a new experience for me, in that many of the most important regressive transference strivings were being reenacted in a separate relationship. On the surface it possessed characteristics that could be described as acting out. It was interesting that the elements of the transference bearing the stamp of a repetition were more involved in the relationship with me, whereas those possessing attributes of a new experience were incorporated in the attachment to the nurse. The totality of the experience appeared to be providing the representational background that was enabling her ability to symbolize, and the overall picture suggested that the patient had been driven unconsciously to seek out this particular configuration in order to reach a sufficient level of regression to heal the splits in her self. It was on this basis that I supported this development, in spite of a nagging internal reluctance. The main alliance surrounding the therapeutic work continued to remain within the therapist–patient interaction.

At the height of her regression the patient could feel the internal fragmentation of her advanced world of psychological functioning, the inexorable movement toward and deepening of her involvement with regressive infantile longings expressed in a relationship, and the active mobilization of the defensive structure designed to prevent the attachment and compelling her into seriously self-destructive acts. She began to express a deep inner conviction of the circumstances she needed to enable the full flowering of her profound regression. Her description was of being completely immobilized, so that the activity within her mind could move unchecked by the distractions created when her body seemed driven to impact against the environment. She visualized this position as being necessary in order to feel and communicate all that transpired within. I was reminded of the cold-packs that had been utilized some years before in containing psychotic patients. When I expressed this vision aloud the patient's face lit up for it fit her need exactly. Arrangements were then made to institute the procedure, introducing another extension of the therapeutic framework.

While she was in the cold-pack I sat at her side with my hand on her forehead. The experience of direct interpersonal contact allowed her to communicate without feeling the threat of being disconnected and plunged into a bottomless void of lost self boundaries. She brought forth a progressive spiral of archaic images, with their symbolic properties revealing the body ego experiences and their object impression counterparts that were at the foundation of her pathology. My interpretative reconstructions of these infantile, preverbal experiences were then validated by the return of childhood memories carrying similar qualities. Coincidentally, not only was the bond between us becoming strengthened by the therapeutic work that was being accomplished, but the infantile strivings incorporated in the relationship with the nurse were also beginning to appear in her relationship with me—at first symbolically and then directly and without undue anxiety. At precisely this point the nurse precipitously withdrew from the relationship, consciously stating that she was fearful of the intensity, the responsibility, and of an inner feeling of inadequacy. Although this reflected her anxiety over unconscious psychic content aroused by the depth of the patient's regression, it was probably also due to some preconscious or unconscious recognition of the shift in the patient's attachment, making it possible for her to pull away. The loss was experienced by the patient as a devastating blow. It elicited reactions that indicated an early infantile, preverbal loss was being repeated, and became a spur to more intensive integrative work.

The patient was now in a totally regressed state in all aspects of her psychic functioning, moving toward integration with a totally different perspective. She needed a world surrounding her that could both foster constructive growth and provide appropriate care, as she maneuvered her way toward advancing levels of psychic structuralization. After a year of hospitalization her insurance was running out, and there were no more funds available. Furthermore, the entire atmosphere of the hospital environment began to change in response to her regressive state. It was no longer an appropriate setting, making it essential to find the proper environment for supporting her continuing growth. I explored every possible facility, without success, and then an unthinkable alternative slowly began to take shape. I had the idea of bringing the patient within my home environment, with arrangements for the care that would be required for her healing and integration to progress. At first this was strictly a fantasy, and reflecting upon it seemed to bring depth to my understanding of the patient's internal state.

In defining the specific ingredients needed for her care I was gaining a deeper grasp of what had gone awry in the course of her development. I utilized these insights in looking for a proper place, but as every avenue was exhausted the idea of moving her into my home became stronger. It was finally transformed into a possible plan of action. Such a move would also involve significant others in my life, and their willingness to participate had to be explored. I outlined for them as clearly as possible the extent of the commitment, the need for honesty and directness in all communications regardless of the consequences, and most important of all, whether they all had a genuine desire to join in the venture. My family was surprisingly receptive, which strengthened my resolve to consider the idea as a serious undertaking.

A great deal of time and energy was expended in self-examination as I searched for a deeper meaning, for any evidence of my acting out some unconscious fantasy. I was concerned about the presence of an unconscious motive that might serve as an obstacle to therapeutic progress, and

I needed to feel some measure of certainty before introducing the idea as a potential reality. Only then could the patient's input be elicited to aid in determining the feasibility of such a drastic measure. I was reminded of my experience with an autistic child (see p. 5) in which I had not acted upon a similar motive. I tried to assess whether the current situation emanated from an empathic resonance with the patient's therapeutic needs, or whether it represented the arousal of compensatory needs within me.

On this occasion there was no sense of relief at the idea of relinquishing the responsibility, but rather a sense of anguish at the idea of unnecessarily abandoning a human being in distress at a critical juncture in achieving integrative functioning. I reviewed the history of her treatment in order to gain some distance and perspective on the urgency of the moment. The manner in which responsibility had been delegated to others, and especially the division that had occurred in the transference relationship, was particularly noteworthy. It seemed that this new move might consolidate the responsibility back under my aegis and conceivably offer some ingredients that were lacking in the new experiences she was representing. This might facilitate a full working through of the original preverbal trauma, involving the self-fragmenting loss of an infantile symbiotic partner that had been repeated with the pulling away of the nurse in the present.

With this possibility firmly in mind I was prepared to present the idea to the patient. I could then listen to whatever responses were evoked, thereby adding another dimension of information before reaching a decision about implementing the move. I mentioned it to her as a possibility, and her initial reaction was one of startled amazement and disbelief. She trembled as she spoke of a privately held fantasy of becoming a part of my total world, and of growing within it. To have had it interpreted would have been surprising enough, for it would have made her feel I was reading her mind. To have it presented as a real possibility, however, made her whole body shake with excitement, anticipation, and anxiety.

The next month was spent examining her internal reactions, while the hospital became increasingly unresponsive to her unique needs. In part the hospital was no longer receptive to supporting her treatment because the staff knew the time for her leaving was imminent. Her hopes, fears, longings, wishes, and fantasies were all expressed on a background of excitement, which gave me pause for reflection about the enormity of the undertaking. Although a pathway was now being defined, it seemed fraught with risk and danger, and I was deeply worried about the potential damage that could ensue. The possibility and even likelihood that I was colluding with an unconscious fantasy of the patient's constantly loomed in the shadows, stirring grave doubts about the consequences. The need for me to discriminate between an unconsciously empathic response and a countertransference-based expression of acting out was essential. It was equally vital to ascertain what the move unconsciously represented to the patient. If it meant living out a new experience to foster constructive growth we were on the right track; but if it was acting out an unconscious fantasy or reenforcing a pathological defense, we were headed for failure.

I noted that my internal reactions carried no sense of urgency or compulsion, and there was considerable internal exploration associated with the active involvement of my intellectual functions. Although these secondary process activities could very well have been an effort to rationalize the decision, they did direct my attention to an overall view of the treatment. One consistent theme involved the patient's reliability in selecting directions. Her sense of what she needed turned out to facilitate therapeutic progress, in spite of appearing out of tune with generally accepted treatment principles. In addition, I now had the opportunity to gather together all aspects of treatment responsibility and focus them into one relationship. Perhaps most important, it felt "right" to me. I was reminded of my earlier experience in backing away from a similar circumstance for all of the wrong reasons. Finally, there was the affective resonance, wherein my idea exactly matched the patient's unarticulated fantasy. I anticipated a number of unspecified problems, but the therapeutic alliance seemed strong and solid enough to work them out and accomplish the imposing task of furthering her progress.

The material from the patient suggested that there was an intermingling of her unconscious perception of what she needed in order to grow, along with the existence of a powerful unconscious fantasy of attaining exclusive possession of a loved object to compensate for her severe, devastating, and inarticulable preverbal trauma. The other consideration involved uncertainty over how the treatment would be affected by conducting sessions in the office while at the same time being in direct contact with her and others in an overall life situation. The assessment of her ability to maintain this divided relationship was supported by the division of her transference experience with the nurse, which had been such a vital feature during her hospitalization. The shift in the patient's mood from one of total despair to joyous excitement and anxiety could have represented her reaction to an impending leap forward into a destructive interaction, or conversely into a growth-promoting experience.

The time for the move became imminent and neither the patient's reactions and associations nor my responses made the distinction totally clear, which probably reflected the presence of both factors operating simultaneously. The lack of clarity was openly acknowledged, and we both began this new and risky venture with great trepidation. The actual date set by the hospital for her leaving turned out to be the day of her birthday. The patient's emphasis on the coincidence seemed to be a hopeful note.

Within my home setting she required a great deal of physical care. She was incontinent, had no bowel control, could eat only baby foods, lost almost all of her advanced functions, and could speak only in baby talk. When she was brought to her appointments, a separation was made between the two areas of involvement. During the therapeutic sessions she explored her internal world of feelings, sensations, and fantasies, with my participation exclusively verbal and interpretive. At home, however, I was involved with her care much like a paternal figure—reading stories, playing games, being accompanied on trips, and so on. Within my home environment she was provocative, occasionally "naughty," possessive, and jealous of others in my life. These feelings were expressed both behaviorally and verbally. All aspects of her previously dominant "false" self had dissolved, and a genuine, infantile, and "true" self was manifested.

She gradually learned various skills, and assumed increasing responsibility for her own care. She was visibly growing without the overuse of autonomous functions that had characterized her previous mode of adaptation. She attended classes at a simple level, taking adult education courses in crafts and other hobbies. She learned to read with comprehension for the first time, and even displayed some talent in her drawings. Her pictures were extremely revealing and expressive of her emotional states. It was striking to see the emergence of life, vitality, and affect in all of her interactions. Treatment continued to be occupied with understanding her internal world. She spent a great deal of time reviewing her hospital experience, linking it to both the actual events during her childhood and the fantasies they elicited. Instinctual drives now instigated intrapsychic conflict and mobilized somewhat archaic prohibitive responses, all of which were new to her. They were experienced with a sense of beginning mastery and delight at feeling intact. She could contain feelings, be ambivalent, and struggle with anger and sexuality without fragmenting, withdrawing, or entering into her private autistic world. She slowly became ready for an independent life, and after a period of one year moved into her own apartment, with a feeling of excitement and hope. Ambitions and goals, which she had previously kept carefully guarded inside, came to the surface as a motivating factor in her life.

For many years she had harbored a secret ambition to become a doctor. Earlier it had been fueled by omnipotent compensatory fantasies, and later was fused with an identification with me. She returned to school, and work, determined to find out just how genuine and realistic that ambition was. The use of her unique talents and skills gave her an avenue for the mature development and realization of an integrated self, and she started to achieve success in negotiating her way toward an "impossible dream." The restructuring of her personality was evident in the transference relationship, which was both stable and object related. Unconscious instinctual wishes engendered intrapsychic conflict, but the nature of her attachment to me over the six years of her treatment interfered with their resolution. It became apparent to both of us that it was time for this treatment to end, and that she needed the experience of being independently involved with reaching her life goals. She had developed the capacity to engage in an effective process of self-examination, though further therapeutic contact might be of benefit later. She has since gone on to a medical career, and continues to maintain contact with me but now only as an extended family member.

From a retrospective viewpoint the leap in this case appeared to be essential for enabling intrapsychic growth. The patient was totally trapped within her schizophrenic illness, and did not possess the wherewithal to bridge the gap that prevented her from reaching highly valued and split-off aspects of her personality. These had to be integrated if she was to attain a viable life. My willingness to leap into the darkness of the unknown, fully knowing its potential for catastrophe, appeared to offer her something she had been lacking—the concrete experience of another's total commitment and responsibility to promote growth in a relationship. The mental representation of that percept could then be structuralized, facilitating the integration of a previously split-off infantile world. These infantile experiences contained the core of her instinctual life, gave impetus and viability to a new synthesis with advanced functions, and created the necessary foundation for healthy psychological growth. It is impossible to predict with any degree of certainty what might have occurred had I desisted from such a drastic departure from standard therapeutic conduct, but there is every likelihood that she would have developed a sense of abandonment that could have mobilized life-threatening behaviors. Considering the severity of her disturbance, and the manner in which early preverbal traumas were being reenacted, my decisions and actions could be encompassed within sound psychoanalytic principles, which were adapted to the structural organization of her personality.

Another significant feature of the treatment concerned the almost consistent trustability of her unconscious perceptions. They provided me with direction and guidelines for discovering the specific qualities in this relationship that were conducive to her growth. Even in the presence of a particularly powerful, distorting internal saboteur, whenever she successfully enlisted my collusion in supporting a pathological structure she became intensely distrustful. This would inevitably be followed by dream material pointing to both the collusion and the necessary direction that had to be taken. Thus when healthy and pathological forces were most enmeshed, the patient's basic inner core of integrity was constantly operative and served as a beacon light for my management of the treatment. It is this latter attribute that is so difficult to assess with any degree of certainty. It often depends upon a therapist's willingness to be guided by intuitive and unconsciously empathic responses. On the surface this may seem to be dangerous and risky, but it is balanced by a therapist's consistent effort to engage in an internal process of self-exploration to identify and filter out defensive or pathological reactions. It is further aided by a careful assessment of the patient's associative productions, behavior, and entire manner of functioning in the interaction.

The Need for Flexibility in Applying Psychoanalytic Principles

Leaps must always be taken with great care, after thoughtful deliberation, and only when there seems to be no other avenue. When traumatic preverbal experiences are embedded in pathological defenses, they may become accessible to therapeutic influence only within the arms of a secure, unyielding framework. A great deal seems to depend upon the extent to which good self-experience has been structured within the personality, so that firm, well-managed ground rules, boundaries, and conditions can elicit their containing influence. Generally speaking, most efforts to modify the conditions of the treatment are motivated by a search for reenforcement of pathological defenses. Therefore, the pressure must be received by a therapist in order to understand the unconscious meaning of the interaction, and gain the information required for formulating an effective interpretive intervention.

It is quite a different state of affairs when a patient is desperately seeking to gain a concrete experience of contact that can provide the necessary groundwork for inaccessible, unthinkable, and inarticulable psychic content to enter the realm of mental representation and ultimately have access to expression. These are individuals for whom the only means of eventually achieving psychic growth is through successfully engaging a therapist into reenforcing a pathological defense, or even participating in the living out of an unconscious fantasy. This usually involves very primitively organized and structurally deficient patients whose little good self-experience is preserved and protected by being split off from any attachment to an object. The resulting unrepresented, and hence not symbolized, infantile experiences may be reachable only through the vehicle of the pathological structures designed to guard them. Under such circumstances it is essential for a therapist to be alert for any hints as to the emergence of these vulnerable strivings for growth, so they can be given the support required to enable them to be experienced within a relationship.

There are times when a therapist's strict adherence to sound psychoanalytic principles may be a product of defensiveness, thus interfering with the flexibility required to adapt them to the structural organization predominant in a patient's personality. A therapist may then recognize the patient's urgent appeal for help in controlling a regression, but misinterpret the accompanying pressure to alter the framework as being solely motivated by demands coming from pathological defenses. The push may be arising from the patient's reaction to the impossible limitations imposed by conditions unresponsive to his needs, and be exaggerated by his inability to overcome a therapist's unrecognized resistance. In this way a therapist may be coerced into behavior that ruptures the containing properties of the relationship, though it may eventually lead to a clarification of what is lacking and needs to be supplied. The therapist has then been pressured into a leap that might not have been necessary had there been an openness to receiving the patient's unconscious communications, especially those expressing an unconscious perception of the unempathic qualities of the relationship.

It is, of course, important to make these various distinctions in order to become more discriminating in defining the specific circumstances needed by a given patient. Whenever the view of what constitutes a secure, effective treatment framework is obscure, there is a potential for entering into detrimental or destructive collusions with a patient. However, a therapist can be equally harmful or disruptive by responding to this difficult problem with the introduction of rigid rules.[8]

---

8. Stone (1961) stressed how all sorts of ancillary techniques have their place. The failure to intervene in such a manner, when indicated by the patient's impairments, can be detrimental to the analysis. It is questionable whether a distorted picture of the therapist is a better technical basis for the development of transference fantasies than a natural outline picture of the therapist, limited by clinical judgment as to what to reveal. Finding the therapist to be human, even when revelations reflect technical errors, is less detrimental than stiff, inconsiderate, unreal attitudes and practices. The therapist's willingness for involvement, even at the risk of introducing an error, is even more pressing and acute with more primitively organized patients.

Winnicott (1963), in defining the significance of the extreme dependency of borderline and psychotic patients, called attention to the dimensions of the problem. The hope was to keep the dependence within the confines of the transference, the sessions, and the setting. However, there was no way of telling in advance, or even to make the sort of diagnosis concerned with the assessment of needs. When the patient is without mental nursing, the psychoanalyst doing psychoanalysis must find the patient is not only daydreaming of being taken over by the analyst, and into his or her home, but also actually needing to be taken in.

Giovacchini (1974) outlined the maneuvers essential to further analytic treatment in psychotic patients, which might be considered by some therapists as parameters of such magnitude that they transcend analysis. However, he felt they differed from parameters in a very important and essential respect. The purpose of the intervention was to preserve the analysis, and it was often instituted so that the therapist, rather than the patient, achieved the ego integration needed to function analytically. By contrast, parameters are designed so the patient can feel sufficient security to become engaged in an analytic relationship, and are in effect a preparation for analysis.

Stolorow and Lachman (1980) gave a developmental perspective on the effects of limitations in the therapist's ability to respond empathically, which are due to the constraints imposed by the usual conditions associated with psychoanalytic treatment. Understanding the origins and consequences of interferences with, and arrests in, the developmental lines leading to the differentiation, integration, and consolidation of self and object representations, provides a broader and more embracing view of psychopathology than was possible within the framework of classical conflict theory. This has crucial implications for the framing of analytic interventions, and for conceptualizing the course and therapeutic action of psychoanalytic treatment. A variety of psychological products may not only express psychopathology, but also signal the attainment of developmental steps in the structuralization of the representational world. The possibility of reversals to pre-stages, which may occur either as a regression or as a disintegration of newly acquired representational structure that is as yet insufficiently consolidated, remains ever present. The therapist must be attuned to these shifts, which may result from minute failures in empathy or in reaction to the arousal of intrapsychic conflict. Analytic exploration must not be complicated by a failure to recognize or acknowledge empathic lapses.

2

Abandoning the Sound Principles of Psychoanalytic Treatment

The Characteristics of a Psychoanalytic Intervention

The criteria for analyzability to a large extent depend upon the particular definition of psychoanalysis that is given. In almost all instances, however, they include the capacity to engage in a relationship based upon an interpretive mode of communication. In order to be considered psychoanalytic the therapeutic relationship must be guided by the basic principles of free association, abstinence, anonymity, and neutrality. A free-associative process is designed to facilitate the expression of psychic contents in the deeper layers of the personality. A therapist's abstinence refers to the avoidance of reenforcing pathological defenses. Anonymity and neutrality enable the unfolding of the transference without interference from a therapist's projections or impositions. In addition, specific developmental tasks that have not been adequately negotiated must be re-created in the transference relationship, with interventions—ultimately interpretive in nature—grounded upon the unconscious meaning of a patient's communications.

The framework of a psychoanalytic treatment environment fosters growth and developmental progression, as the therapist is guided by a patient's unconscious perceptions of what is needed to accomplish this task. An ideally functioning therapist presents the combined good-object qualities of optimal gratification and optimal frustration, and those of a transitional object. Optimal gratification includes those elements in the therapeutic interaction that favor autonomy, independence, insight, and perspective. Optimal frustration is the result of abstaining from the gratification of regressive cravings, which are a manifestation of pathological defenses that obscure embedded unconscious transference wishes. The qualities of a transitional object allow room for the regressive demands dictated by a particular personality to be openly expressed and welcomed, thereby fostering the free flow of projective identifications necessary for the unfolding of the transference. The basic psychoanalytic principles and the qualities of a good object are intimately intertwined, and they provide a firm, contained framework with well-regulated boundaries and ground rules. Within this context an effective therapeutic alliance can evolve: a bond between a patient's unconscious perceptions of what is growth-promoting and constructive, and a therapist's unconsciously empathic interpretations, appropriate silences, and management of the framework.

Expanding the Conditions of Psychoanalytic Treatment

There are many clinicians who believe a given treatment modality cannot be considered psychoanalytic unless the therapist's interventions are exclusively interpretive in nature. What then is required of a therapist, when by virtue of maintaining a psychoanalytically directed stance the necessary ingredients for structural change leading to developmental progression do not involve interpretations as such? In such a situation a therapist is confronted with a difficult determination. The very conditions enabling a benign therapeutic regression point to gaps in psychic functioning, or in the underlying structural organization of the personality, that can only be bridged by some specific noninterpretive intervention. A therapist's movement into this unknown territory is seemingly antithetical to sound psychoanalytically derived principles. Yet by virtue of presenting a pathway for gaining contact with otherwise totally inaccessible psychic content, it is psychoanalytic in scope. The subsequent constructive structural change has depended upon the use of sound psychoanalytic principles.

These kinds of circumstances were undoubtedly behind the concept of parameters, first formally introduced by Eissler (1953). It directed a therapist to utilize modifications whenever a patient's ego deficits or distortions interfered with or did not permit adapting to the demands of a classical psychoanalytic situation. These deviations were designed to strengthen the patient's ego, in order to ultimately develop the capacity to adapt to the conditions of psychoanalytic treatment. It was emphasized that they should be reduced to the very minimum, and the reasons for their use and the effects they produced had to be interpreted until they could be relinquished. Parameters were thereby a different concept, in that they were selected by the therapist as a means of gaining the patient's cooperation in adapting to the conditions of psychoanalytic treatment. They were not thought of as growth-promoting in and of themselves, and were not viewed as a vehicle for providing either new mental representations to establish a foundation for deficient psychic functions, or as a means of enabling preverbal transferences to be articulated. Instead, they were seen as a stop-gap measure—often as an emergency procedure—and even as a necessary obstacle until the patient's cooperation could once again be enlisted. It was subsequently recognized that some modifications could not be reduced through interpretations. Therefore their use might present permanent limitations to what could be accomplished in psychoanalytic treatment.

The Application of Psychoanalytic Principles with Primitively Organized Patients

Manifestations of early deficits can be brought under the influence of a psychoanalytic treatment process by changing the manner in which the basic principles are applied, without in any way altering the essential nature of the principles themselves (Mendelsohn 1987b). Serious failures in negotiating developmental tasks often demand concrete experiences of involvement with a therapist— which are specific to what is lacking in the patient's representational world—before growth and progression can continue. Interpretations depend upon the viability of symbolic processes, and thus cannot be effective when they cannot completely reach what has not been symbolized.[1]

---

1. Milner (1952) indicated the ways in which symbol formation is both a means of dealing with anxiety and a means of adapting to realities. It has aspects

This problem is best exemplified when addressing the treatment needs of an autistic child, who displays the most primitive level of psychic organization and is least accessible to the minimum requirements of what could be considered psychoanalytic treatment. However, even in this situation psychoanalytic principles define the therapeutic environment. The dearth and fragmentation of good self-experience, the abundance and destructive impact of a bad object's influence, and the extremely primitive level of psychic organization require that the therapeutic relationship offer a new concrete empathic experience if progress is to take place. The therapist must be directed by a patient's unconscious perception of a good object's qualities in order to enable the healthy symbiotic attachment that has been lacking. Previously absent mental representations are then formed, which facilitate the consolidation of defined self-entities. A foundation allowing self-individuation to be initiated is present for the first time, and an autistic organization is no longer in evidence. The treatment relationship is the means for creating a new experience, rather than re-

---

of a regressive phenomenon and also serves as a means of taking a step forward. However, there are particular conditions in which symbolization is nonfunctional. The primary and secondary objects are fused and felt as one and the same, and the person believes for the moment that the secondary object is the primary one. Most narcissistic transferences that result in such a situation have important implications for the role of interpretation.

Modell (1976) defined the differences between narcissistic and neurotic transferences, with each posing different problems for the establishment of a holding environment. Neurotic transferences appear only after a certain degree of ego growth and consolidation has been accomplished, require a capacity for illusion and symbolization, and tend to be changeable and different in every patient. Narcissistic transferences tend to be relatively uniform, are based on the externalization of self or self object, and do not require a condition of basic trust for their emergence. With narcissistic transferences interpretations function primarily as a sign of the therapist's empathy and understanding, and consequently a part of the holding environment. They are therefore not mutative until there is maturation of the ego and acceptance of self–object differentiation.

Gedo (1984) called attention to a critical aspect of therapeutic functioning when confronted with a regression in the presence of severe developmental deficits. He believed that whenever the self organization has been disrupted, so that the patient is unable to sort out priorities among a multiplicity of conflicting aims, urgent external assistance is needed to overcome the confusion. The treatment modality appropriate to such states aims at a unification of the self organization, which must be achieved before interpretive interventions can be effective.

creating an old one, and it does not consist of a transference repetition of a developmental distortion resolved through the effect of interpretive interventions. The impressions of an object are overwhelmingly destructive and the only repetitions are in response to empathic lapses. At such moments the extent of autistic withdrawal is so extreme that an alliance—necessary for therapeutic influence—is impossible. Thus, although the treatment is guided by psychoanalytic principles, it would be difficult to think of it as psychoanalytic. The paucity of good self-experience and the primitive nature of defenses do not permit the treatment to meet conditions considered to be psychoanalytic in the usual sense. In addition, interpretive interventions must be concretely expressed in behavior (Mendelsohn 1987b).

There are individuals, however, who have achieved advances in psychic structuralization but continue to have remnants of an autistic core operating internally. If this primitive mode of functioning prevents symbolic communication, treatment may have to be approached by offering more concrete noninterpretive interventions. This may also be the case when traumatic experiences from the preverbal period exert a continuously debilitating effect. On the other hand, early developmental arrests, deficits, and infantile traumas may become bonded together with later, more structured editions of intrapsychic conflict, which is reflected in continuity of experience being well structured in the personality. Extra measures are then not only unnecessary, but would be infantilizing and an obstacle; an interpretive mode of communication is most conducive to growth. The differences in opinion amongst psychoanalytic clinicians as to whether these preverbal, regressive transferences require concrete experiences of involvement, rather than unconsciously empathic interpretations, may to a large extent be a consequence of differences in patients.[2]

---

2. Bion (1967) felt that real progress with psychotic patients was not likely to take place until due weight was given to the nature of the divergence between the psychotic and nonpsychotic personality, and in particular the role of projective identification in the psychotic part of the personality as a substitute for repression in the neurotic part.

Deciding When to Maintain a Firm Framework and When to Introduce Changes

A great deal of confusion arises when considering factors that may in fact be somewhat different in differing patients. Thus two separate patients carrying what appears on the surface to be a similar psychic makeup, and suffering from the effects of traumatic preverbal regressive transferences, do not necessarily require a similar therapeutic approach.

In the presence of primitive mechanisms of splitting, continuity of experience and processes of symbolization are seriously obstructed. The effect upon psychic functioning makes it extremely difficult to ascertain when the exclusive use of an interpretive modality is most facilitating to constructive growth, and when additional measures must be taken. The problem is further complicated in such individuals, since there is frequently an admixture of healthy and pathological processes at work. The most important aspect may reside in a therapist's willingness to be open for guidance from the best intuitive reading of a patient's communications. At times, the significant element involves the patient's reactive

---

Modell (1976) observed how many authors have called attention to the weakening of an analytic holding environment if active measures are introduced. This holds true especially with neurotic individuals, with individuals displaying narcissistic pathology and having maintained continuity of experience, and even in some more serious narcissistic disturbances. In so-called classic cases the analytic setting functions silently as a holding environment. Where there is ego distortion the analytic setting as a holding environment is central to the therapeutic action.

Stolorow and Lachman (1980) considered it to be of utmost importance to distinguish between defenses warding off intrapsychic conflict, and mental activity that is a remnant of a developmental arrest. This distinction makes it more possible to recognize when an interpretation of defense is called for, and when more active involvement is required to support constructive growth.

Etchegoyen (1982) was concerned with the way in which early preverbal experiences, childhood intrapsychic conflicts, and actual conflicts occurring in the present can be simultaneously linked to the same structure. The childhood conflict tends to express itself by means of neurotic mechanisms, and the early conflict by means of a language of action and psychotic mechanisms. He believed that since early infantile experiences could become integrated to the personality they could thereby be reconstructed and hence analyzed, although with great difficulty, using classical technique.

awareness of the therapist's level of commitment and responsibility in relation to the patient's treatment needs. This commitment may represent the missing concrete experiences. In general, the primacy of interpretations recedes into the background with severely disturbed patients, and it is the therapist's management of the boundaries, ground rules, and conditions of the relationship that then takes precedence. These nonverbal communications express the nature and degree of a therapist's commitment and responsibility to the treatment, and his openness to receiving primitive projective identifications.[3]

There does continue to be uncertainty as to how much the conditions of the treatment must be modified, in what specific ways these modifications should take place, and even whether they are necessary at all. The discrepancy may in part reflect the differences in personality and perspective of a given therapist. However,

---

3. Winnicott (1963) related the regressive dependence in the psychoanalytic transference to the dependence at various stages of infant and child development. However, since a patient becomes wary due to previous experiences, it may take a long time for the patient to get there because of all the tests that have to be made. It is very painful to be dependent unless one is actually an infant, and the risks that have to be taken are very great. The risk is that the therapist will suddenly be unable to believe in the reality and intensity of the patient's primitive anxiety, which is a fear of disintegration and annihilation or of falling forever. The therapist is holding the patient by conveying in words at appropriate moments that the therapist knows and understands the deepest anxiety being experienced. Occasionally holding must take a physical form, mostly because of a delay in the therapist's understanding. Probably there are times when a psychotic patient needs physical holding, but eventually it will be understanding and empathy that will be necessary.

Kinston and Coen (1986) believed that if the absence of structure developing from preverbal traumas and manifested in primal repression is approached, the potential for death, disintegration, or madness previously absent or unimaginable by both patient and therapist is sensed as a possibility. In order for growth to occur the therapist must make direct contact with the patient in a state of primal repression. This is possible only in the presence of primary relatedness, which is the direct, valuing, nurturing, confiding, and reflecting relationship with others that every person absolutely and objectively needs. It is characterized by an intense mutual attachment and deep empathic communication. Primary relatedness, though officially minimized, is intuitively appreciated and deliberately fostered by psychoanalysts. The move to primary relatedness and emotional growth is blocked by the habitual self-protective reactions to the underlying traumatic state, and overcoming the blocks may be gradual or dramatic.

it also seems to be a product of a particular patient's overall level of psychic structuralization. Some clinicians advocate an adequate and rigorous handling of the transference relationship, within a stable and secure treatment framework, believing that the pressure exerted to alter these conditions must be absorbed and interpreted (Bleger 1967, Bott-Spillius 1983, Dorpat 1974, Green 1975, Langs 1975a, Loewald 1960, Modell 1976, Segal 1981a). They consider it possible to analyze these early conflicts, deficits, and ego distortions without resorting to any type of active therapy or controlled regression; and they believe that to alter the conditions of psychoanalytic treatment in any way will lead to unhealthy collusions, and obviate against their integration.

Others consider these early conflicts, deficits, and distortions to be analyzable only by changing the technique. The relationship must be capable of providing concrete experiences of involvement, thereby replacing interpretation as the primary therapeutic instrument (Allen 1956, Balint 1968, Dickes 1967, Gedo 1984, Little 1981, McDougall 1979, Searles 1975, Sechehaye 1951, Stolorow and Lachman 1980, Viderman 1976, Weigert 1954, Winnicott 1963). These clinicians believe that serious failures in early development demand technical changes, because only actual experiences can alleviate them. Interpretations, being a specifically symbolic act, can never reach what has not been symbolized.

Both approaches appear to have validity, since a firm therapeutic framework is an essential ingredient for any treatment and the conditions must be flexible enough to not limit the range of regressive experiences that can be responded to in a therapeutic fashion. However, an exclusively interpretive mode of communication operates on the assumption that regressive reenactments in the transference relationship—which take the form of action and behavior—are accessible to representation and hence eventually to symbolization. This would have to be the case for interpretive words to surround the experience and make it amenable for integration.

Over time it has become increasingly apparent that there are some patients whose preverbal experiences continue to have a detrimental impact on their psychic functioning. These usually involve early traumas that have remained split off from access to either representation or symbolization, and consequently are unable to be influenced from the effects of a relationship unless special conditions are introduced. The conditions are designed to provide an opportunity to internalize a new experience, which establishes the mental representational foundation necessary for processes of symbolization to become functional, or which resonates with the split-off experiences in such a manner that they can be included in the transference relationship. It is only then that an interpretive mode of communication can be effective and support the growth-promoting forces in the personality. Once this is achieved the reasons for altering the framework can be subjected to analytic exploration.[4]

A therapist's selection of what is considered to be an appropriate intervention depends upon an accurate assessment of its

---

4. Gaddini (1982) discussed the differences between nonintegration and disintegration. A primitive fantasy expressed in the body can hardly be further elaborated in the course of development. It is the result of a gap in the process of integration, not of a splitting mechanism. It is fragmenting and representative of a mental functioning that precedes the integrative process, and through reactivation prevents integration. In the suffering of nonintegration there is no place for conflict, since for the fragmentary self no object can exist *as* an object. Thus it cannot give way to wishes and drives, but instead must only obey necessity and need.

Kinston and Coen (1986) pointed out that, from a developmental viewpoint, needs must be met before mental representations in the form of a wish can be elaborated. A failure in need mediation results in a persistent absence of associated wishes (internal self–object relations), and thus a gap in emotional understanding (psychic structure). Such a failure is the essence of trauma and the resultant absence is primal repression. Wishes often need to be frustrated and this is not traumatic, but failure of the environment to meet needs is to be avoided. The failure is traumatic and results in a persistent hold in the psyche. Hole repair is what psychoanalytic therapy is all about, and the transition to primal repression is of the utmost significance for therapeutic effectiveness. Primal repression has a dual and paradoxical function. It is the site of catastrophic, unthinkable, past but ever-present trauma, terror, hopelessness, and loss of self-preservative functions; while at the same time it can serve as a nidus from which growth occurs. A person is forced to express needs and inner states through action, and through provoking the therapist to act. This special type of self-transformative action in relation to symbolization is termed *developmental acting out*. Developmental acting out differs from acting out, which is defensive, impulsive, or gratifying. It refers to action, which by virtue of the absence of wishes is the only means available for achieving some perspective, some awareness of needs and experiences, or for affirming identity and separateness.

suitability for furthering therapeutic progress. One vital aspect in that determination is the nature and quality of a patient's affective responses, which often serve as a reliable guidepost in the midst of confusion. Thus when infantile and preverbal traumatic experiences accrete to more advanced intrapsychic structures, they become embedded in unconscious wishes. Consequently, any modification of a therapist's interpretive posture, within a well-managed therapeutic framework, would only serve to strengthen repressive forces and work in opposition to their integration. Furthermore, if these psychic contents are transformed into action and behavior with the purpose of avoiding remembering, any attempt to live out an unconscious fantasy or reenforce a pathological defense requires the containing influence of clearly defined boundaries and ground rules. The information contained in these defensive efforts can then be utilized to offer appropriate interpretive interventions.

There are special circumstances in which the therapeutic relationship, as we have come to understand it in our present state of knowledge, is not sufficiently receptive and responsive to assessing the possibility of introducing unusual conditions to facilitate growth. In most instances these would involve infantile and preverbal traumas that have no other way to attain expression except through behavior. Early experiences that have been totally split off, or that are otherwise inaccessible to processes of symbolization and verbalization, must often be expressed in action if they are ultimately to become integrated. This makes it mandatory for a treatment relationship to have room within it for innovations and creative interventions to be used whenever they seem called for and appropriate.

To enable the full reenactment of an early trauma, and achieve a new solution to an impossible developmental dilemma in the present relationship, unique ways of participating may have to be found by a therapist.

Rigidity Forcing a Leap, and Flexibility Making It Unnecessary

The derivatives of a patient's unconscious perceptions are an invaluable aid in guiding a therapist toward creating a well-contained environment, and in recognizing the indications of an empathic lapse or failure. These derivatives are more freely available and more easily identified in the cohesive personality, making the task less confusing. In the primitively organized individual it may be a much more complex and difficult determination to make. Efforts to provide safety and containment may lead to the introduction of rigidities, causing a patient to pressure a therapist into modifying the therapeutic framework in a way that would otherwise be unnecessary.

Clinical Example

This was illustrated in the treatment of a 12-year-old schizophrenic boy, who was convinced that he needed to be physically held by the therapist in order to establish the kind of contact that would enable split-off facets of self-experience to be fully integrated and healed.

After the initiation of therapeutic contact, the early months were spent in identifying the nature of his pathology, and in creating a therapeutic environment capable of supporting the emergence of powerful regressive experiences in a manner that was safe. The patient had indicated the existence of a world of infantile experience, operating in the deeper layers of his personality, split off from any attachment to an object. At the same time, his psychic functioning was dominated by an uncontrollable distorting defensive structure, serving as an internal saboteur to prevent any engagement with an object and to preserve and protect his vulnerable infantile yearnings. An advanced, instinctually depleted realm of experience was operative at the interface of his contacts with the external world, which was gradually relinquished in response to the regression induced by the therapeutic relationship.

During this time the fluid cathectic shifts and condensations associated with primary process thinking were strongly in evidence, and he frequently spoke of ghosts, devils, and strange internal events. He was alternately terrified, enraged, and dominated by internal forces he could not understand, and with great trepidation he revealed how he was dominated by the voice of the devil. He was constantly reacting to the devil's accusatory and enticing voices, either luring him into homosexual acts or accusing him in vicious ways. The devil also directed him to balance himself on a chair with a rope around his neck, challenging him to jump. He had to fight with all his will to quiet the voice, only to have it return, making him fearful that he might kill himself. He became preoccupied with searching for a name for these experiences, stating that *hallucinations* did not seem to be the right name because he could feel them coming from inside. He wanted me to give him a name that could help him surround the experience and contain it. I gave him a name, *hypnogogic fantasies*, and he loved it.

Although he experienced the voice of the devil as an alien presence, he also knew that it emanated from within. It stood in the way of his being able to find what he needed in a relationship to heal those infantile experiences that had been split off from any attachment to an object. His recognition of the internal nature of the devil's voice was indicative that a considerable dimension of good infantile experience remained split off and preserved, and I anticipated that this defensive structure would function to maintain the split by provoking me to behave in a pathological, or defensively distant manner. Characteristics resonant with the qualities of a pathologically symbiotic object would in all likelihood be projectively identified within the therapeutic relationship. His potential for self-destructiveness was constantly in the background, becoming more alive when attachment to an object was imminent. Therefore it was vital for me not to be drawn into reenforcing this pathological defense, but also not to avoid it. The treatment task was to internalize the input of his projective identifications, determine their source and function, and offer an interpretive intervention that was capable of diminishing the distortions while at the same time presenting his conditions for an adequate symbiosis.

When the patient had asked me for something to surround and contain the devil's voice in order to bring it under more control, I had responded by giving him a name, thereby letting him know how I would manage his psychic productions. Symbolically, then, the patient had requested that I process this defensive structure and then return it to him in a more usable form with its distorting power diminished. I in turn had displayed a willingness to engage in this important venture, and he felt contained by the name. He had given me an opportunity to communicate in a fashion that did not reenforce a pathological defense, was not impinging, depriving, or overstimulating, and could offer containment and regulation without interfering with his autonomy. This quality in the interaction gave evidence of his ability to function within an interpretive process. In addition, it hinted that were I to do otherwise, pathological distortions might be amplified and work against his search for the healing attributes of a relationship. Thus there was enough good self-experience, carefully preserved in the deeper layers of his personality, to resonate with my efforts to develop an unconsciously empathic environment. It suggested that sufficient containment could be created to enable the depth of the regression required to reach and integrate his split-off infantile world. Altering the firm framework he needed would in all likelihood carry with it a disruptive influence. I had intuitively sensed the importance of answering this request for a name; otherwise he would have been left unprotected from the distorting influence of a defensively constructed internal force.

The experience of being understood both excited and frightened him. He became acutely aware of how fearful he was of being exposed as hopelessly bad. At the same time the regressive strivings deep within were exerting a strong pull toward a lack of differentiation. He indicated how carefully he observed me for any signs of defensiveness, and how hungry he was for any evidence of human responsiveness. He was worried lest I hide my feelings, or not trust my intuitiveness, and in this way become a source of danger. He frequently tested to determine whether I could listen and respond to his infantile needs, or whether I would be provoked into behaving like a bad object. He also revealed how overalerted he was to my reactions, keeping constant vigilance for any clues to verify his anticipation that I would impose expectations upon him.

There were other moments when he withdrew inside of himself. On those occasions he felt tiny, almost invisible, and lost any contact with the external world to which he was so attuned. These revelations were accompanied by intense anxiety, as they became so alive he felt enveloped by them. To speak of infantile sensations was to be completely dominated by their effects. He could allow this experience only when he felt some confidence in my ability to maintain contact with him, since the experience made him lose his functional capacities and feel completely helpless. This meant that my emotional responsiveness was apparent in everything I said or did, because it was the sound of my voice, not so much the content of it, that facilitated the connection. It seemed as though the primary function of interpretations was to give concrete evidence of my emotional attitude, and only secondarily to convey the nature of my understanding. In this way the influences of a good object could echo within him. Any alteration in the conditions supporting this mode of interacting would have been received by him as an enveloping imposition.

As stated earlier, a good object possesses an interwoven amalgamation of the qualities of optimal gratification and optimal frustration along with the qualities of a transitional object. A therapeutic relationship that is managed and conducted in accordance with the basic principles of psychoanalysis possesses these attributes, when the psychic structuralization of a given patient's personality is the determining factor in how these principles are applied. The deeper layers of this patient's personality were composed of the split-off and preserved representations of good infantile instinctual self-experience. Therefore the fundamental principle of free association, which is designed to facilitate the expression of these deeper layers, was applied by providing the particular ingredients of an adequate symbiosis. The patient had clearly indicated that for him an adequate symbiosis would embody the safeguarding of his autonomy and the encouragement of regressive longings, within an emotional atmosphere of understanding and acceptance. In this way an infantile instinctual attachment could ultimately be made, with the resulting experience of optimal gratification initiating the healing of the original split in the self. The principle of abstinence guided me in refraining from re-enforcing his pathological defenses, which were embodied in an internal saboteur. The distortions created were in the process of being eliminated through the vehicle of my interpretations. This in turn was evocative to the containing forces in his personality, by providing the experience of optimal frustration. With this patient the principles of anonymity and neutrality were of special significance, in that it was vital for my emotional responses to be openly evident at the same time that the interaction had to be free of my projections or impositions. The free flow of primitive projective identifications, essential for fueling the transference, was thereby ensured. The resulting experience had the attributes of a transitional object. It was the combination of these good-object qualities that was fostering his movement toward a therapeutic symbiosis, and thus advancing therapeutic progress.

Gradually it became possible for him to talk about the infantile realm of experience that had remained split off in his internal world. At night or on rainy days he often curled up in a fetal position; with the outside world quiet, he became disengaged from perceptual contact with all external stimuli. He was uncontrollably drawn into the deeply buried inner parts of himself; this was an experience he both welcomed and feared. He spoke of the regression as comforting and attractive, but simultaneously it was ominous and his vulnerability was overwhelming. He often felt starved, empty, and as though he could die. Most disturbing was his inner sense of being disconnected: when he was most functional he was most unreal, but when he was most real he was totally vulnerable. Although he was too unprotected to live when he was real, he did not live when he was most protected. Thus he was disconnected from the most vital and infantile parts of himself, and worried that these varied facets could never be united.

He loved to exercise his intellectual abilities and his interest in science and literature, yet this was totally divorced from his infantile experiences. While wanting desperately to be a part of the external world, he felt isolated from it. He was constantly reacting to the two separate and disparate worlds that could not be brought together. The split-off infantile world exerted a constant demand for attachment to an object, which in turn mobilized a self-attacking defensive reaction; and the world of underdeveloped, advanced functions was empty and depleted. The pressure of one obviated against the other. The energizing effects of instinctual activity were excluded from the advanced realm, and when enveloped by infantile instinctual strivings, he was totally helpless, vulnerable, and detached. He was very much aware that an infantile instinctual attachment to me would have to occur for the split to be healed, but he was fearful that I would be defensive, unempathic, and a source of destruction. He was also fearful of my empathic responses, because they evoked and resonated with his split-off infantile yearnings and activated his internal saboteur.

He noted the devil became most powerful whenever he felt drawn to making an infantile attachment. This inner struggle was intensified as my understanding and responsiveness became increasingly important to him. He then began to exert subtle pressure upon me to alter the firm framework within which this profound regression was taking place, and thus I received frequent calls from his school, family members, and doctors asking for information. His illness had become more overt in all aspects of his life; the family blamed his involvement in the treatment, which they had not expected to be more than temporary. He had become more withdrawn and seclusive, but also more violent and explosive, and was no longer the compliant child they had known. However, he was emphatic in directing me not to respond to their calls because any information I passed on to or received from others was experienced by him as extremely disruptive. He needed a contained space in which he could allow himself to be exposed, and the requests for information had the impact of a pathological force invading that space. I maintained that stance, which was reassuring to him, but shortly afterward he began to call me whenever the devil emerged.

I was drawn into being a participant in this deviation, since the phone conversations decreased the devil's influence. It was relatively easy to rationalize this at first, due to the seemingly positive effect in diminishing a destructive, defensive, distorting internal force. Extensions of the therapeutic framework are often necessary, particularly with such a seriously disturbed, potentially suicidal patient. In conjunction with previous experiences in which such behaviors were essential to facilitate therapeutic progress, and in temporarily losing sight of what had already been learned about this patient's requirement for a firmly contained space, I considered the phone calls as a form of "leap." This did not last long, however, for shortly afterward he called me at home and a family member answered. His name was whispered to me, which he overheard, and he became furious. He demanded an explanation of how his name was known. I stated simply that I had revealed it. Initially, he was enraged that I had ruptured his contained space, and then expressed surprise at being told so freely. He gradually recognized that his anger was more a result of being allowed to invade my private space, and it soon emerged that through his calls he had been giving me a message regarding his need to meet more often.

I was confronted with one of the situations in which a willingness to engage in a leap can in fact lead one into unnecessary deviations that have a detrimental effect. Although my involvement with the calls had lessened the influence of the internal saboteur and the voice of the devil, it had also raised the patient's level of distrust. He was concerned about the ease with which I was pulled into a form of participation, which undermined the firmness of the contained space he required. I acknowledged my mistake, corrected it, and both of us were able to engage in a meaningful exploration of the powerful effects it created. It evoked images in the patient of an enveloping, invasive, need-supplying object, utilizing his infantile hungers as a means of exerting control and undermining his autonomy.

The regression continued with the patient making many indirect references to a need to have physical contact with me. I silently registered it as an expression of his cautious, tentative efforts to determine whether clearly defined boundaries would be violated. He then entered the following session appearing irritable and enraged. He angrily shouted out that he was getting nowhere, and I was not giving him what he needed. He felt like he could kill me. He pulled out a knife and lunged, but in a way that made it easy and natural for me to hold and contain him. He then talked of the depth of his rage, of wanting me to feel the helplessness he experienced so frequently, and, most importantly, of my seeming to be blind to his powerful need to establish physical contact. He had been terrified that he would completely destroy the relationship, but felt compelled to create a situation in which he could be touched and held. He recalled his many veiled references to this need. When there was no response he thought it reflected my defensiveness to its homosexual implications. In the physical act with the knife, which on the surface appeared violent, there was never a sense of danger. It had a profound effect on both of us; it gave me a reason and a way to hold him, and it gave him the experience of feeling his infantile longings in a relationship. His early infantile trauma was re-created, though this time with a different outcome.

The patient had long known of his need to be held, and was afraid to state it openly for fear of it being heard as a homosexual invitation. When his indirect hints were not picked up, he began to feel I was too defensive to respond in this much-needed fashion. In retrospect, I had heard the patient's implied request as having either homosexual or defense-reenforcing implications, and I did have a countertransference-based blind spot. Because of the previous incidents in which the patient had clearly shown his need for well-defined boundaries and ground rules, and since he had a tendency to feel enveloped by an annihilating presence when they were ruptured or blurred, I had not considered these references as emanating from a striving for growth. Consequently, I did not think his seeking a concrete body ego experience of attachment had validity. Yet the need was so alive in the patient that he began to feel increasingly hopeless, and entered the session speaking from the accompanying rage and despair. It was a repetition in the present of a developmental trauma of his past. When he lunged with the knife, he folded himself in my arms and was held. At that moment he became aware that he was giving me an opportunity to overcome my defensiveness, and giving himself the experience of a new outcome to a life-threatening infantile dilemma. He sensed my receptiveness, expressed his infantile longing openly, and a momentary experience of healing resulted. The previously split-off infantile realm established contact with an object under conditions that were not traumatic or damaging. The influence of his internal saboteur was practically nonexistent so that the experience was not distorted; the infantile symbiotic dilemma, wherein what is needed destroys, resulted in a different ending than had occurred developmentally and had been anticipated in the present. A pathway of contact was established, which could be represented to serve as an intrapsychic bridge from a symbiotic relationship to negotiating self-differentiation.

In subsequent sessions this experience of an infantile attachment, along with the merger of his disparate worlds, was repeated often. He no longer required being physically held, since he could now be held by my recognition of his need and its meaning. The devil periodically resurfaced, but could be seen with perspective, had little power, and was not frightening. He was able to further his grasp of the destructive forces operating within him, and to allow the deep regression accompanying the process of healing. He was quite isolated for a time outside of his sessions, until the healing of the split became more solidified.

This treatment situation stressed the importance of maintaining a well-contained therapeutic framework, with clearly demarcated ground rules and boundaries, but also showed the necessity of retaining within it the flexibility to extend to the patient what was required to facilitate growth. In most areas I had been open to receiving the patient's unconscious perceptions of the qualities needed in the relationship, and had utilized them to aid in developing the contained space he required. This was amply validated by his overall reactions. However, when it came to the need for physical contact I clung to earlier evidence of the vital function of a firm framework. It is always a little frightening to consider moving in the direction of actual bodily contact. At that point the question was not so much whether this form of behavioral involvement was actually necesary, but the fact that it was not even considered.[5]

---

5. Allen (1956) discussed the problems arising with any decision to modify the structural arrangements of analysis, stressing that it must be determined according to the needs of the patient's personality structure. Frequently at such times the therapist struggles with introjected figures, but the criteria for such rule changes should include whether they favor a lifting of repression, the releasing of initiative, and the progressive reorganization of the personality. Intuition alone cannot be a safe guide, and the greatest difficulty in making the decision can lie in unanalyzed residues within the therapist. Each basic rule should be considerd solely in terms of freeing the sick patient from the bonds of unworkable human relationships.

Winnicott (1963) also addressed the need for flexibility in a slightly different manner. He believed that good psychoanalytic technique was in and of itself a corrective experience, but the corrective provision was never enough. The patient uses the therapist's failures, perhaps maneuvered by the patient; or the patient produces delusional transferences, and we then have to put up with being misunderstood. The operative factor is that the patient hates the therapist for the original failure that was outside the area of the infant's omnipotent control, but that is now staged in the transference. So in the end we succeed by failing the patient's way. In this manner regression can be in the service of the ego, if it is met by the therapist and turned into a new dependence. The patient then brings the bad external factor into the area of omnipotent control, and it becomes manageable by projection and introjection.

Gedo (1984) indicated that a shared language must evolve between patient and therapist, going beyond words. It must include paraverbal aspects of ordinary speech as well as the transmission of messages without verbalization. In addition to complex, dramatic enactments, meaningful information is often communicated through facial expression, gestures, or the autonomic activities of

This patient had given abundant evidence of how the therapeutic alliance was strengthened by my emotional responsiveness, spontaneity, and willingness to learn from and trust what was expressed from his split-off realm of infantile experience. It is often an extremely difficult task for a therapist to be receptive to, and resonate with, these intense and extremely regressive experiences, since they evoke internal reactions readily mobilizing defensiveness. In order to even think about the actuality of engaging in behavioral interventions, there must be an openness to take into account its potential effects, including some realistic concern about a blurring of therapeutic boundaries. The combination of justifiable concern and deeply regressive anxieties can inadvertently lead a therapist into rationalizing the use of rules of conduct, thereby undermining the containing influence of a firm but flexible treatment framework. Therefore, it is conceivable that had I heard and interpreted the message as one expressing a need for the concrete experience of an emotional attachment, knowing that it could only be communicated if there was a willingness to follow through, the direct physical component may not have been necessary. However, the combination of the patient's need and my defensive lack of recognition forced him into overcoming my resistance. It turned out to be the only way he could find to bridge the gap in his representational world.

Although it could not be determined with any measurable degree of certainty, the physical contact may have been the focal point of a number of dynamic events occurring simultaneously. The powerful internal impression of an enveloping, invasive, unempathic object, apparently modeled after the original trauma, had been utilized to serve a defensive purpose in maintaining the split. He may have required an actual body ego experience of contact, in which his autonomy was protected and he was not either enveloped or imposed upon. This would have made it imperative for me to provide the experience, but in a limited way and for a short period of time, since as soon as he could be held symbolically the behavioral mode would have to be relinquished. Were I to extend the contact beyond its appropriate purpose, the experience would be a repetition rather than a new solution.

---

physiological subsystems. When tension regulation is beyond the integrative capacity of an overstimulated patient, it is incumbent upon the therapist to patch over this deficit by assisting the patient with measures aimed at accomplishing this important task. Only treatment that successfully provides these essential functions will eventuate in the firm symbiotic bond that can form the basis for anything additional.

Similarly, my reluctance to engage in this potential boundary-blurring experience, though it did contain a defensive component, may also have been necessary. It gave the patient an opportunity to be an effective participant in the relationship. He was successful in making enough of an impact that it eventuated in the contact taking place, without damage to either party. These considerations were, of course, only retrospectively available. The patient's capacity to integrate split-off aspects of self experience following this event suggested that the totality of what had transpired was essential.

Contraindications for Engaging in a Leap with a Primitive Personality Who Shows the Effects of Severe Preverbal Traumas

The demand for actual behavioral contact may emanate from a split-off infantile world of experience that reflects the individual's striving for growth, but that fact in and of itself does not mean progress cannot be gained through a verbally symbolic mode of interaction. The unique meaning to each patient of modifying the framework must be assessed and taken into account, before deciding if such a move is indicated. The significant factors center around a therapist's willingness and ability to allow emotional responsiveness to enter the relationship, to be receptive to primitive projective identifications without having them elicit defensiveness, and to provide a containing influence within which new solutions to early infantile dilemmas can be represented.

Clinical Example

This was shown in the treatment of a seriously disturbed young adult woman, who had a number of schizophrenic breaks that required hospitalization at different periods of her life. She was convinced that she had to relive her infancy and be re-parented in order to be complete, and had spent years searching for a relationship that could provide the healing she knew was needed. She had seen a number of therapists in her attempt to find just the right one.

She was extremely bright and talented, and was very sensitive to others' weak spots. Characteristically, she would pressure a therapist into behaving defensively until it reached a point where she provoked a rejection and withdrew. When these efforts were interpreted to her as manipulative and controlling, she would submit to this perception, and after a time leave in despair of being properly understood. She continued her search for a therapist who could offer her the regressive experiences she felt were needed to be healed. She was looking for someone who was sensitive, firm, responsive, and open to learning in a relatively nondefensive fashion. She finally found one who met her conditions, and a firm connection was established. Over a six-year period she was actively encouraged to show her primitive rage so as to reach the inaccessible feelings of a helpless infant. She sensed that her therapist's active encouragement was defensive, reflecting an inability to tolerate a regression, and she was fearful that her therapist would be driven away. Despite feeling impelled to present a picture of herself that matched her therapist's expectations, finally in desperation she brought a gun to her session. It was irrelevant that it was a toy gun, for its intent was to show her therapist the feeling of helplessness that immobilized her. She put the gun to the therapist's head and demanded to be held. The therapist responded with a sensitive interpretation addressing the patient's underlying desire to be comforted; the patient then felt understood and contained, allowed her infantile yearnings to be experienced in the relationship, and could feel herself beginning to heal. But on the following day the therapist had a delayed reaction, became inordinately anxious, scheduled an appointment for the patient and directed her to bring a friend. In that session the therapist was also accompanied by a friend and told the patient, "I can no longer see you, you have overstepped my boundaries in a way that is unforgivable." The patient was then totally overcome; the next thing she recalled was being in a mental hospital. While there she overheard people talking about sending her to a state hospital, was able to communicate her need to see someone, and was referred to me.

Her subsequent treatment demonstrated the efficacy of utilizing sound psychoanalytic principles with serious psychic disturbances. It also pointed out the need for flexibility in adapting their application to be in accordance with the psychic organization of the patient. Following her first session she reported the following:

> I went to see my sister's therapist and she said it was amazing that in one hour she had gotten to know me better than she knew my sister in years. I had a very deep sore on my knee and was showing it to her. When I left her office I thought, "My sore isn't healing." I went to my apartment, went from room to room to turn on the lights,

they didn't go on; I felt frightened, and woke up disoriented and on the edge of losing contact.

This manifest dream reflected her awareness of a severe, deeply penetrating illness, symbolized by the sore on her knee. It was shown to a doctor and was not healing. The dream also pictured a separation from the doctor, along with an unsuccessful attempt to shed light upon her own private space, culminating in a high level of anxiety that extended into wakefulness and threatened her ability to remain in contact with the external world. The dream appeared to give expression to her search for therapeutic understanding, and to her anticipation of an empathic failure. The manifest content implicitly captured the position she was now in. This latest venture toward finding therapeutic help was questionable, she had to once again expose the depth of her disturbance, and when left to her own devices she was totally lost and overwhelmed.

In that initial session I had felt uncomfortable about what I could offer in a therapeutic relationship. I was also uneasy because I anticipated the potential for a malignant regression. The dream seemed to express her unconscious perception of my concern, and hinted at the devastating effects a lack of openness could present. Upon awakening from the dream she was in even greater danger, since the level of psychic structuralization required to construct the manifest dream was less effectively maintained as she entered a waking state. It was indicative that the mental structures underlying the dream were more advanced than those available to her when faced with adapting to the demands of the external world. Thus the construction and reporting of the dream suggested that there might be threads of healthy mental processes latently available. However, they appeared to be so vulnerable to destruction that they could be manifested only under circumstances in which there was no potential for narcissistic injury and no threat of an attachment to an object. These healthy processes would then most likely not be visible in a relationship. They were inadequately supported, highly unstable, and uanble to manage instinctual activity, the effects of impingements, or any adaptational demand.

Under the conditions of sleep she was able to utilize split-off good self-experience and threads of healthy functioning as a foundation for constructing the dream. This was probably possible because of the disengagement from the external world and more specifically from the threat of making an instinctual attachment. In this sense the structural organization behind the dream was much more advanced than was apparent while she was awake. It thereby hinted from the outset that although she exhibited evidence of a profound disorder, a firm, well-managed psycho-

ABANDONING THE SOUND PRINCIPLES

analytic framework might be most supportive to the containing forces in her personality. It further suggested that the integration of even very primitive infantile experiences might be accomplished within a communicative sphere, focusing exclusively upon interpretations. Her implied demands for active involvement might best be understood as reflecting an anxious concern that boundaries could be ruptured, re-creating early developmental traumas, at the same time that they expressed a yearning for a nontraumatic infantile attachment. Her ability to internalize and represent the experience might then bridge the gap of discontinuity in her internal world.

The patient then became involved in probing for the limits in the therapeutic relationship. She expressed her worry that I would be unable to tolerate her regression and respond in a way that she needed. There were many indirect references to the necessity for a firm framework, but also for an openness in receiving and processing very primitive projective identifications. She began to feel both hopeful and frightened, expressing a great deal of uncertainty as to whether she would be injured once again. She held a firm conviction that though she felt understood by me, the regressive attachment she required could be offered only by a woman.

With great intensity she asked if I would refer her to a woman—a female therapist—and convincingly described her reasons. She was apparently giving me an opportunity to send her away with the feeling that something good and constructive had been done. However, I thought she was tacitly asking if I was willing to receive and internalize regressive experiences that could very well be anxiety-arousing. I commented on this understanding of her question, and she made clear that she could not tolerate another mistake. It would be the source of her destruction. She then proceeded to outline the female therapist she was looking for, and in so doing defined the conditions she required to attain healing. It included warmth and sensitivity on a firm background of separateness, with the ability to enhance the autonomy of a helpless, clinging, and dependent infant. While talking about these requirements, infantile longings were aroused that activated a "black Mama" inside of her. This compelling internal presence drove her to urgently demand comfort and reassurance, accompanied by strong pressure for me to hold her lest she go crazy or kill herself.

Primitive non-neurotic transferences face a therapist with internalizing regressive psychic contents that may be disturbing, which increases the possibility of the therapist becoming lost, fearful, and unseeing. A subsequent breakdown in the therapeutic framework, although instigated by the patient, is the therapist's ultimate responsibility. The purpose of the basic psychoanalytic principles is to invite a patient to place all available psychic contents into the relationship, so the therapist can take responsibility for their management. The healthy processes at work in the patient serve as a guide toward determining the conditions of the treatment. When these growth-promoting forces are well differentiated, a relatively clear effective framework can be outlined.

In the more primitive personality, healthy strivings are not only limited and vulnerable but are also poorly differentiated. The manifestations of their activity are hard to discern, and determining what is in the patient and what is in the therapist is often blurred. The therapist's task is to metabolize these experiences and provide the differentiating influence that is missing and necessary. If the therapist's mode of functioning does not allow this interchange to take place the door is closed to the healing power of a benign regression. On the other hand, if the therapist is receptive to these undifferentiated experiences the door is open to both opportunity and mistake. It is crucial to be able to distinguish when a demand for direct contact is absolutely essential to enable symbolic processes to become viable and functional, and when such a demand reenforces a pathological defense, re-creates an infantile trauma, or has the effect of limiting the necessary regression. In one set of circumstances this form of involvement must transpire before the constructive influences of an unconsciously empathic interpretation can be utilized, whereas the other requires an appropriate interpretation in order to maintain the therapeutic properties of the relationship.

The differences center around the degree to which good self-experience, though split off and buried deep within the personality, has at least some continuity with other facets of psychic functioning. Most likely it is a reflection of some temporary or transient movement toward individuation, which had been established developmentally before the disruptive impact of splitting mechanisms came more forcefully into play. In those situations where there are virtually no mental impressions of good self-experience capable of being amplified by an interpretive mode of communication, words will only emphasize the distance and unavailability of a therapist, thereby intensifying a patient's despair. Conversely, when there has been even some small measure of continuity within the personality, a therapist's ability to stand on firm, separate ground—while consistently keeping the framework of the treatment intact and offering interpretations empathic with unconscious communications—is vital. This stance serves to strengthen limited strands of autonomous functioning and further the process of symbolization. An admixture of these two opposing psychic constellations can add to the confusion, and then it is the manner in which a therapist addresses the confusion that is critical.

The basic psychoanalytic principles as originally defined were attuned to the containing needs of individuals having fairly advanced levels of differentiation. When that degree of differentiation is not available, the application not the essence, of the principles must change. In order to discover the proper conditions for supporting a benign regression in primitively organized patients, it is essential that a therapist relinquish any defensive use of rules. At the same time, however, a well-contained therapeutic framework with clearly defined boundaries and ground rules is essential. Otherwise a rupture is created equivalent to the traumatic events of early development. It is reminiscent of the violations of psychological boundaries by nurturing figures, which are so prevalent in the history of narcissistic disorders. The most devastating aspect is the loss of trust in a relationship needed to foster constructive growth. A therapist's errors of commission, in not strengthening the experience of containment and in having impinging or overstimulating qualities when the patient has been led to expect otherwise, re-creates these developmental failures. Establishing pre-formed ground rules with non-neurotic individuals protects against invoking these kinds of errors, but it obstructs the free flow of projective identifications and prevents the internalization of much-needed information. In addition, the defensiveness embodied in such a position results in errors of *omission*, which in a silent and subtle way can be equally destructive.

In the case under discussion, I did not think the patient—despite her protests to the contrary—had to be physically held in order to heal the splits in the self. She did, of course, need to feel held by the words and emotional attitude of a caring figure. The viability of her symbolic functions could then be facilitated, allowing the destructive, defensively distorting forces raging within to become accessible to interpretive influence. I considered her infantile demand to be motivated by an internal saboteur, and consistently interpreted her attempt to enlist my participation in the destruction of her autonomy. I also reflected upon this being the only way she could test the trustability of the relationship. I actively encouraged her to hold on to the feelings that frightened her, and pointed out the various means she utilized to distract herself. In this way I was presenting my view of the autonomy-supporting responses that characterized the "woman" she had to find in a relationship.

She became more adamant in insisting she could not find what she needed with me. She felt she had to be touched by a woman who was a mother, and repeatedly expressed her conviction that a man couldn't possibly have such knowledge available. She worked hard at making me believe that the healing regressive experience she sought could only be found with a woman, and that my attitudes were admirable but ineffective. Yet there were brief moments of doubt about this, when she felt something important was happening inside of her. This was a very crucial period for she successfully instigated moments of uncertainty in me. I wondered at times if I was making a mistake, and considered the possibility and implications of following her directions. She so loudly portrayed touching as necessary for her survival as a total person that I began to waver.

Much support could be gained for leaning in this direction, both from previous experiences in which it had turned out to be an effective curative factor, and from readings in the literature where other clinicians faced with similar dilemmas had apparently responded helpfully in this way. Her symbolic processes were periodically nonfunctional or at best could function only in a limited fashion, and my interpretations appeared to have little effect at moments of profound regression when the intensity of her demand was at its height. In addition, the severity of her disorder seemed to point to a need for more active measures. In this case, however, a strong therapeutic alliance was almost continually present, and there did seem to be a silent background sense of safety. I was not at all convinced about the validity of her demand, and her vague feeling that something important was happening to her encouraged me to hold my interpretive posture.

The patient then had a series of somewhat obscure dreams in which she was lying on a couch but could recall nothing else. This made her think of why she couldn't use the couch: it was too distant, I would be disconnected from her, and she could get lost in an uncontrolled regression and end up in a hospital. It seemed too frightening to her to have me out of sight, for she felt she would lose all contact with the external world. Her words reminded me of statements I had heard as to why psychoanalytic treatment was contraindicated in the schizophrenias. I commented that I had an entirely different view of the couch—that I felt it would bring me much closer to her internal experiences, more in touch with the deeper parts of her; and that her present position of face-to-face contact felt like it was holding me at a distance where I was often out of touch with what was happening inside. In the following session she described feeling dizzy after she had left, as though she were spinning around with no thoughts to explain it. I remarked that I was reminded of our talk about the couch, which made me think she was spun around by my words toward looking at it in a different way. She then recalled a dream from the night before.

> I was on a couch and a woman was my analyst. I became smaller and smaller and was surprised I wasn't frightened and felt I was in the right hands.

The symbolic imagery of this manifest dream pictured the evolution of a profound regression under conditions of safety and containment. I heard it as a statement that my interventions were enabling the necessary movement toward a therapeutic symbiosis. Her defensive attempt to re-create a relationship based upon a pathological dependency seemed to have had a two pronged motive, first to protect and preserve a split-off realm of infantile experience, and second to test my ability to recognize and facilitate a growth-promoting infantile attachment. This situation suggested that my interpretive attitude was lessening the distortions produced by her internal saboteur, and echoing with her conditions for an adequate symbiosis. It looked like a benign regression was accelerating.

This was subsequently borne out in later sessions, when it became patently evident that she had found the right "woman" in me but could not completely allow the necessary regression until she was certain its significance was appreciated. She could move into the therapeutic symbiosis portrayed in the dream only if she was consistently shown by my interpretations that I had a grasp of how to "hold" her within the arms of an unconsciously empathic relationship. For her this meant maintaining the necessary and proper distance so as not to be impinging and overstimulating; not too close, which she experienced as enveloping, and not too distant, which she experienced as abandoning and depriving. Her loudly proclaimed need to be physically held, and specifically by a woman who was a mother, appeared to encompass the totality of her dilemma.

She did need to have a new experience of being held within a relationship, particularly in a way that could support and foster her autonomy and independence. Severe early preverbal traumas had created a gap in her mental functioning, which resulted in her being able to make attachments only in a pathologically dependent fashion, preventing her from integrating the impact of the trauma. Her latent resources had been vulnerable to destruction from even the slightest nuance of a lapse in empathy, because of the resonance with traumatic ruptures in the holding properties of a maternal relationship. These infantile traumas lurked as a silent, inarticulable but powerful background presence, and could not begin to be verbalized until the therapeutic relationship offered the sensitive "maternal holding" she required. She had to hope that the distorting defensive forces operating within and creating confusion, doubt, and the destruction of understanding, would be successfully internalized by me and returned to her in a form that she could use in fostering the regressive attachment she needed.

The Status of the Therapeutic Alliance: A Prerequisite for Considering a Leap

Webster defines the word *leap* as moving oneself from the ground by using one's leg muscles to spring or bound from one position to another. As used in this book, it is a metaphorical expression referring to the use of the therapist's self, in either some behavioral action or concrete expression of involvement, in order to provide an experience that makes it possible to bridge a gap in a patient's mental functioning that is unreachable by any other means. It implies that an area of firm, constructive contact has been established with the patient in one position, which then can serve as a point of leverage to propel the therapist into reaching an area of contact in another position. The ultimate goal is to unite the two points of contact. Therefore, it is imperative to carefully delineate the ground upon which contact is initially established, before it is in any way possible to even consider the slightest movement away from that ground—much less a leap into new and uncharted territory. The groundwork refers to an effective therapeutic alliance. Individuals with whom a leap should be considered are those who possess marked limitations in their ability to engage in a therapeutic interaction with the degree of confidence and trust required to construct a stable bond of mutual constructive purpose. Thus in most instances it takes a long period of arduous therapeutic work to develop a solid enough position for such an undertaking to be considered. Hence it is essential to have a clear view of what constitutes an effective therapeutic environment.

The manner in which the boundaries, ground rules, and conditions of the treatment are introduced must be gradually interwoven into a fabric that fits the unique therapeutic needs of each individual patient. The treatment framework provides a background of safety within which a therapist's interpretive interventions can be addressed to the unconscious significance of a patient's communications. To the extent that they are accurate and well timed, they are evocative to a patient's unconscious perception of what is needed to promote growth, thereby strengthening the therapeutic alliance. The therapist's management of the framework slowly recedes to occupy a silent presence of containment, as the influence of interpretive interventions rises into the ascendency.

When both parties are confronted with a regressive gap in the therapist's psychic functioning, so that interpretations cannot be effectively received, management of the framework assumes primacy. A variety of measures may then have to be introduced in order to produce the necessary experience of containment. These must clearly be validated and be consonant with sound treatment principles before being incorporated into what is now an extended treatment framework. Any elements that are resonant with a patient's deepest anxieties and most powerful unconscious experiences will tend to be highlighted, and the way in which they are woven in to ensure the therapeutic properties of the relationship adds an ever-expanding view of the patient's total personality. The vital information gleaned from a patient's response to the conditions of the treatment furthers a therapist's unconsciously empathic understanding, and it is within this context that the boundaries of the relationship are established.[6]

---

6. Winnicott (1960b) sought to explicate the developmental background upon which the holding properties of a therapeutic relationship are based. It includes the management of experiences that are inherent in existence and is a stage of absolute dependence, in which the infant cannot control what is done and can only gain profit or suffer disturbance in response to it. The mother's reliablity and empathy in meeting the child's physiological needs is most important and these functions are crystallized in the concept of holding. It protects from physiological insult, takes into account the infant's sensitivities and lack of knowledge of the existence of anything other than the self, and responds to the moment-to-moment dangers within the infant. It is the special form of loving in which ego organization is crucial, rather than instinctual gratification or object relationships. There are important parallels between this type of maternal care and the functioning of the therapist especially in the treatment of borderline and psychotic patients.

Bleger (1967) described the psychoanalytic situation as including all phenomena in the therapeutic relationship, both process and nonprocess. Nonprocess is the frame that is made up of constants within whose bounds the process of analysis takes place. The process can be examined only when the same constants are being kept up, and these silently maintained protective elements in the frame must ultimately be analyzed. The frame is part of the steady relationship with objects, out of which the ego is built; it has a strong basis in the bodily ego and early symbiosis between mother and child. It works as a bulwark that is fulfilled in the usual analysis in which there are no modifications in technique. The frame contains the symbiotic elements in the relationship acting as a support, and it is perceived only when it is incomplete, changes, or breaks.

3

Leaps and Empathic Responsiveness

Redressing the Necessary Imbalance in the Therapeutic Relationship: The Role of Empathy

Clinical Example

A 7-year-old boy, desperately seeking help for the terrifying thoughts that made the whole world appear dangerous, was guarded and agitated as he tried to communicate with me. He struggled to find a position in which he could feel comfortable enough to bare his innermost thoughts, but no matter where he placed himself he could not find the comfort he sought. He sat in an easy chair at the side of my desk, but from that angle he felt too small and insignificant and I seemed too large and imposing. It was impossible for him to think, much less speak. He then tried reversing his posture, and once again became fearful for this time he felt too high, too much on his own, and unsteady—while I looked too small, and in his eyes therefore too weak and helpless to offer the support he was seeking. Thus he continued to search for the position that would allow him to feel safe enough to articulate his concerns. Then one day I grasped the meaning of his internal dilemma. I did so by virtue of feeling what it was like to alternate between being small, inept, and ineffective in influencing a potential need-supplying object, and conversely to perceive that same need-supplying object as being incapable of receiving and aiding in the management of powerful emotional states. I allowed this feeling to surface, and was also able to fantasize what I would look like to the patient. I then integrated the information gleaned from the feeling and the fantasy into an interpretation that was couched in language resonant with the patient's unique style of communication. At this point I had recognized that the child's struggle to find a comfortable enough position in the relationship mirrored his efforts to attain the same end in his internal world.

The child responded to this recognition of his internal dilemma by revealing the content of his consciously held fears. He also presented derivative associations reflective of their unconscious significance, indicating that the relationship possessed the specific attributes necessary for therapeutic influence to evolve. At the end of the session he paused, became pensive, and in a very soft voice said, "My gosh, we're both the same size!" The way he experienced the change in the interaction was striking, in that both parties were seen as the same size only after a proper imbalance was established. He was allowing regressive sensations and experiences to fill him, thereby being smaller; whereas he received help from my being bigger through my ability to process his input and return it to him in a more integratable form. Thus his statement about being the same size captured the way in which the surface imbalance created by a therapist's warranted authority is redressed.

My previous interpretive comments to the patient had come from an objective, intellectual perspective, emotionally distant from the experience in the interaction. My words had been infused with theoretical constructs, and were based upon an internal resistance to the revival of unwelcome infantile feelings and memories of helplessness. Although these interpretive remarks may have had a dimension of correctness in their content, they were not empathic to the immediacy of what was taking place.

A therapist's authority is based upon an accurate, sensitive reading of the patient's unconscious communications. This includes the unconscious perception of what is required of the therapeutic relationship to promote growth, which gives the ultimate authority to the patient. No position felt right to this child until my empathic responses led me to an accurate interpretation of the unconscious meaning of his distress. In this case words alone could accomplish it, but in other situations an empathic response may be expressed through the management of the ground rules and boundaries of the relationship, through appropriate silences, or even at times through noninterpretive interventions. The conscious imbalance in the therapeutic relationship, necessary to facilitate the free flow of projective identifications that fuel the transference, has to be balanced by a therapist being guided by the patient's unconscious perception of what is needed to promote growth. Both parties are then of the same size.

The Significance of a Therapist's Subjective Responses in Determining the Therapeutic Needs of Primitive Personalities

There are some narcissistic individuals for whom the task of establishing the proper conditions for a well-contained therapeutic framework, and a clear set of ground rules and boundaries, is extremely confusing. With these more primitively organized personalities the activity of unconscious perceptions emanates from a realm of psychological experience that is basically inaccessible and excessively vulnerable. Such patients often find it dangerous to express the psychic contents occupying this sector of their internal world, because the act of communicating elicits a profound regression and could result in destruction if the proper conditions are not present. Therefore, a therapist's primary beacon light for guidance is carefully guarded and protected by a defensive force devoted to successfully obscuring the nature of these required conditions. A picture could then emerge that was both inaccurate and disruptive, as an effort is exerted to enlist the therapist's participation in the destruction of the meaning of the relationship. A therapist must be capable of receiving and processing the patient's input, and of recognizing the distortions, in order to locate a pathway to the proper conditions. Subjective responses may play a greater than usual role in determining what is called for, although they must be consistently exposed to a process of self-examination.

Good intentions and compassion can motivate a therapist to behave in ways that do something for a patient—believing that it will be of benefit—but they can also lead a therapist far astray. It is vital to include an overall understanding of the individual's disturbance and difficulties and how they are manifested, so decisions can be based upon therapeutic needs beyond the urgency of a given moment. A therapist's subjective responses are crucial in making the assessment. However, those reflecting an empathic appreciation of the patient's unconscious communications must be clearly distinguished from conflicted or regressive countertransference reactions. A therapist's emotional responses can operate either as an obstacle to effective integrative work, or be the greatest of assets. From an empathic stance they are not only a source of information but also provide guidance for being able to act judiciously. By contrast, emotions arising out of conflict and defensiveness prevent expansion of the therapist's knowledge of the patient. When acted out they operate as an impediment to developmental progression.[1]

It is impossible for a therapist to sustain adequate functioning while excluding emotional responses. Such responses are necessary for a full understanding of the patient's internal world, and are an integral part of the therapeutic properties of the relationship. The therapist's task is to contain feelings arising out of intrapsychic conflict, narcissistic needs, or regressive identifications until they can be filtered out enough for empathic resonance to be manifested. Conversely, it is important to recognize when empathic resonance activates conflicted countertransference-based reactions. Inappropriate emotions are associated with defensiveness, creating "blind spots" that stand in the way of identifying the specific interpersonal qualities essential for facilitating a benign regression.

---

1. Beres and Arlow (1974) delineated the role of fantasy and identification in empathy when ideas in the form of conscious fantasies present themselves to a therapist as inner perceptions. Beyond the therapist's efforts to cognitively organize the patient's data there may be an immediate noncognitive sharing with the patient of a fantasy, the basis of which the therapist is initially unaware, which then enables comprehension of the derivatives of the unconscious fantasies expressed in the patient's material. The therapist's fantasies in response to the patient's associations may represent shared unconscious fantasies, which is an aspect of empathy. Empathy is the projection of one person's personality into that of another in order to understand him better. It can be traced back to the infant's sensitive response to the mother's affective state, and can tend to be more primitive and archaic. However, being with a patient, for all its implications of human warmth, may be detrimental to therapeutic process. Being with a patient is not necessarily empathic, and may indicate countertransference projection or a merging form of identification that can interfere with therapeutic work.

Bettelheim (1974) discussed the difference between projection and empathy. Projection is essentially self-centered, whereas empathy, through drawing on one's inner experience, is centered on the other. In projection one sees one's self in the other; in empathy, one feels the other in one's self. This is not total as in introjection but only as the other is feeling at the moment. Approaching the work by understanding the patient's psychological problems results in decisions based on what is needed in the long run rather than the moment, allowing compassion to be more effectively channeled.

Often the same attributes that make it possible for a therapist to be receptive to primitive projective identifications expose the relationship to a blurring of boundaries and destructive deviations, and it may be a fine line from one to the other. When this dilemma evokes the therapist's withdrawal, this response obviates against effective therapeutic influence. In not being open to internalizing primitive projective identifications, a therapist may construct a firm but inflexible therapeutic framework. With some this can be destructive and even life-threatening; with others it may lead to solidifying an adaptive style based on conformity. Years may then be spent strengthening an empty, depleted realm of functioning, deepening the despair of finding a much-needed new solution. If a therapist presents an unyielding barrier to the experiences required for healing to take place, a patient may be impelled to go to extremes trying to penetrate the wall of defensiveness in order to make meaningful contact. A therapist has to engage in a continuous process of self-examination so as to maintain a clear focus of attention upon a patient's therapeutic needs. This involves an ability to allow regressive fantasies and experiences to surface, to re-invoke advanced psychic functions that have been suspended in order to achieve this internal state, and to utilize the ensuing understanding to come closer to the patient's experience of the moment.

The conditions of the treatment environment are managed and regulated by the therapist, and the manner in which they are presented reflects the therapist's healthy or pathological modes of functioning. Some aspects are fixed and unyielding, while others are flexible. The determination of which are fixed and which are flexible is an area that reveals the therapist's mode of operation. It is a conveyor of unconscious motivations, and is a powerful stimulus to a patient's unconscious perceptions. The posture of a therapist will of necessity vary with each patient, since it must be attuned to how the relationship is unconsciously perceived. An ideal therapist's responses are predicated upon an empathic reading of the patient's unconscious perceptions, and they direct attention to the manifestations of transference distortions or of developmental deficits, defects, and arrests. An action-discharge therapist's responses are based upon an inability to contain and process the stimuli of the interaction; this mobilizes the need to engage in defense-reenforcing forms of behavior, to gratify a patient's regressive cravings, or to unnecessarily modify the appropriate boundaries or ground rules of the treatment. A distantly observing therapist's responses are based upon a withdrawal from the impact of the relationship, and they will be primarily intellectual in nature. It is important for a therapist to delineate as clearly as possible the indications of ideal functioning, because an ideal response for one patient may be an action-discharge response for another or a distancing response for still another. The principles of analytic anonymity and neutrality do not mean that the therapist's personality is not revealed, but that it is utilized in offering empathic responsiveness to a patient's unconscious communications.

An ideal therapist is consistently engaged in monitoring internal reactions, is receptive to the derivatives and other signs expressive of unconscious mental activity, and is capable of recognizing the processes involved in an ideal, an action-discharge, and a defensive stance. The loss of ideal functioning will be revealed by the specific nature of the available derivatives, accompanied by a blending of regressive fantasies and memories with defensive configurations. Momentary lapses are inevitable, but they must serve as a spur for self-analytic work. The handling of the therapeutic framework is guided by the basic psychoanalytic principles and gives expression to the therapist's personality. It is much like the outline of a picture, with the therapist regulating the boundary of the relationship. It is a boundary because the personality of the therapist differs from that of the patient. The manner in which the basic principles of psychoanalysis are applied will then change as continually progressive levels of psychic organization are manifested by a patient. Ultimately, the conditions evolve into approximating the more familiar psychoanalytic model when addressing the neurotically structured personality.

Engaging in a Leap on the Basis of an Empathic Subjective Response to a Nonverbal Communication

A therapist's internal reactions must be examined so as to identify those emotional responses that are based upon empathy, but the input of a patient is crucial for attaining validation. This becomes especially relevant when a patient is either unable to communicate, or when the material necessary for achieving validation is not articulable. The therapist may then be confronted with emotions and fantasies carrying the attributes of an empathic response, but dictating the introduction of actions and behavior that from a surface view may appear to alter the conditions of a secure therapeutic framework. It is not until the patient's overall reactions have been fully assessed that a determination can be made of its appropriateness.

Clinical Example

This was demonstrated in the treatment of a 3½-year-old autistic child. In the early sessions he paced the room endlessly, posturing and gesturing as he did so, and stopped only to engage in some self-stimulating activity. He seemingly paid no attention to my words, and no language was discernible although incomprehensible vocalizations were periodically expressed. The only indication of any experience having meaning for him was his apparent terror of my physical proximity. He often indicated through his actions that he needed space, and when it was narrowed he gave the impression of being panic-stricken. He did, however, enter the office willingly, and appeared to be reassured when I sat myself at a distance.

The first evidence of some communicative intent in his behavior emerged as he ran around the office touching all of the reachable objects, sensitively determining which could be damaged, and proceeding to occupy himself specifically with just those. He quickly identified which ones were off limits and which were not. He had no words and communicated this entirely through his actions. He climbed on a table (that was O.K.) and rapidly pushed at a lamp (that was not); he went on in this fashion until he had tested each item in the room. He then went from one object to another that was not O.K., and I struggled with the question of how to communicate with him and make myself understood. His behavior with the forbidden objects posed some risk to himself, as well as potential unwanted damage to my belongings. I wanted to hold him, but at the same time to allow him the space for his behavioral communications to be expressed. His actions were understood by me as expressing a need to be held and contained, and I wondered if my actions were the only means of doing so. In addition, I had a serious concern as to what it would mean for him to be physically touched, since he had already indicated how frightened he was of that eventuality. Although he identified through my words what was and wasn't O.K., and appeared aware of and responsive to this verbal communication, it did not seem that an interpretive intervention would possess the symbolic meaning capable of evoking body ego experiences of containment.

I had little idea of what powerful internal experiences were occupying his mind, much less how to offer a verbal interpretation capable of facilitating his ability to communicate. I voiced my best understanding of his behavior by referring to his need to be held, but he did not respond in any noticeable way at that moment. However, when he came to his next appointment he put his head in the office and then turned to run out. He ran to a plant in the hallway, pulled off its leaves, and began a high-pitched screeching. The sound elicited the image of a young, helpless victim being confronted with imminent destruction. He ran back to the office and poked his head in the door. Aware of an important communication taking place, I started to talk; at my first word he bolted out, only to repeat his behavior. His facial expression and body mannerisms became increasingly wild in appearance. I remained silent; he put his head in the door once again and this time beckoned me to follow. When I did not do so immediately he ran to the plant, pulled off more leaves, and screeched again. I got out of my chair to follow him and just as I arrived he placed his hand on the stem while looking directly into my eyes. Utilizing the fantasy aroused by his screech, I spoke of his seeming to ask whether I wanted him to kill the plant. I added that it looked as though he felt if I didn't come to hold him and protect the plant I might also stand by and let him die. His reaction was startling. He threw his arms around my neck, buried his head in my shoulder, and molded his body closely.

The conditions that constitute a growth-promoting therapeutic environment are unique for every individual. In some measure what constitutes an ideal, action-discharge, or distantly observing response is determined by how a given patient is affected. With this as a background the manner in which the basic psychoanalytic principles are applied will depend upon the contents of the deeper layers of a patient's personality, the predominant organization of pathological defenses, and a therapist's capacity for empathy with unconscious communications. A therapist must be able to remain in a well-contained introjective mode long enough to gain a grasp of the patient's unconscious communications, and then gradually shift to a projective mode as interpretive interventions are formulated and expressed. In an introjective mode a therapist is occupied with internalizing a patient's productions, intermingled with and associatively connected to memories, fantasies, and derivatives accompanying the process of free-floating attention. During the shift to a projective mode these mental contents are exposed to the therapist's secondary process thinking, in order to monitor their readiness for integration and synthesis. In a projective mode a therapist's attention is concentrated upon formulating and expressing an interpretation that is derived from a patient's unconscious communications, and that is consonant with the patient's demonstrated capacity to utilize the intervention constructively. However, there are situations in which an empathic response cannot be presented in the form of a verbal interpretation, since the patient's capacity to function in that symbolic modality has either not developed or is seriously enough interfered with as to be inaccessible. With the autistic child under discussion, for example, when I was hesitant to follow his direction and instead began to talk, he could only run out, pull on the plant, and screech.

A therapist must be in an introjective mode for the stimuli being presented to be internalized. A patient's input can then resonate with parallel memory traces and fantasies, after which what is experienced can be exposed to more advanced integrative functions in order to achieve the necessary understanding to find an appropriate intervention. There are many clues for ascertaining whether a patient's productions are eliciting defensiveness or provoking action-discharge modes of interacting. The shift into a projective mode is generally gradual, and is accompanied by an emerging and deepening grasp of what is implicit in communications rather than what is explicit. If the shift into a projective mode is sudden, abrupt, or associated with a sense of urgency or compulsion, this is indicative that a patient's communications are not being effectively processed.

I was in an introjective mode, letting the child's behavior reach me, and filled with memories and fantasies involving the similar theme of a young infant in distress. The screeching noise evoked an image of a child being threatened with destruction, crying out for its life. The screech followed his pulling leaves from a plant, which seemed to verify my image. The patient's behavior, however, indicated that I was functioning in a distantly observing fashion, and further implied that he perceived my behavior as having destructive intent. I understood his behavior as expressing a conviction that making an attachment exposed him to destruction, and that he needed something from me to feel safe. My first attempt at offering interpretive words, without an accompanying action, seemed to be experienced by him as distant and unempathic. I then shifted my posture and followed his lead, while conveying my understanding in both actions and words.

The time I took to process his input—for I did not immediately respond to his door behavior—created a space perceived by him as dangerous. Although he obviously felt threatened I thought it was important not to interfere with this moment, by either being unwilling or unable to allow myself to be experienced as destructive. If I moved quickly it might very well have been averted. This time lapse, which was necessary to formulate a therapeutic response, was seemingly experienced by the patient as having murderous intent. This gave expression to what could be considered as a manifestation of an extremely primitive transference. The combination of my willingness to act on his behalf and my words expressing how I understood his behavior had a positive influence, as a consequence of which he made direct physical contact. It seemed to evoke a feeling of containment, since he could permit himself to be held closely. In all likelihood my intervention possessed the qualities of a good object and the body ego experience of molding himself to me was registered and represented, because shortly thereafter he spoke his first communicative words. Apparently my understanding had been conveyed in a modality he could internalize, so that my concrete action functioned much like an interpretation.[2]

---

2. Alexander (1954) underlined the importance of the therapist behaving in ways that are not reminiscent of the earlier experiences that have contributed to the patient's pathology, in order for interventions to be usefully received. If the therapist can control the more subtle manifestations of countertransference and maintain an objective, helpful attitude, he can adopt the principle of contrast in which he behaves in a manner opposite to the behavior in the original situation.

Kanzer (1961) considered the patient's ability to verbalize thoughts to be a sign of available integrative capacities, which may be limited for a number of reasons. Nonverbal communications therefore play an important part in a therapeutic interaction, and the ground rules of analysis operate as nonverbal communications from the therapist that ultimately contribute to the use of interpreta-

Contact must be established in a relationship for therapeutic influence to be effective, and the basic psychoanalytic principles give direction to the manner in which this crucial factor can be carried out. With this patient my immobility was experienced as a threat, and had it been sustained it would have been unempathic. An ideal posture required an empathic response expressed through a concrete action.

Unconsciously Empathic Responsiveness and the Introduction of a Leap

A therapist's empathic responses to a patient's internal experiences are in most instances a source of creativity, but at the same time

---

tion. Interpretation and noninterpretive interventions occur along a continuum, and are introduced to be consonant with the patient's therapeutic needs. The idiom of the patient varies not only with his own character structure but with the dispositions of the therapist, and the therapist's capacity for empathy is especially important.

Balint (1968) noted how inequalities between patient and therapist must be reduced to better the chances of a benign regression. At such moments, since for some regressed patients words are experienced as disturbing impositions, the therapist's attitude and behavior assume predominance.

Little (1981) described the total and complete responsibility a therapist must take for responses to a patient, even though they arise from unconscious processes. The responsibility can be delegated or shared, but the decisions as to how and when are the therapist's. There are also many patients for whom any kind of delegation is extremely difficult and often impossible. It is here that the therapist's responsibility can be seen most clearly, and management is most important. Every patient needs at some point to become aware of the responsibility the therapist is taking. Stability in analysis depends upon it, and the patient's ultimate capacity for taking his own responsibility depends upon having a reliably responsible person with whom to identify. Eventually the form it takes has to be verbal and interpretive, but an object can have an effect like an interpretation and be linked later when the capacity to use symbols has been far enough developed.

Joseph (1983) noted the way patients who have reached the depressive position are able to use understanding, compared with patients who are in a paranoid-schizoid position. In the latter, understanding is avoided by splitting and projection, and attempting unconsciously to draw the therapist into a type of acting out in the transference. It is important for the therapist to listen to the patient in terms of the position from which he is operating, so that contact can be achieved, and with it real understanding as opposed to subtle acting out and pseudo-understanding.

they may elicit defensive opposition that interferes with its expression. The arousal of regressive experiences has the potential of expanding a therapist's perspective as well as the potential of activating infantile conflicts.[3] A therapist's ability to know a patient's internal world can be enhanced by these affect-laden subjective responses; this in turn broadens and deepens the range of therapeutic interventions that can be offered. Sometimes an otherwise unobtainable and effective pathway to understanding can be provided, particularly when it involves rearranging or altering elements already built into an established treatment framework.

Clinical Example

This was shown in the treatment of an 11-year-old girl. She was originally referred because of her family's concern about her lying and stealing, which she steadfastly refused to acknowledge. Her biological mother had died of cancer when she was 6 years of age, and she had been adopted by her present family. Her mother had selected this family prior to her death, because she believed her daughter would be well taken care of by them. The patient had two older sisters who were married and living independent lives at the time of their mother's death. This child had been close to her mother, participated in her care during the terminal phase of her illness, and lived with the imminence of the loss for some time. Her adopted family had been members of her mother's church and were

---

3. Stone (1961) considered countertransference to be an integral part of all good analytic work, and acknowledged that it was difficult to know where the usefulness of an unanalyzed reaction would end and difficulties begin. Countertransference is an affirmative instrument facilitating perception, and must always be included in the understanding of a therapist's technique.

Bettelheim (1974) referred to empathy as an oscillating movement from primary process thinking and feeling to an integration of these feelings, in order to come closer to the core of the other's experience of the moment. In order to mature emotionally, children must identify with characteristics they do not as yet possess but wish to acquire. When a therapist identifies with the immature parts of a patient it leads to a stalemate, since the immature person cannot relinquish those parts which are the essence of the adult person's attachment. Such identifications represent an immature object choice by the adult, narcissistically pleasing but not suitable for a constructive relationship. Only those whose commitment is to supply the patient with something that is missing succeed in helping him to achieve autonomy.

respected for their warmth, sensitivity, and high moral values. The patient then entered a new family with two boys, ages 4 and 2, who were cherished and idealized by the parents.

After a brief period of time, during which she appeared cheerful and animated, difficulties began to emerge. The parents experienced her as greedy, determined to have her way, and erupting in either overt temper outbursts or silent pouting whenever she was thwarted. She complained about injustices, and confronted her new parents with unacceptable behaviors. She was sloppy and undisciplined, and when corrected she would cry about being unloved and unfairly treated. Although they understood her behavior as emanating from the death of her mother, both parents began to feel more and more helpless in their efforts to form an attachment to her. There were periods of time when she would appear warm, friendly, and charming, and at such moments the parents would reassure themselves that in time she would be more incorporated within their family; but she would always revert to her former negative behavior. In the year preceding her treatment they had discovered some valuables missing. This occurred more frequently; money would disappear, and several missing articles were found in her bedroom. When faced with evidence she denied having anything to do with it, and was hurt at their refusal to trust her. This was the last straw for both parents, who placed a high value on truthfulness and trust; it instigated their decision to seek help, which represented a narcissistic blow to them. She in turn was eager to see a therapist, for she was quite troubled about herself.

In the beginning almost all of her thoughts, fantasies, and feelings centered around the themes of the pain involved with the loss of an attachment, or the anxious anticipation and excitement in forming a new one. Like a broken record in her mind, it occupied her both awake and asleep. She readily recognized the connection to the loss of her mother at age 6, and also to the emotional losses she had experienced at an earlier age. At first she spoke with intensity about the resentment she felt at her parents' restrictive attitudes, their inability to trust her, and their blindness to the various flaws she saw so clearly in her adoptive brothers. The hostility she expressed only barely concealed the underlying hunger to be loved and approved of, and served to guard her vulnerability were she to openly acknowledge their importance to her. She slowly began to recognize the impact of moving from where she had been the center of her mother's universe and yet was unable to hold onto her, to a world in which she was a disconnected outsider with others trying in vain to hold onto her. She entered the therapeutic relationship by re-creating her original world, looking to me as the mother she had once lost and now had rediscovered. Much of the impetus for therapeutic work rested on this silent background, which would rise to the forefront only when exploring her extreme reactions to inevitable separations, silences, or occasional empathic lapses. It was through these transference experiences that she came to fully appreciate the significance of her relationship with her biological mother, the deeply ingrained need to protect and maintain a positive image, and her fear of expressing any aggression.

Mourning the loss of her mother became an active, viable process within her, and she found herself more receptive to forming an attachment to her present parents and especially her adoptive mother. Her sessions were then filled with the constant pain she experienced when, upon reaching out to her, she was met with open contempt, rejection, and penetrating criticisms concerning her dishonesty and stealing. She could think of nothing else. My attempts to explore the meaning of the tenacity of this internal state, and its linkage to unrecognized aspects of the transference, were all received but did not elicit any new material or revelatory information. Her explanation was that she felt so impacted upon by the impenetrability of her parents' attitudes about her that she could not proceed into any internal exploration as long as it persisted. It was not that she didn't want to or that she didn't sense there was much more going on inside of her that could usefully be expressed or understood, it was more that these events in her external life were so imposing that her mind was totally involved with them.

After some time I began to imagine the entire family within the office as she spoke, and could visualize the patient's total inability to get through the armor of defensiveness that surrounded each family member. I wondered if it reflected some budding awareness on my part of a wall of my defensiveness that she was unable to penetrate. The imaginative internal picture expanded to include me as a participant in the gathering, pointing out the defensiveness much as I had just done with myself, only to meet a flurry of objections from the fantasied family members that I was approaching it in the wrong way. The fantasy shifted to playing a game with all family members, in which their fixed attributes were mirrored in a way that made their defensiveness unmistakable. The sense of humor I knew each family member possessed became a force that overcame the barriers. At precisely this point the patient interrupted my reverie. She had noted my preoccupation and asked what I was thinking. I told her I was imagining her family meeting together with us to try and help them all communicate more freely, and she immediately became excited about the idea.

She remembered being concerned earlier that I might reveal personal information to her parents, particularly about her relationship with her original mother. However, the thought of meeting to talk exclusively about her current family interrelationships felt exactly right to her. At that moment I conceived of an idea, which I conveyed to her, of inviting her family to come in and play a game in which they all had to secretly decide whether they could be a truth-teller or a liar. I would be the only one to know which was which, and by a series of questions each was to determine the identity of the others. The winner would be the one who was most successful in correctly naming the liars and the truth-tellers. The patient was delighted with the idea. I called the family, explaining that I would like them to come in to play a game. They were intrigued and curious, agreed to participate, and the meeting was scheduled.

The session itself was striking. After an initial period of awkwardness they all eagerly entered into the spirit of the game. Each member wrote on a slip of paper whether he or she would be a truth-teller or liar, and gave the papers to me; they then asked each other questions and from the answers they determined what decisions to make. The game was played twice, for on the first go-around everybody won. They knew exactly what questions to ask that would reveal whether the respondent was telling the truth or lying, based upon their knowledge of the individual's likes and dislikes. On the second go-around there was an additional rule. Each member always had the option of answering a question with "I don't know." This could either fool the asker into believing that the answer was designed to hide the truth, or conversely to make one think it was correct. The knowledge of specific characteristics as a source of information was thereby eliminated.

This time everyone became acutely aware of the impossibility of determining accurate answers. All had to simply guess. It turned out that the patient won easily by basing her guesses on her reading of an attitude or tone of voice. There was a short silence as the game ended, and the parents wondered if there was anything else I wanted to discuss. I said there wasn't, but the youngest brother tearfully stated there was something he wanted to say. He then hesitantly poured out a confession of having been responsible for the stolen items. He had placed some of these among the patient's belongings, and had harbored this guilty secret for a long time. The patient ran over to hug her little brother, as everyone was stunned by his revelation. The parents reacted at first with chagrin, and then with some sensitive, concerned questions to him as to why he had done it. They were shocked by his statement that he knew the patient would be blamed. The meeting ended with the various family members talking rapidly to each other, expressing in one way or another how shook up they all felt by what had happened.

The experience of having me intervene on her behalf had an immediate, positive influence. Although there continued to be short periods of time when she felt closed out by her family, this no longer occupied her attention in the same way. She was able to explore the significance of her preoccupation, and to recognize how much it echoed with having been closed off from contact with her mother particularly during the last years of her illness. This was also silently at work in the therapeutic relationship. She felt all along that she had been making an indirect appeal to me to understand her plight and call it to the attention of the others, just as she had cried out to an unhearing mother in the past. She now had available an actual experience that aided her in discriminating between the feelings emanating from repressed infantile experiences, and the circumstances she was engaged with in her everyday life. In subsequent sessions there was no further indication of any need to alter the treatment framework.

Whether the lack of therapeutic movement would eventually have been alleviated through my interpretive understanding of the unconscious forces at work, and especially its transference implications, is, of course, impossible to ascertain. The strength of the therapeutic alliance would suggest that had I been capable of interpreting the unconscious meaning of her appeal for help, it would have been enough to facilitate ongoing progression. However, there was also a hint that she needed some actual experience of my acting on her behalf before she could go on. My unconsciously empathic response, translated into a meeting with the family that addressed the powerful forces at work impinging upon the patient's growth, added a very strong dimension of positive support to both her internal and external world. It did point out the importance of leaving room for creative interventions within the established framework of a therapeutic situation.

Such measures must always be considered, but their potential for disrupting the containing influence of the framework must also be kept in mind. When a therapist's interventions modify or deviate from the well-established ground rules, boundaries, and conditions of a psychoanalytic treatment situation, in some measure it serves to strengthen a defensive posture. However, not all defenses are pathological, and it is crucial to remain open toward assessing when or if the framework can be extended to reach otherwise unavailable traumatic infantile experiences or developmental deficits, defects, and arrests. A question can be raised as to whether such interventions can be considered psychoanalytic, for in all of their surface appearances they are not, and it is untenable to base the determination on the ends justifying the means. Yet although the interventions encompassed in a leap are outside of the ground rules, boundaries, and conditions of a psychoanalytically conducted relationship, if they facilitate the integration of what is otherwise unreachable it would be antithetical to psychoanalytic principles to refuse to consider them.

An Infantile Trauma Dictating the Necessity of a Leap, and the Importance of the Therapist's Subjective Response

Empathy and countertransference incorporate an affective component that can either foster or obstruct therapeutic progress. Both offer a potential pathway for a deeper understanding of the hidden and most significant aspects of a patient's internal life.[4] It is part and parcel of a therapist's function to engage in a constant internal dialogue, in order to distinguish between the empathic and counter-

---

4. Wolf (1983a) depicted the way in which prolonged empathic immersion into the mental life of another yields introspective data just as reliable as the extrospective data that we depend on in ordering our daily lives. Although empathic understanding can be put in the service of resistance, sooner or later any therapist who is willing to listen with prolonged empathic immersion will apprehend the same introspective data. It is what the therapist does with it that depends upon a theoretical framework, which then guides how it is processed into an intervention.

Basch (1983) made note of the assumption that others resemble us sufficiently that we may attribute feelings, emotions, characteristics, and attitudes to them that we would have had under similar circumstances. He felt it should not be thought of as a projection, but as a normal function, since projection is defensive and unconscious. Generalization is a normal part of cognition in which the knowledge of the process of attribution is not lost.

Berger (1987) emphasized how a therapist pays close attention to inner experiences on the assumption that personal imagery, emotions, and visceral sensations have been activated by the patient's inner state. The therapist can then reach for available aspects within, which may involve archaic, painful, and usually unrecognized emotions and conflicts.

transference-based facets of affective experience. Impositions, projections, and idiosyncratic personal reactions have to be consistently filtered out to keep from impacting on a patient's transferences. Ultimately, it leads to interpretive interventions that are empathic with the unconscious meaning of a patient's productions. On some occasions a therapist's empathic response to a lack of therapeutic movement, to manifestations of deficits in psychic functioning, or to hearing an unconscious appeal for help in gaining access to otherwise inarticulable psychic content, may dictate the introduction of actions or behavior seemingly in opposition to a well-contained therapeutic framework. These interventions, though noninterpretive in nature, are designed to enable the inclusion of an essential experience within the growth-promoting attributes of the therapeutic interaction.

Almost invariably when this situation arises there is something about the interaction that is resonating with an infantile or preverbal trauma, or is making an impossible demand by requiring the use of psychic functions that have not yet developed. Thus the conditions of the relationship serve to prevent the integration of warded-off psychic content. The task is to create a framework, consonant with sound psychoanalytic principles, eliminating the particular component echoing with deficits or traumas until the source of the trouble is identified. Difficulty is encountered when the only available material comes from the patient's conscious directions. In the absence of any demonstrable evidence of an unconscious motive, a therapist can be guided only by whatever the patient has to offer in conjunction with the empathic or intuitive responses that it evokes.

Clinical Example

This problem was exemplified in the treatment of a 7-year-old girl who was originally referred because of her school's and her parents' concern over her compulsive masturbatory activity. She came to her sessions reluctantly, each time hesitantly entering with a sullen, pouting expression on her face. The only communications she offered were angry monosyllabic protests against coming to her appointments, interspersed with occasional denials of having any feelings whatsoever. Whenever I spoke, whether it was to wonder about the meaning of her attitude or to ask a question in order to gain some understanding of what was happening, her response was to look agitated and to forcibly withdraw her body back into her chair. At the same time she seemed tense and restless as if she could hardly bear to hold herself in this immobilized position.

I was puzzled in trying to find a way to shape the environment in order to create an atmosphere of safety, since she appeared threatened by whatever meaning the current circumstances had for her. Any attempt to interpret her anxiety was rebuffed by this outwardly hostile attitude. It was therefore somewhat surprising when I suggested it might be best to postpone the idea of meeting until she felt more ready to engage in the experience, and she emphatically shook her head *no*. I remarked that this was a very helpful piece of information, because it told me that she was communicating something extremely important in her attitude. I added that it seemed to be the only way she could show me what she meant, and I would try to understand. A faint smile crossed her lips, which then quickly disappeared, and her previous demeanor once again surfaced.

In spite of the overt absence of openly verbal communications, and the obvious barrier preventing a free flow of therapeutic dialogue, the emotional atmosphere was neither frustrating nor adversarial. However, with each passing session her restlessness and agitation increased. She could no longer stay in one place, and she began to pace in a manner that seemed designed to discharge tension. She finally turned to me and with an exasperated tone blurted out, "Do we have to stay in this room?" This was her first spontaneous utterance, and it had within it the potential for a multiplicity of implied meanings, but she seemed to demand an immediate reply. Tacitly, it suggested that at some level she felt controlled by me. Some as yet unclear motive was pushing her to give me a direction, yet I had no idea of what wishes or desires underlied it and she seemed to anticipate that my agenda would take precedence. These were all matters that could be determined only by a process of inner exploration. However, up to this point at least she could only react negatively to such a process, as my efforts to encourage introspection always seemed to mobilize some powerful internal force and strengthen her defensive posture.

Her protesting question made me realize just how much the conditions of the treatment had been established by me without her participation. Now there was an opportunity for both of us to shape the framework to be in accord with what was necessary to promote growth. I wanted to communicate this to her in a simple fashion, and to underscore that it did not necessarily mean acceding to her consciously expressed wishes or demands. I was hoping to introduce a way of listening for the derivatives of her unconscious perceptions of what was needed, and thereby be guided to an appropriate answer. However, my intuitive feeling was that she could not wait too long, could not tolerate ambiguity, and that she had to feel my support of her autonomous, independent gesture. In addition, I had periodically thought of how confining the room was for this patient, and had considered bringing in some form of play activity to facilitate an easier flow of communication. I had even imagined some leisurely undemanding situation, as though the imbalance in the present relationship was too extreme to be useful.

After a pause, during which I reviewed all of these considerations, I stated that from my point of view the room was a place to create the conditions of safety she needed in order to know and communicate her internal experiences. In addition, I added, if there were a better way it would be important to discover it, and it sounded as though she had some ideas. For the first time her hostile facade melted away. She spoke in an anxious, tremulous voice of her feeling that if she could only go for a walk outside she knew she could talk more freely, but she was worried that I wouldn't want to do it. I told her I thought it was worth a try, and for the next several months our biweekly sessions were conducted while walking in the confines of a nearby park.

I agreed to modify the therapeutic framework on the basis of the patient's conscious, somewhat desperate request, in combination with an empathic, intuitive response. The enclosed space of the office almost totally immobilized her, while my interpretive interventions had little or no observable positive influence. It looked as though powerful unconscious drives were constantly threatening to be unleashed. Her request could be seen as a consequence of material now becoming available, and a question did arise in my mind as to what it would mean to her to engage in an interaction that implicitly encouraged action and discharge. This was especially relevant for this patient, who had as yet not been able to articulate what were apparently intense instinctual conflicts. I considered the possibility that I might be fostering a form of acting out. If this was the case I might be avoiding the chance to unravel the unconscious meaning of her request, but more importantly it would reenforce defenses, rendering the underlying instinctual wishes inaccessible to therapeutic influence. However, it was conceivable, and in this situation con-

sidered more likely, that to interpret her request solely as a defense or to hear it only as material to be analyzed would in some as yet unseen manner operate as a traumatic repetition further entrapping her in an unmovable position. The patient's request so matched my empathic intuitive response that it appeared worthwhile to engage in this leap. At the same time I was alerted to look for signs that it might represent an unnecessary or harmful deviation, and be ready to rectify any injurious or untoward effects.

Initially, the patient utilized the walks in a way that made me question the validity of the decision. She behaved like a caged animal having just been freed as she romped excitedly to explore different parts of the environment. However, she stayed within range of me and began to talk about things that caught her attention. It soon became apparent that her observations were noteworthy; they symbolically reflected the internal meaning of the changed conditions of the treatment, giving some measure of validation to how it was being conducted, and thus encouraging me to continue. On one of our walks she found the remnants of a cocoon, eagerly described what it must be like to grow enough to be able to change and fly off, and then speculated about how confining it must have been to be stuck in such a narrow space. Similarly, she wondered how the squirrels could stand to be cooped up all winter, and how eagerly they must await the time when they could be free to run. She laughed when I translated these metaphors into her current experience, but gradually started to walk alongside of me. It looked like we were on the right track, for her attention turned to trying to find words to express what she was feeling.

She spoke with mounting vehemence of her place in the family. She was the oldest of four children, resented the favoritism shown to her two younger brothers and was jealous of the attention shown to her baby sister. Her life consisted of a constant series of demands and expectations. There were frantically paced outside activities, in which she tried to be the best at everything she did and felt terribly frustrated when she failed. My only comments to this material were my being able to better understand how she must have viewed coming to see me as an extension of these expectations; this seemed to encourage her to elaborate further. Later I commented that I could also see how the walks enabled her to speak more freely, but I could not yet see what made the office appear to be such an oppressive setting. Her face lit up, but then she lapsed into an embarrassed silence. She indicated that she knew why but did not know if she could talk about it. With that she once again darted off on some independent venture, this time with less enthusiasm and with an awareness of avoiding an important topic.

I wondered if it was now time to stay in the office where she could more easily be with the feelings that were aroused indoors, and she readily agreed. Once inside she slowly brought out how for as long as she could remember she had sought solace in masturbatory activities. In the privacy of her room her mind was filled with wild and confusing erotic fantasies of being tied down and tickled. Although her fantasies were not present when she was in public places the urge to masturbate persisted, particularly when she was under any tension. It exposed her to a great deal of embarrassment and humiliation, and she tried to hide or mask what she was doing from others. She now revealed for the first time that when she was 4 years old she was brought to a doctor for this problem. He injected alcohol into her genital area with the intent of deadening her sensations there, thus curing the problem. During the procedure she felt totally invaded and humiliated, and afterward the numbness only drove her more frantically to rearouse the sought-after genital sensations. She had not realized it before, but coming to see me had touched off a feeling of fear and anger that she connected to this earlier experience.

From this point on the patient engaged more fully in the treatment relationship, and a benign therapeutic regression gradually unfolded. The transference relationship reawakened repressed early childhood memories, and an inordinately conflicted oedipal constellation became evident. Her symptom of compulsive masturbation represented a means for giving expression to these conflicted unconscious instinctual strivings, while at the same time defending against them. The experience with the previous doctor had a traumatic impact in part because of its linkage to these powerful unconscious fantasies. In a way that she could not articulate at the time, she knew that she needed to have control over what happened in the relationship with me. The circumstances of the treatment were continually echoing with her previous trauma, preventing her from being able to talk or even think. My willingness to be directed by her was sufficiently divorced from what had happened before that she was able to gain the necessary perspective to enter into a process of internal exploration, which might otherwise not have been possible. It was equally essential for me to recognize when the usefulness of the walks was changing, for in supporting a defensive posture the walks could readily be received as seductive and overstimulating. There was no further need to alter the conditions, and the treatment was thereafter conducted within an exclusively interpretive mode.

Empathy or Countertransference: A Crucial Distinction

The definition of a leap has implicit in it that the necessity has been determined in part by an assessment of the accuracy of a therapist's unconsciously empathic responses. One reason it is referred to as a leap into the darkness to find the light centers around the ease with which a therapist can confuse empathic responses with conflicted or regressive countertransference-based reactions, which obscure rather than enhance unconscious perceptiveness. This is particularly the case when the crucial component of a patient's input, for aid in validation, is rendered unavailable or unreliable. Yet these are exactly the times when such a step is usually contemplated, since therapeutic progress has been stalled as a consequence of the impact of infantile and preverbal traumas or by the effects of developmental deficits, defects, and arrests.

The problem is compounded further when the patient's defensive pattern is devoted to obscuring or distorting those unconscious perceptions that are expressive of what is growth-promoting in a relationship. This vital source of information, which is needed to make an accurate assessment of specifically what is required to facilitate therapeutic progress, is thereby unobtainable in a direct and immediate fashion. However, a therapist's unconscious perceptions may be receiving the necessary directions, eliciting affective responses, fantasies, sensations, and ideational activity. Provided that they are identified correctly they may be the only reliable source of guidance. A missing experience may then be offered that either allows symbolic processes to become functional, alleviates inordinate defensive opposition, or bridges a gap in psychic structuralization. This paves the way for interpretations to serve as the major therapeutic instrument.

A therapist's empathic response to a patient's unconscious communications is essential for any treatment, but under these circumstances it may be the only avenue for gaining access to what otherwise remains unthinkable and unexpressable. The outcome of the treatment may depend upon it. In the construction of a therapeutic framework, room must always be granted for a therapist's unconscious perceptions and empathic responses to occupy a place as a source of creativity. The door may then be open for countertransference-based errors to be more overt, but they also become more noticeable and hence correctable.[5]

---

5. Wolf (1983b) defined empathy as an introspective, perceptual mode that can be processed by any theory, and comes prior to theory. By contrast countertransference phenomena, based upon a therapist's needs, are observed and formulated differently by each theoretical perspective. He approached countertransference from a self-psychological theory, in which all of the psychological needs that are mobilized in the therapist's subjective experience by participating in the analytic interaction are included. It was the exact counterpart and the natural complement of, but not necessarily a reaction to, the patient's transference. He felt there were some countertransference responses that rather than being destructive to analysis can be a necessary condition for the analytic process to unfold. These were responses that supported a patient's strivings for growth, and were in contrast to countertransference responses that interfered with the patient's realizing self potentials. Thus when there are persistent signs of an impending or actual disruption in the treatment, and the therapist cannot explain them, countertransference possibilities should be considered before the possibility of the patient's resistance to analysis.

Basch (1983) utilized a developmental perspective to illustrate the problem of distinguishing between empathy and countertransference in an immediate way. Affective sensation is processed so rapidly that consciousness of what is taking place occurs after the fact. Therefore autonomic sensation is experienced as something that happens to us, and often we do not know either the source or the reason. Cortically mediated sensation, being slower, seems to be directly related to consciousness, is understandable, and under our control. However, the participation of consciousness in cortical perception is illusory, and consciousness is as much after the fact in cortically mediated sensation as it is in autonomically generated affective sensations. In neither case is perception equated with consciousness. The stimulation of the autonomic nervous system is as likely to come from the outside as is that of the cortex, and it is usually the two systems working synchronously that define inner and outer reality. In principle, since neither is direct, one form of perception is not inherently more reliable than the other. In neither case can we rely with absolute certainty on our perceptions.

Nathanson (1986) termed empathy the affective linkage that is forged during psychotherapy, and believed that empathic perception was experienced as emotion because of our associations to the particular affect transmitted. The psychoanalyst is thus a paradigm of the "good audience," and for many people therapy provides the first life experience in which they are heard and are able to feel real. Both therapist and patient value so highly this feeling of being known, on an affective level, that there is a tendency to consider the absence of empathy normal and the presence of it special. In fact the presence of empathy is normal, whereas its absence is a product of defensiveness.

4

Leaps and Countertransference

The Interrelation and Distinctions between Empathy and Countertransference, and the Significance of a Patient's Unconscious Perceptions

Empathy and countertransference are closely related subjective phenomena. Both depend upon the evocation of a therapist's affective responses, and present a potential pathway toward a deeper understanding of the unconscious dimension of a patient's experiences. An empathic stance is predicated upon the activation of temporary trial identifications, consciously invoked by a therapist in order to gain an appreciation of how the patient perceives the internal and external world. The resulting experience is then exposed to higher order functions that have been held in abeyance, leading to the formulation of an interpretation empathic with the unconscious meaning of a patient's communications.

Countertransference serves the same purpose of grasping the unconscious meaning of a patient's psychic productions, particularly when the concept is broadened to incorporate all of a therapist's responses and reactions. Although it must also be understood by suspended secondary process functions, the experience does not encompass the use of trial identifications. With countertransference the focus of attention is centered upon a therapist's reaction to the stimuli of a patient's input, thereby expanding the view of its unique unconscious significance and enlarging the range of a therapist's self-awareness. However, if countertransference elements evoke defensiveness in a therapist they create blind spots that pose an obstacle to that very understanding. A therapist's unrecognized unconscious fantasies, regressive identifications, or narcissistic needs will lead to a patient's transferences either passing unnoticed or being misidentified. A transference–countertransference interchange is an integral facet of every therapeutic interaction, and when there is no obstruction it is a source of ongoing information that helps translate the encoded unconscious significance of a patient's communications. Depending upon how countertransference is dealt with by a therapist it can either constitute an opportunity for growth in both parties, or introduce an empathic failure. Unless the trouble is recognized and corrected it can lead to an impasse, to the development of detrimental collusions with a patient's unconscious fantasies or pathological defenses, to disruption of the treatment, or to the patient's ongoing exercise in submission and conformity.[1]

It was because of the ease with which a therapist's emotional responses can shift into activating personal difficulty that Kleinians in general are uneasy about widening the concept of countertransference. Of course the analyst's feelings are a source of information about the patient, but Kleinian analysts tend to feel that the definition of countertransference as the analyst's unanalyzed

---

1. Racker (1957) thought that the transference became intense not only as a resistance to remembering but as a defense against the danger within the transference experience itself; and that the same was true for countertransference. The greatest danger was in suppressing and repressing countertransference, for when the therapist is not aware of countertransference responses he may make the patient feel exposed once again to an archaic object, and thereby perpetuate a vicious cycle.

Schwaber (1983) addressed the tendency to be overconcerned about the distortions created by the transference, and to overlook their importance in calling attention to the impact of the therapist's mode of functioning. Rather than viewing the transference as a distortion to be modified it should be seen as a perception to be recognized and articulated, facilitating a deeper entry into the patient's inner world. Although the impact of this perception, and the meaning assigned to it, will be a reflection of the analytic moment, it does not mean we must question the validity of the perception. We still need to check the patient's perceptions and view of reality against our own, but this is primarily to maintain vigilance against the imposition of our own view. Utilizing this point of view as a way of listening leads to a heightened attention to the therapist's contribution, and deepens what we can see of the experience inside, bringing certain nonverbal phenomenology under increased illumination.

transference to the patient should be kept. However, the idea of empathy as the analyst's awareness and understanding of the patient's projections should be added (Bott-Spillius 1983). Nevertheless, a patient's unconscious perceptions are a vital source of help in preventing or alleviating roadblocks in the treatment caused by a therapist's loss of ideal functioning; it is important to always search for their manifestations in determining the unconscious significance of the therapeutic interaction. A therapist's willingness to receive a patient's messages in this fashion strengthens the therapeutic alliance, gives impetus to strivings for growth, and furthers a therapist's ability to distinguish more clearly between empathic responsiveness and countertransference-based failures in empathy. At such moments the patient functions briefly as the therapist's supervisor, and provided these failures are not too frequent or long-lasting they ultimately foster therapeutic progress.[2] Thus, although there are differences, empathy and countertransference are closely interrelated and it is important to delineate their varying manifestations.

Countertransference in its narrow definition is limited to those feelings and reactions that are a product of conflict, defensiveness, and narcissistic needs, thereby obviating against an empathic response. All of a therapist's subjective responses are encompassed

---

2. Searles (1975) stressed that the crucial element in a treatment process is that of a patient's therapeutic strivings being received by a therapist in a useful fashion. This is then reflected in a return of successful therapeutic functioning. The consequence for the patient is in individuation becoming free of its connotation of a murderous dismembering or lethal abandonment of the mother, for whom the patient has not only been made to feel responsible, but whom the patient has loved and wanted to make whole and fulfilled.

Langs (1975c), although concerned about the negative impact of the therapist's errors, observed how a frank acknowledgment of the error, along with an exploration and working through of the patient's reaction to it, could provide a unique and growth-promoting, insight-producing experience for both patient and therapist.

Etchegoyen (1982) noted how essential it was to elucidate what happened in the present to clear away the past. In this way the analysis of transference delimits the past and present, and discriminates between objective and subjective. When this is achieved the past need not be repeated, but remains as a reservoir of experience that can be applied to an understanding of the present and to forecasting the future.

in its broadest definition, including empathy. Empathy and countertransference are inextricably intertwined, since it is virtually impossible for a therapist to be completely free of the residuals of intrapsychic conflict or defensive opposition to the emergence of regressive fantasies, identifications, and narcissistic strivings. In addition, the ability to empathize requires that a therapist have access to the derivatives and their affective components emanating from the unconscious realm. Receptiveness to countertransference-based reactions is integral for a therapist's free-floating attention. Consequently, an accurate assessment of the therapeutic value of an intervention must always take into account the effect that it has on a patient's unconscious perceptions or, if this is not recognizable and available, on a patient's overall response. This is especially a problem in treating those non-neurotic individuals whose transferences are poorly differentiated, and in whom the derivatives of unconscious perceptions are seriously distorted or have no direct avenue for expression. Therefore, a combination of a therapist's empathy, intuition, and countertransference may have to be almost exclusively utilized to determine what constitutes a growth-promoting intervention, at least until the reliability of a patient's reactions can be established, and the manner in which unconscious perceptions are expressed can be identified.

With more primitively organized and structurally deficient patients there is a greater potential for a therapist to introduce serious errors of commission, especially when intense demands for action are implicitly or explicitly in the picture. The arousal of regressive identifications and rescue fantasies may lead to a blurring of therapeutic boundaries, or to a rupture in the containing properties of a well-managed therapeutic interaction.[3] Conversely,

---

3. Bleger (1967) defined the non-ego as the background or frame of the organized ego. It was the most primitive part of the personality and consisted of a fusion of ego–body–world on whose immobility the formation of ego, objects, and body images depended. It may be critical for the therapist to accept the frame that the patient brings, because of the unsolved problems of primitive symbiosis it contains. This does not mean that the therapist should abandon his own frame, through which he is able to analyze the process and transform the frame itself into a process.

a much needed form of active participation may be required of the therapist, in order to enable a patient to gain the lacking mental representations at the foundation of deficient or absent crucial psychic functions. When a therapist defensively withdraws from bridging the resulting gap in the relationship, a serious error of omission is introduced.[4] Thus countertransference can be an ally

---

Rosenfeld (1971) distinguished between the projective identification used for communication and that used for defensive purposes, and in addition identified a third form observed in the transference relationship of psychotic patients. This is based upon a very early infantile type of object relationship that leads to a fusion with the therapist and to anxiety related to a loss of self. The patient's projection of parts of the self and internal objects into the therapist gives an opportunity to truly understand the immediacy of the transference.

Segal (1981a) noted that the powerful impact of primitive projective identifications have the potential of eliciting counterproductive responses in the therapist. The therapeutic interaction contained the constant presence of a nonverbal dimension that acted upon the therapist's mind, and took many forms. It may be integrated with other forms of communication, giving them depth and emotional resonance; or it may be the predominant form of communication coming from preverbal experiences that can be expressed in only this way; or it may be meant as an attack upon communication. The nearer to psychotic processes, the more this form of acting takes precedence over symbolic or verbal communications.

Rosenbaum (1987) discussed the problem of certain psychotic patients who act out as a consequence of their total conviction about a delusional belief concerning the therapist. The psychotic transference is not manifested openly, but the acting out is hidden or silent and detectable only from its effects.

4. Alexander (1954) noticed the problem in handling what he called the ever-present dependent component in the transference. Although his approach was questionable he did observe that by satisfying a patient's dependent needs, a regression goes beyond unresolved conflicts into pre-conflictual phases of development. His approach was to avoid this development through somewhat manipulative measures, and he consequently missed an opportunity for understanding and/or healing early deficits. However, he emphasized that both too detached and too intense transference involvement can retard the treatment.

Stone (1961) brought out the negative effects of a therapist's arbitrary authoritarianism, and the generally detrimental influences of severe frustration or lack of gratification. He also highlighted the destructiveness of attitudes based upon general principles rather than therapeutic need.

Gedo (1984) suspected that the inability of a given therapist to overcome technical difficulties was related to an insufficient appreciation of the true exent of his aversion for a particular patient's conduct at the climactic phase of the treatment. In an effort to curb disapproval we may adhere too scrupulously to a position of "neutrality," thereby leaving others to feed the patient's symbiotic needs. Conversely the prerequisite a patient has for maintaining a therapeutic relationship, without unmanageable anxiety about the loss of a sense of autonomy, may put intolerable demands upon a therapist.

or an enemy, an obstacle or a facilitator, but at all times is an essential feature at work in the interaction.

An Unconsciously Empathic Response Leading to a Leap, and Arousing Conflicted Countertransference Reactions Preventing Another Necessary Leap

A therapist's unconsciously empathic responses can sometimes be misidentified, usually because they activate an intrapsychic conflict. The subsequent defensive reaction may be noted, which leads to attributing the empathic nature of the affective experience to a countertransference-based regressive identification.[5]

These situations generally arise in patients with very primitive psychic states, especially those for whom the therapist's conduct is largely dependent upon subjective sensitivities as to what is required. On most occasions these are patients whose capacity to symbolize is either severely deficient or absent, and in whom a verbal communicative modality is unreliable or interfered with by gaps in psychic functioning. A patient's input plays an essential part in distinguishing between the effects of empathy, which is growth-promoting, and conflicted countertransference reactions, which result in projections and impositions and is debilitating. Under these kinds of circumstances it is the patient's overall manner of engaging in the relationship that can call attention to a therapist's lapse in empathy.

---

5. Racker (1957) referred to this therapeutic difficulty by noting that countertransference was not a source of pure truth, but that our unconscious is a personal receiver and transmitter and we must reckon with frequent distortions of objective reality. Therefore the therapist must get to know his personal equation, and the danger of exaggerated faith in messages from the unconscious is less than that of repressing and denying them any objective value. One must critically examine one's deductions from perceptions and from countertransference.

Berger (1987), in describing the relationship between regression and empathy, observed how the therapist occasionally may experience a state of merger with the patient. In such situations it is likely that the therapist's ego and superego have relaxed their hold on the id, and in order for such experiential states to contribute to empathy a therapist must exhibit the capacity to resist needing to know.

Clinical Example

The critical importance of a therapist being able to unravel the origins of these subjective responses was exemplified in the early period of treatment of a 4-year-old autistic child, who ultimately was able to gain fairly advanced levels of psychic structuralization over a period of fourteen years of intensive, psychoanalytically derived psychotherapy. In the later years of his treatment, after he had attained a considerable degree of developmental progression, my inevitable empathic lapses or occasional empathic failures served as a spur to growth in both parties. They elicited derivatives of his unconscious perceptions, aiding me in identifying their source; and in being acknowledged and rectified they fostered the patient's efforts to further integrative processes by gaining a deeper view of their effects.

In the beginning phases of therapeutic contact, however, his remarkable sensitivity to even the slightest nuance of my introduction of depriving, impinging, or overstimulating attributes had the effect of eliciting a dramatic response—his total autistic withdrawal. This made my lapse in empathy very noticeable and unavoidable. It was essential for me to be unencumbered by defense-inducing attitudes, and for the relationship to be free of my projections or impositions, since they were perceived by him as having annihilative intent. The basic psychoanalytic principles guided the interaction in providing a background of containment; I had to carefully monitor the shift from an introjective to a projective mode of communication—when movements were made from listening to intervening—and it was crucial to identify the existence of an ideal posture, and to discern when action-discharge or defensively distant attitudes threatened to surface.

The very essence of the principles guiding a psychoanalytic process are especially relevant in the treatment of an autistic child. Good self-experience is so profoundly deficient that its vestiges must be protected and held in the deepest layers of the personality, and the only available defense against the noxious stimuli of the internal and external world is of an extreme withdrawal. Therefore contact must be established in a relationship for therapeutic influence to eventuate; and for contact to take place, the environment has to be empathic in a consistent manner and in a form that is capable of being internalized. This means that the application of the basic psychoanalytic principles will vary markedly from what is required in the more structured personality. Interventions that would be intrusive, infantilizing, defense-reenforcing, and debilitating with more advanced levels of psychic organization may be called for in this circumstance. Furthermore, a determination of what is appropriate is extremely difficult, since it depends to such a large extent upon a therapist's subjective impressions.

With neurotic transferences the structural foundation for ongoing constructive growth has already been established. The pathology centers around the effects of fantasy distortions; symbolic processes are actively functional, and an exclusively interpretive modality is essential for attaining the realignment of the existing forces ultimately leading to ongoing self-expansion. The therapist's management of the ground rules, boundaries, and conditions of the treatment serves as a background presence of safety and containment, needing to be addressed only when it has been disrupted by an empathic lapse. It is easy to lose sight of the developmental line upon which containing experiences are based, for in the neuroses their symbolic meaning is predominant. In the treatment of individuals manifesting non-neurotic transferences, and most particularly with an autistic child, the role of concrete, body ego experiences of contact with a good object's influence is more clearly emphasized.

The 4-year-old boy was referred after being diagnosed on several occasions as being autistic, brain-damaged, and/or retarded. The family had been advised that institutionalization was necessary; the only question was when. He was seen in a series of diagnostic sessions to determine whether psychotherapeutic intervention was feasible, or to aid the family in deciding his future. In the first two sessions this wizened-looking boy, with no identifiable communicative speech and only occasional singsong vocalizations, wandered unendingly from place to place submissively complying with external physical direction. He occasionally stood silently gesturing, his fingers undulating under his poorly focused eyes. He seemingly paid no attention to me as I sat silently, trying to grasp any possible meaning from his behavior.

The problem of establishing communication was immediately apparent, as any understanding would have to be almost totally based upon my subjective responses. Even though whatever emerged may well be a product of nonverbal communications, effected through body language and subtle emotional interchanges, nevertheless it would be very difficult to attain validation. There was also much uncertainty as to whether verbal communications were capable of evoking body ego experiences, and it was most likely that this task could be accomplished only through something concrete in the relationship. My tone of voice and body movements, the starting and stopping of a session, the points at which I spoke, the significance of silences, and the like would probably be the most powerful stimuli and the most effective vehicles for conveying meaning. The patient's behavior could then be watched to attain some measure of validation. In this situation I was attempting to establish some groundwork for a relationship, while being aware that the qualities of a good object are best presented nonverbally, an area with the least amount of conscious control. I was in an introjective, listening mode, allowing my nonverbal reactions to be openly revealed, and the patient was seemingly disengaged from any connection to me.

In the subsequent session I began to sense that the empty outer shell of the patient's mannerisms and singsong vocalizations surrounded an inner experience he was either unwilling or unable to communicate. After sitting in silence for some time, unable to extract further meaning from his behavior, I fantasized that the patient was yelling at his fingers, threatening them with punishment were they to reach out and touch me. The fantasy suggested that some dimension of meaning was emerging, so I told him what I understood. I stated that for myself fingers were a means of reaching out to touch the outside world, and I sensed the patient was admonishing his fingers to keep them from being drawn to exploring.

I identified the interpretation as originating within myself by reflecting upon what I did with my own fingers, in order to acknowledge an awareness of the potential my words had for representing a projection. The intent was to facilitate the patient's ability to express himself by implicitly encouraging him to reach out and explore the environment. The patient, however, continued to wander aimlessly, gesturing with his fingers, apparently unaffected by this communication. His lack of an observable response elicited a feeling in me of being ignored, as though I did not exist. I began thinking about my next appointment; this made me aware that I had become disengaged and withdrawn from the patient. At precisely this moment the patient turned to me and asked, "Are you listening?" I was startled at the nature of this immediate reaction. He seemed to have tacitly reached out by mobilizing all of his resources into this one gesture of communication. It suggested that a nonverbal, primitive form of communication had been taking place, and that I had been more in contact with him than I realized. When the contact was withdrawn it invoked a level of functioning the patient was unable to continuously sustain. Implicitly, it appeared to be calling out for a return to the conditions taking place prior to my disengagement, and in this way he validated that he had been communicating in his own unique manner.

The interchange called attention to the simultaneous existence in the patient of a sensitivity to, and withdrawal from, the external world. It was evident in his looking as if he were totally unaware of my presence, yet he reacted sensitively to a change in my attitude. His question also revealed a latent potential for achieving a higher level of functioning. It certainly underscored how much more control a therapist has over the way a patient's productions are processed, and how much larger the capacity is for monitoring and validating therapeutic interventions, when communications are verbal. For this child the nonverbal aspects of communication were predominant, and it was interesting that a more integrated response was instigated by a loss of contact with a good object rather than in its presence. I speculated that the momentary consolidation of good self-experience necessary for this communicative expression occurred at a point of loss, because he was making an effort to retrieve the influence of a good object that he had been experiencing. It suggested to me that my sense of being ignored by the patient, which had aroused the uncomfortable feeling of having no existence, was an unrecognized unconscious empathic response. For a brief moment I had received a glimpse of what it was like in the patient's internal world to feel like a nonentity.

I responded to his question by stating that he was right: I had not been listening. I had felt rejected, and had turned my attention to other thoughts. The patient then became somber and started to explore the chair with his fingers. This introduced a long period of time during which he spent the entire session exploring other objects in the room, and then tentatively touched my body with his fingers. It looked as though his initial question had expressed an unconscious perception of my withdrawal, and when it was acknowledged he engaged in the exploratory actions that were implicitly encouraged by the interpretation.

Much later, at age 12, the patient recalled this moment, remembering only that my voice had made him feel safe. On the surface, my active encouragement for him to reach out and touch, along with my openness to that exploration, might appear to violate the psychoanalytic principles of abstinence, anonymity, and neutrality. However, when abstinence is defined as refraining from reenforcing a pathological defense, and anonymity and neutrality are defined as not projecting or imposing onto a patient, my receptiveness to his touch was in accordance with the essence of these important principles.

Autistic withdrawal was this patient's predominant defense, elicited by the depriving, impinging, or overstimulating qualities of a bad object. Had I displayed any of these attributes it would undoubtedly have reenforced this pathological defense. Anonymity and neutrality does not mean hiding or withholding personality traits or emotional responses, and the patient had already shown his enormous sensitivity to projections. An interaction that was discordant with his internal responses appeared to be experienced by him as potentially dangerous, and resulted in a total discontinuation of all communication. The developmental failure at the root of his disturbance made an adequate symbiosis essential for attaining any movement toward psychic growth, and emotional responsiveness is a vital ingredient of a therapeutic symbiosis. I had to be capable of revealing my emotions to aid him in determining whether they matched his need. This is in striking contrast to those individuals for whom the open expression of a therapist's emotions can act as an imposition, and contaminate or have a detrimental influence upon transference-based experiences. It thereby illustrated the very different manner in which the basic psychoanalytic principles are applied with such a child, since in this situation a therapist's self-revelations are within their guidelines.

The patient periodically returned to gesturing and posturing, as he would alternately explore and retreat. Finally, he brought two toy soldiers to his sessions; one was wounded and bandaged, another intact and upright. Nonverbally he portrayed their interaction. While he played I slowly became aware of a silent countertransference-based defensive response to the relationship. I could see the patient's damage, but was ineffective in knowing what to do in addressing it. The situation made me feel stiff and helpless. The patient's play seemed to mirror the emotional interchange that was taking place between us, and hinted that he was making a continuous effort to establish contact with me only to be rebuffed as he came in touch with the silent echoes of my defensive reaction. With this dawning realization I talked about the hurt and damage inflicted upon the one soldier, and the stiff, ineffective efforts of the erect soldier in tending to the other's wounds. I went on to say that I thought the patient was trying to call my attention to the rejection he was experiencing, as my feeling of helplessness made me pull away. It was apparently creating a gap between us. There was no immediate response, but the following morning he awoke very early and spoke his first communicative sentence to his parents: "Take me to ferapy." He wanted to see me right then. The parents called, and I arranged to see him as soon as I could get to the office.

The patient arrived looking entirely different. His face was worn and haggard and he looked terrified. He was restless, agitated, and irritable. Periodically he made sounds that were alternately whining and anguished. The picture was of a child being viciously bombarded by some internal process, and helpless in managing the onslaught. I spoke to what I sensed was happening inside of him, and as I did I felt my stiffness dissolving. It made me acutely aware of this patient's need to be physically held, comforted, and buffered, and of my resistance to spontaneously doing that. At just this moment he approached me, at first tentatively. He gradually allowed himself to be held close, molding himself to my body. I simply held him in this fashion for several sessions. He slowly indicated, at first behaviorally and then with monosyllabic verbalizations, that my voice was too loud or the lights were too bright or the surrounding noise of the street too intense. Everything hurt, for he was totally vulnerable to the impact of all stimuli. Light, sound, and touch were very painful, and internal stimuli seemed equally painful.

It was apparent that his autistic defenses were no longer operative and he felt little buffering. The lights were turned out, the shades drawn to diminish the noise level, and I found a way to gently hold and comfort him. The number of sessions was increased, sometimes to twice a day. This went on for a period of seven or eight months, during which time he was sleepless and in a constant state of terror. He spent many sessions in my arms, while I was either silent or occasionally talked. My voice was soft, my actions loving and gentle, and I spoke of his need for buffering from the impact of both internal and external stimuli upon him. There were several sessions in which he slept the entire time. Then he began to talk, first from the position of being cradled, and later when moving around the room. At times he was contained and at other times agitated. He started by describing the internal creatures that assaulted him, and the occasional figures that were comforting. When he spoke of being assaulted his agitation mounted; when he spoke of being comforted he appeared contained. He also spoke of mischievous and fun-loving creatures and smiled. Although he had previously exhibited a variety of facial expressions, this was the first time that he smiled.

My awareness that the rupture in the relationship was created by my own defensiveness, in conjunction with acknowledging the patient's unconscious perception of this failure in empathy, communicated the openness that was now present. It enabled the patient to experience being heard. He had thus been effective in producing a change in my attitude, and this was followed by his relinquishing the primitive defense of autistic withdrawal.[6] The patient's inability to tolerate the effects of sound, touch, and light seemed to reflect a deficient capacity to buffer the stimuli of the external world. The traumatic impact of internal stimuli was inferred from his behavior. This difficulty with buffering stimuli was not observable until his autistic defenses were no longer functional, suggesting that this may have been a major factor in his pathology. The question of some organic deficit almost always arises in the assessment of autistic children, and it is likely that some organic determinants may have contributed to this deficit. There was much to suggest that from birth onward he had been confronted with this weakness, which may well have profoundly distorted his developmental experiences. The inordinate needs of an incipient autistic infant are often beyond what can be offered by the usual adequate maternal environment, or may intensify latent pathological tendencies in nurturing figures. Perhaps with an exceptional maternal presence, empathic to his special needs, a different outcome might have resulted. It was interesting that the patient had a right-sided hemiparesis, which had been diagnosed as evidence of a neurological deficit. Shortly after this period being described, the hemiparesis disappeared. It had been on the side held close to the mother, and also the side held close to the therapist. This only highlights the uncertainties as to the nature of organic impairments and their particular effects upon mental development.

---

6. Winnicott (1960b) likened the professional attitude to symbolism, in that it assumes a distance between therapist and patient. The therapist is thereby objective, and is not a rescuer, teacher, ally, or moralist. An important effect of the therapist's analysis is in strengthening his own ego in order to remain professionally involved without too much strain. It might be better to let the term *countertransference* revert to its meaning of that which we hope to eliminate by selection and analysis. This would leave us free to discuss the many interesting things that therapists can do with psychotic patients who are temporarily regressed and dependent. There is much to be said about the use a therapist can make of conscious and unconscious reactions to the impact of the psychotic patient, and only muddle can come from stretching the word *countertransference* to cover all of this.

Loewald (1986) reflected upon analytic neutrality as a continuously regenerating product of transformations, in which the power of motivational dynamics is contained and channeled. He noted how defenses are necessary for an individual to remain sane on returning from immersion in the irrational unconscious. They are needed to protect ego organization, and at times must be supported even though or because analysis goes beyond them. The holding qualities of the analytic situation then often allow us to return to the trouble spot later, when therapist and patient are both less in need of protective defense.

Although I was offering interpretive words, the primary experience affecting the relationship involved my holding and comforting the patient. My behavior was designed to provide a concrete, body ego experience of containment. After a sustained and continuous span of time the relationship began to take on the characteristics of a symbiotic attachment. The patient's appearance of comfort and safety gave the impression of a blurring of self and object images, and the frequent episodes of sleeping were consonant with this aura of fusion and merger. His emerging capacity for verbal communication gave evidence of the growth-promoting properties of the interaction. Previously fragmented representations of good self-experience were beginning to consolidate into a functional entity. This was in contrast to his initial communicative expression that was unable to be sustained.

The patient continued to speak in a quiet voice with many words difficult for me to understand. However, the names he assigned to the mental objects populating his mind were spoken very clearly. His descriptions were accentuated by his whole manner, and captured the particular effect these internal objects were having upon him. The "Make-a-dos" were the most variable. They changed from mischievous, fun-loving, impish characters to angry, hostile, troublesome creatures, and finally to very frightening, provocative figures who escalated in size. They were always associated with a feeling of overexcitement or irritability. The "Big Black Pops" were dark, partly hidden, sticklike figures that were extremely explosive and frightening. His whole being was immobilized in their presence, and their prohibitive qualities were unmistakable. The "Big Pain" was a weak maternal figure who suffered intensely with anything that involved conflict or psychic pain. This figure was constantly whining and commiserating. "Pa'ba" was an undernourished, underdeveloped, deprived, and helpless infant. Interspersed with his portrayal of these internal objects was the gradual emergence of the figure of the soldier. This figure alternated from being firm, steadfast, reality-bound and insisting on performance, to being soft, understanding, and warmly responsive. In revealing the makeup of his representational world, he was now displaying a capacity for symbolization. His initial question, "Are you listening?" was undoubtedly based upon these fragmented mental representations that had been silently forming.

The figure of "Pa'ba" seemed to represent the ravages of oral deprivation that were the consequences of a pathological symbiosis, and reflected the destructiveness of its impact. The "Make-a-dos" possessed anal instinctual qualities ranging from mastery, autonomy, and control, to hostility and sadism, to becoming overpowering and ominous. In giving the same name to objects possessing such variable attributes, it suggested that they emanated from the same source. Their fluctuating instability expressed his difficulty in sustaining contact with good instinctual self-experience, and underscored the tenuousness of any movement toward consolidation. The name also shed some light on his lifelong episodes of severe constipation. There had been two occasions when he had not had a bowel movement for as long as one month. It looked as though he had established a symbiotic attachment to the body functions associated with anality, and utilized them to represent instinctual experience. The "Big Black Pops" were patterned after his father, a very obsessive man with periodic outbursts of rage, and the name captured the sense of explosiveness that frightened the child. The "Big Pain" represented his experience with mothering, which exaggerated his deficiency in buffering painful stimuli. The image of the soldier was represented during the extended period of lack of differentiation, embodied the influence of the treatment relationship, and possessed the combined qualities of a good object. There was always an aura of containment in the presence of the soldier.

The patient's attitude in being held gradually changed. He was quiet, contained, and molded himself to my body with little animation, irritability, or expression of any noticeable intensity. He developed a pattern of entering the room and passively establishing physical contact. After this went on for an extended period of time he gradually stopped talking. He then brought in the injured and erect soldiers once again, playing with them in a listless manner. Wordlessly, he indicated the interchangeability of the two soldiers. As I held him and witnessed this change in his behavior I felt somewhat uncomfortable. It was reminiscent of his description of "Pa'ba," the injured infant, and I did not want him to be helpless and undifferentiated. My eyes were opened to the possibility that in continuing to offer the concrete experience of buffering and containment I was reenforcing a newly developed pathological defense.

The patient had become verbally communicative, utilizing functions that were previously unavailable, and was no longer manifesting autistic defenses. An emerging capacity for self differentiation was clearly in evidence. In directing his communications specifically to me he was showing his newfound ability to consolidate good self-experience into a functional entity, and to maintain a connection to the mental impression of a separate good object's influence. Consequently, a shift was required in the application of the basic psychoanalytic principles so as to be in accord with his progression to this more advanced level of psychic organization. Holding and comforting him was no longer fostering his growth, making me realize that I was not taking these changes in psychic structuralization into consideration by altering the manner in which the relationship was conducted. I was concerned, however, that my discomfort might be a product of some lingering countertransference-based conflict around the extended involvement with nurturing experiences. I knew from my earlier period of defensive withdrawal that this potential existed within me. Although my feeling was seemingly verified by his behavior, I was worried that a change in my attitude might be premature.

Nevertheless, I told him that it looked like he needed me to be like the erect soldier who knew when it was time to encourage the injured soldier to use his strength. I had noticed how he had sought the comfort of being held at the expense of losing his ability to talk about his disturbing experiences. At first there was no observable response to these words, as the patient remained listlessly in my lap. Suddenly he arose, walked to the other side of the room, and spoke directly to me. Referring to an upcoming interruption in therapy necessitated by my vacation, he asked, "Doctor, go way?" His questioning tone seemed to express the anxiety he felt in what had just happened. The interpretation was indicative of a shift in my therapeutic posture, and expressed an unwillingness to comfort him if it interfered with his growth. His question, "Doctor, go way?" communicated the fear he experienced at the prospect of separating from a symbiotic attachment. However, my intervention did not result in either fragmentation or withdrawal, but in an adaptive response. It tended to verify the empathic nature of my internal feeling, although a lingering sense of uncertainty remained. In a larger context the potential for growth implied in the patient's initial question, "Are you listening?" appeared to be in the process of being realized.

The patient greeted my return from vacation by releasing a month's accumulation of feces. My initial response was one of warmth and concern, as I felt the urge to hug him and clean him up. However, instead of acting upon this feeling I withheld it, thinking it was inappropriate and a manifestation of a regressive countertransference-based identification. In its place I talked about his anger at being abandoned. The patient then ceased to communicate for an extended period of time, making it apparent that he had been misunderstood. After considerable self-exploration I was able to recognize the source of my inhibition in a much more specific way than had previously been possible. A conflict over feminine identifications had affected my initial feeling of warmth and affection, blocking me from expressing this understanding behaviorally. I informed the patient of my realization, and he was then able to describe his experience. He explained that while I was gone he had refused to evacuate his bowels.

Then as soon as he saw me, after my extended absence, he had let go of this tenacious hold on them. Instead of feeling welcomed by me, he was hurt by my defensive use of words.

I thought the patient had reestablished a symbiotic attachment to his own bodily products during the time I was away, an attachment which could be relinquished only with the continuation of our relationship. Thus, had I hugged and cleaned him it would have acknowledged the importance of the attachment, and in all likelihood supported his unsteady movements toward growth. Had the process of symbolization been consistently available to him when I was away he would not have had to retain his feces. The interweaving of my empathic responsiveness with regressive countertransference-based conflicts operated as a reappearing obstacle during this phase of the treatment. In the beginning it had been much easier for me to overcome any defensive opposition to nurturing him, because his regressive, infantile state was so clearly a factor in the interaction and the need for nurturing responses was patently obvious. When he was able to progress, the unresolved aspects of my conflict became more of an imposing barrier. It interfered with my ability to shift flexibly so as to be in concert with the fluctuations exhibited by the patient. Later in the course of his treatment, when psychic structuralization was more firmly established, his unconscious perception of my empathic lapses did not invoke an autistic withdrawal and could be more readily expressed through derivatives. This made it easier for me to identify and correct an empathic failure, and deepened his understanding of the negative effects upon him.

The Admixture of Empathy and Countertransference Resulting in a Silent Leap

When a patient is unwilling or unable to engage in a verbal interchange, or is unduly silent for extended segments of time, it heightens the tendency to attribute unconsciously empathic responses to conflicted countertransference-based reactions. This is often the case even with individuals possessing more advanced levels of psychic structuralization. Silence gives a surface appearance of being in opposition to the therapeutic process, and places greater emphasis on a therapist's subjective responses for guiding the conduct of the treatment. This makes it relatively easy for the underlying meaning to be misidentified and misinterpreted. Silence is an important form of communication, at times expressing powerful unconscious fantasies.[7]

The most effective means of exposing the unconscious significance of a silence may not reside in an interpretation. Instead it may be in a therapist's willingness and ability to be guided by subjective responses, which after all are a consequence of how the relationship is received and understood. In this sense a therapist would be engaging in a leap by introducing a noninterpretive intervention without overt validation by a patient, moving into the darkness to find the light. Ultimately, it will be the patient who verifies the appropriateness or inappropriateness of the intervention, whether it be silent or active in nature. It may not be until the patient's input is available that a clearer distinction can be made as to whether the therapist's subjective response was a result of unconscious empathy, or a countertransference-based projection.

Clinical Example

This was illustrated in the treatment of a 12-year-old girl who was originally referred because of her parents' concern about her sullenness, isolated behavior, refusal to participate in family gatherings, general aura of unhappiness, and a multiplicity of psychosomatic symptoms.

The parents had been divorced when the patient was 5 and the mother was immediately married to a family friend. Both mother and stepfather were very tall, gaunt, somber people. Before therapy began,

---

7. Arlow (1961) discussed how silences are not simply a resistance but have content and express a wide range of unconscious fantasies including transference fantasies. The ambiguity affords the patient an opportunity to invite the therapist to share in the fantasies, and provides moments during which the therapist can be accurately observed. Silence may also represent an effort to control or frustrate the therapist, and may induce a reinstinctualization of the process of empathy. In this way silence can stimulate countertransference. However, silence may represent a living out of a fragment of an experience with an earlier object, and may serve as an invitation for a shared acting out and joint repetition rather than recollection. The mood that the patient's silence evokes in the therapist can yield important insights into the nature of the silence. Silences may also represent both intrapsychically determined defenses and a transference repetition that is designed to preserve the relationship with an object.

when they had been describing their worry about the child, they had portrayed her as being very ugly and obese and said that they felt this contributed to her poor self-image. I had unwittingly formed an internal image of the patient's appearance, injecting a strong emotional component into the first moment of therapeutic contact and creating a somewhat dramatic beginning to the relationship. I walked into the waiting room at the time of the scheduled appointment with the expectation of greeting an obese preadolescent girl, only to discover a slim, very attractive child who immediately noticed the brief expression of surprise that crossed my face. She laughingly commented upon it as she introduced herself, referring to her awareness of how her parents perceived her and therefore must have described her to me. Matter-of-factly she noted that she had become accustomed to people being surprised upon first meeting her, but she was delighted that I did not mask my reaction. She emphasized the importance to her of knowing how people reacted, and joked about my surprise strengthening her self-image. She also made an indirect comment about her distrust of people who try to hide their feelings.

I was immediately given a strong direction for my conduct of the therapeutic interaction. Explicitly she was stressing the importance of being able to see my emotional responses, and implicitly stressing her need for me to carefully listen to her input for help in identifying any subtle countertransference-based obstacles that might arise. She spent the early months painting a painful picture of her current life, but remembered practically nothing about the period of time prior to the divorce. She recalled only that the family's next-door neighbors had been very good friends, and had switched partners. The friend she had previously called "Uncle" became her father, while her father moved next door to marry the mother and become the father of the other children. It all made her feel extremely confused. She had the impression that there was a dramatic change in her mother, because after they moved to another city it felt for a time as if her mother was a stranger. Meanwhile her father had two children with his second wife. At first she visited him occasionally, finding him to be harsh, strict, and extremely protective of his wife. The visits were very painful, and she had since refused to go. She dwelled on her relationship to her one-year-younger sister, who seemingly could do nothing wrong in her mother's and stepfather's eyes, and toward whom she felt very jealous. In addition, she was furious about the destructive influence her mother and stepfather were having upon a baby brother born of their union. She was fond of him and concerned about his welfare.

She hated being in her home. The anger and resentment she constantly felt made her sick, triggering severe headaches and stomachaches. Talking about the atmosphere in her home environment aroused these very feelings, which led to her not wanting to come to her appointments or at least trying to push these things out of her mind. She emphasized how very much she valued her isolation, and how speaking to no one was her only protection. It seemed like she was always hurt and angry, particularly in relation to her mother who unerringly invaded her space at all the wrong times. When she wanted her mother's time and attention she was unavailable, and the moments when her mother intruded upon her were inevitably when she was not wanted. With mounting anger the patient elaborated on how, to her mother, everyone else came first, in preference to her; she complained vociferously about her mother's weakness and her worry about others' opinions. She was especially enraged when her mother was too afraid to stand up for her in confrontations with the stepfather. With a deep sigh, and a tone of resignation, she stated that it was safer and better to want nothing rather than allow yourself to want something and be repelled. Immediately following this statement she lapsed into a prolonged silence, looking as though she had withdrawn deeply inside of herself.

I was considering the transference implications of what she had been talking about, wondering about the proper timing and content of an appropriate interpretation. On the surface her silence appeared to be reenacting the scenes she had described with her mother in the transference relationship. She was displaying what looked like a resistant defensive attitude, perhaps waiting for me either to reach out to her or to ward off an expected intrusion. Either way an interpretive intervention was apparently called for. However, I remembered her early comments about the significance of my emotional responses being visible to her, and my feeling was one of quiet comfort with the silence. It felt like it would be important not to interrupt, for though her external appearance looked sullen there was an aura of containment that was difficult to explain. As we both sat in silence I began to question whether somewhere deep inside I welcomed her pulling back from the hostile elements of the transference; but keeping the early sessions in mind, I stayed with my internal sense of comfort. The silence became more protracted and I started to think my comfort was the product of some unidentified defensive attitude. I then made some tentative transference interpretations concerning the defensiveness of her silence, attributing it to her attempt to protect herself against a wish for closeness with me and the conflicts this aroused.

She first ignored these interventions, but later made a remark directed to a statue of a dog on my desk. She spoke of the dog being very crabby and needing someone to pet him, and chastised him for his impatience. It did not dawn on me that she was giving me her interpretation of my inability to sit in silence. Instead I heard it as a projection of her internal state. An interpretive comment to this effect elicited an immediate return to her silent posture. Finally she brought a book to each session, reading it almost the entire time.

Again I was somewhat surprised at my internal feeling of comfort with the silence. It was accompanied, however, by a nagging sensation that I ought to be offering some interpretive help. Whenever I began to talk her physical movements would show annoyance. I commented that her reaction to my words seemed similar to the experience of her mother's being available at the wrong time. The patient's irritability increased as she started to angrily attack me for talking. Right in the middle she paused, and in a soft voice noted that far back in her mind she had been thinking about a beloved grandfather. In the beginning this was just an internal impression of comfort and warmth. It gradually expanded to what was like a daydream of being on a warm, sunny beach, and it evolved into a memory of very special times spent with her grandfather at his summer home at the ocean. He would frequently hold her on his lap reading books that she loved, and she felt cared for and safe. She suddenly recognized how much solace she found in the memory. My words, which had intruded on this internal sense of comfort, had also made her aware of its source.

My feeling of comfort with the silence was in tune with her silent, inarticulable grandparental transference. It was serving as a background of containment, and preparing the way for disturbing intrapsychic instinctual wishes and conflicts to emerge. This mental representation of a good object's influence must have been activated by my initial surprise in reacting to her attractiveness, allowing an almost immediate therapeutic alliance to be established. In this situation my silent presence was thus unconsciously the most empathic response possible. From her outward appearance, and the material she communicated, it seemed as though a resistant, oppositional defensive stance was in the forefront and that she needed some interpretive help to further therapeutic progress. My misidentification of an empathic response, by attributing it to a defensive countertransference-based reaction, resulted in interpretive words that were unempathic.

The patient had made a brief effort to help me by speaking to the crabbiness and impatience of the dog, but it was unsuccessful. My ability to remain in a silent listening posture could not be completely sustained, because of a lack of clarity concerning the meaning of my comfort. However, it was there long enough for the underlying transference to unfold and become known. My words mobilized an adversarial interchange reminiscent of the struggle with her mother, and she was thus able to see how it protected her from being aware of a loving attachment to a caring figure. Later this positive element of the transference was linked to an inordinately conflicted oedipal attachment to the (original) father, which had assumed traumatic proportions centering around the events associated with the divorce. The angry, hostile battles with her mother reenforced defenses against her unconscious instinctual wishes. My empathic lapse was relatively minimal so that it ultimately turned out to be a spur toward identifying the unconscious meaning of her silence. *My silence—to the extent that I maintained it—represented a leap, for I was in an area of darkness guided only by my sense of comfort.*

A Leap Emanating from a Countertransference-Based Regressive Identification

A therapist's acting upon regressive identifications tends to be counter to therapeutic progress, since this form of participation usually re-creates an infantile trauma or reenforces a pathological defense. This almost universal truth makes it mandatory for a therapist to contain such motivations toward action, and to identify their internal source through a recognition of the meaning of accompanying derivatives, eventuating in a deeper grasp of the patient's internal experience. A therapist's projections and impositions must be filtered out, while inappropriate encouragement of acting out is eliminated. A patient's regressive strivings can then more readily enter into the treatment relationship. However, all patients may act out to some extent, and some patients to a major all-encompassing extent, in order to discover what is otherwise intolerable or unrepresentable.

There are many infantile or preverbal traumas that are either split off or unable to be included within the representational world, even in the form of fantasy. They can be expressed only through various impulsive actions and behavior. A therapist may then be compelled to become a participant, for more primitively organized patients are prone to having no other available connection to an object. Unless this avenue is utilized the individual is left alone, cut off from contact with potential therapeutic influence.[8] The risk of participating in a patient's acting out, particularly if it is continued beyond the limits of necessity, is that it possesses manipulative, exploitative qualities that readily rupture the very bond of trust essential for maintaining the therapeutic properties

---

8. Bion (1961) depicted the functioning of patients who have developed the capacity to transform sensorial experiences so that they can be stored and used to form memories. It permits dreaming, thinking, and maintaining the differences in the conscious and the unconscious. Patients who have not developed this capacity cannot use sensory experience to form thoughts. They can only be evacuated through projective identification, and appear in the production of acting out.

Little (1981) focused attention upon the vital importance of a therapist's total response to a patient's needs, particularly when confronted with more primitive personalities. When a limit is reached and the patient becomes aware of it, and aware of the impossibility of going beyond it even though needs and demands go further, it elicits an awareness of separateness. If the ability to bear separateness is small, every limit will be reached too soon. The demand on the ego is then too great and a reaction will follow, usually some violent acting out or physical illness. However, limits within the ego's capacity provide growing points and places where the ego can be strengthened.

Kinston and Coen (1986) described the problem of encountering the traumas associated with primal repression, for it is then that fear due to real danger—rather than anxiety based on fantasy—occurs. Whenever the traumatic phase of primal repression is activated, death or near-death events become a real risk.

Arvanitakis (1987) gave a developmental perspective on the evolution of symbolic functions, and the difficulties that arise in patients who have not been successful in achieving this capacity. Developmentally the mirroring function of the mother provides a frame for fragmenting instinctual overexcitement, and also for the overwhelming external excitations impinging upon the organism. The ego will find its foundation here at the interface of the two body surfaces. The interface serves as the boundary between inner and outer, between fantasy and reality, but it also serves as a surface of exchange and of object relations. It is the locus where symbols arise to shield against the disorganizing primitive anxieties; where symbols act as a buffer against the exciting, enveloping object and the creation of things novel and different. This reflecting surface that provides boundaries is defective or absent in the psychotic, due to constitutional or environmental failures, or both. The individual is thus left open to the tyranny of the body or of the sensory object.

of the relationship. However, avoiding this form of participation can also create discontinuity in the relationship, and it may only be through a therapist's regressive identifications that the necessary linkage can be established.

Engaging in such a potentially dangerous interaction requires careful consideration, for being carried blindly in this direction can become an end in itself and hence support primitive, archaic, and destructive modes of adaptation. Nevertheless, there are situations wherein this may be the only visible alternative, which tests a therapist's willingness to take a leap into unknown territory and communicates the degree of commitment to the treatment relationship. This pathway may have to be traversed before previously split-off psychic contents can be integrated, thereby enabling interpretations to be internalized.

Clinical Example

The treatment of a schizophrenic young woman presented me with this dilemma. The only avenue I could find to develop a workable therapeutic alliance was to actively support a pathological defense for a period of time. I was confronted with the need to implicitly encourage an acting out in the transference that was potentially destructive, with the emotional components of my position originating from a regressive identification.

The initial contact was made by a family member who called in desperation, describing the patient as "psychotic." She was delusional, irrational, had not eaten, acted bizarre, and would not communicate. She had been in psychotherapy on two prior occasions, and after a short time angrily refused to continue. I asked to talk to her, and she was brought to the phone. I repeated what I had been told, asking if she would like to make an appointment. Her voice was very hostile as she stated there was no reason to do so, and there was nothing wrong. I replied that it seemed like there was a lot of trouble and that I would give her my phone number in case she changed her mind. She coldly said she wasn't interested and did not want to see anyone. This made me aware that I was strongly affected by the family member who had called and was trying to entice her to come in. I informed her of this awareness and thanked her for calling it to my attention. She said good night and hung up.

In this brief interchange much was communicated. The patient displayed a surface compliance in coming to the phone. I ultimately recognized how I had been influenced by a third party and I thus expressed a willingness to listen and be guided by the patient. In that way I showed some respect for her autonomy. Several days later she called and asked for an appointment, entered her first session, and immediately lay down on the couch. I expressed surprise and she related her action to an earlier contact with an analyst, explaining that when she saw the couch here she just thought that was what she was supposed to do. I remarked that in the initial call she had let me know it was destructive for her to follow someone else's directions. She laughed, sat up, and began to describe why she came. Thus even at this early stage there were hints of an attempt to distort the relationship into one that demanded submission, and by implication her hope that it would be unsuccessful. My intervention, in expressing surprise about her lying on the couch, was followed by an interpretation of the destructiveness of her submissive act. Her response seemed to validate this impression.

She then bitterly remarked that talking seemed useless to her. She had spent her entire life analyzing her feelings and it led her nowhere. She thought of her life as made up of empty words and of experiences of conformity. She constantly made lists of things to do or remember, or of places to go, and could never be spontaneous. She was acutely aware of what others expected of her, and she produced. She did well in school and her family was proud of her. Her mother seemed totally enveloping, like an octopus with tentacles that surrounded and squeezed the life out of her. She never had the feeling of making a decision of her own. She then recalled frequent episodes of not eating as if that were her only choice. This reminded her of a recent decision she had made to not move, eat, or have any bodily function. She had felt that if she moved or her body functioned she would be in jeopardy of being occupied by whomever happened to be in her vicinity; she felt completely open to being invaded and taken over.

The patient had reacted to my interpretation by describing the depleted existence of her childhood years, along with her constant battle against regression. She made a reference to a pathologically invasive object, and revealed her enormous fear of fusion and merger. It suggested that there was a powerful defensive force operating inside of her that could readily transform whatever I did into a threatening re-creation of an engulfing, annihilative object. The importance of my respect for, and encouragement of, her autonomy and decision-making powers was thereby underscored. It also indicated the need to diminish the distorting effects of this pathological defense, and determine her specific conditions for an adequate symbiosis.

During the next several months she continued to emphasize how foolish it was to talk, but then proceeded to talk about herself. As a child she had been mechanical, could never play, felt no joy, and was fearful of spontaneity. Yet she was successful in school and had decided to go to college. She thought of it as an escape from the unbearable temptation to be enveloped by a relationship. She felt as though she was two separate people and living a lie. She could also feel another presence inside her searching for someone to love, and was terrified that she might find someone, and also that she might not. She graduated from college, got a job, met an artist, and fell deeply in love, but experienced the man she loved as totally undifferentiated from herself. He was spontaneous, playful, immature, irresponsible, and motivated solely by whim and fantasy. He was all of the things she had never been but wanted to be. When with him she felt exhilarated, unsure of her boundaries, confused, and at times disoriented. She began to feel that she was merged with everyone. Any conversation she heard entered her, she became increasingly frightened and felt like she had no skin. She began to hear voices and to have vivid fantasies that she could not separate from memory—one of which was that she was a criminal and the police were after her. She became increasingly terrified, finally deciding that the only way to hold on to herself was to stay in one position, totally immobile, and not exercise any bodily function.

My dilemma was now coming clearer into focus. On the one side, to pay exclusive attention to formulating interpretive words had the potential of amplifying her pathology. This kind of intervention resonated with a depleted "false self" that had dominated during her developmental years, making her feel trapped. The end result would be to avoid the infantile instinctual attachment that was so frightening but necessary for growth to transpire. On the other side, encouraging her spontaneity and the active expression of her deeply protected fantasies, and of her powerful wish for an instinctual attachment, threatened to activate fusion and merger experiences, eliciting a psychotic episode. I would have to be guided by the patient's unconscious perception of what was required to facilitate constructive growth, and to thereby negotiate between those two extremes. Hopefully, an alliance could be formed that was strong enough to allow her experiences to be contained within the confines of the therapeutic relationship.

I commented that she had originally come into therapy under duress and had believed that talking did no good. I agreed that talking, the way she defined it, did no good, and wondered why she continued to do so. She appeared surprised and wanted to know what I meant. I described meaningful lessons I had learned in various relationships with dogs and infants, who used no words in their communication, adding that it was my impression she needed this kind of talking. She became tearful as she spoke of feeling caged and needing to be free. She had to fly like a bird, and asked if I believed in magic. I answered that I didn't think she could survive without magic. I then defined magic as the capacity to be so profoundly in touch with the laws of nature that it seemed supernatural. She was intrigued and excited by this idea, but wondered if it meant I thought she might be able to fly. I remarked that I wanted her to be able to fly and it appeared to me as though she couldn't get off the ground.

I understood and interpreted her words as a defense against infantile preverbal experiences, thus explicitly encouraging this form of communication. Implicitly I was directing attention to the threat associated with it. The patient was continuing to give brief glimpses of her conditions for an adequate, growth-producing symbiosis, which involved the encouragement of regressive infantile longings within a containing relationship capable of supporting her autonomy. I perceived her questions about magic and flying as a subtle attempt to transform me into an enveloping, restrictive representative of reality. At the same time they offered an opportunity simultaneously to diminish the distortion and to present the attributes of a good object.

My empathic response was fueled by a regressive identification, which enabled me to appreciate the patient's internal experience of wanting to fly freely. I am sure my words carried the emotional accompaniment of my identification. I thought of the symbolic meaning of flying in my answer knowing full well that this was an area of confusion in the patient's mind. It thereby carried with it the risk of encouraging her to translate her wish into potentially dangerous and destructive actions. Yet to curb the emotional aspects and explain my response would have introduced a more distant, somber attitude, readily leading to my being perceived as an autonomy-eroding, controlling object. I was trying to find my way through this difficult and complex maze, with an acute awareness that the patient's deficiencies in symbolization tended to create a situation in which she received my input in a literal context. The resulting encouragement of her fantasies might easily lead to behavior outside of therapy that might have serious consequences. Conversely, to in any way act as a representative of what for her was an annihilative external reality could serve only to drive her away from the therapeutic relationship. She would then defensively and successfully avoid the infantile attachment that would be necessary for integration to take place. It was this very attachment that was both terrifying and necessary for her to be able to symbolically fly.

I was trying to give her an opportunity to represent a new solution to the developmental failures of her past, but was concerned that the regression would get out of control before a therapeutic symbiosis had been solidly established. My interpretations were designed to intervene with the distorting influence of an internal saboteur, while encouraging the vestiges of her autonomy that were still viable. She had clearly indicated how much she had functioned as a slave to the wishes and expectations of others, and I heard her questions asking if I would be able to guard her autonomy when she was in a state of lack of differentiation. She needed something to assure her that her autonomy would be respected in negotiating a symbiotic relationship; and in telling her how I thought she would be able to gain the ability to fly, I was telling her she could be separated and differentiated.

The patient began to express her awareness of the cages she had erected inside of herself, even as she continually wanted to run away and to fly. I indicated my alliance with her wish, along with a concern that she might embark on such a journey prematurely before she was ready to "spread her wings." I was utilizing this mode of communication to reflect upon her need to engage in a therapeutic symbiosis, as a vital prerequisite for achieving self differentiation. In addition I was interpreting the destructiveness of her defensive flight from the regression. I was quite concerned that she would act upon the urge to fly, in order to avoid the overwhelming anxiety associated with the regressive pull toward envelopment in a symbiosis. Her developmental solution to an infantile dilemma would then be repeated. However, we had a common understanding that she was in treatment to gain the strength to fly. Her "crazy behavior," which frightened her family, was identified by her as "rattling her cage." She recognized that much of the behavior was motivated by a powerful need to provoke her "jailers" into invoking more extreme restrictions upon her, thereby reenforcing her defensive stance.

She noticed that she could not control her cage-rattling, which dominated her whenever she was moving closer to me or whenever she felt good about herself. A telephone call to me was prescribed as her medication, to be taken for the impulse to rattle her cage. At this point she revealed a secret fantasy that had kept hope alive in her. It grew from a time when as a child she saw a portrait of an Indian woman, and had elaborated a fantasy of the woman as a mother who encouraged autonomy and independence. With mounting intensity she described her need to fly to India to find this woman, and hence herself. She did not want to fly there in her imagination; she had done that all her life and it meant nothing. She had to have the actual experience. She started to act upon the fantasy, making numerous efforts to board an airplane, but was stopped when she had no ticket. My reaction was to emphasize that although she had the right idea she was going about it in the wrong way, and at the wrong time. *Right* was defined as direct and straightforward, *wrong* as twisted and distorted.

I was walking a narrow line with the patient, trying to strengthen the part of her that was seeking the concrete experience of an adequate symbiosis, which was the right idea. At the same time I was gently interpreting the distorted direction her motivation was taking, distorted in that it kept her from making the very attachment she needed. I related this to her effort to create the right conditions with me, so the treatment relationship could make the fantasy real. My regressive identification with her frantic attempt to hold on to her autonomy and freedom, albeit from a narcissistic and magical position, enabled me to empathize with her experience. The strength of my support was focused upon diminishing her need to flee from the very conditions required to accomplish the goal of autonomy and independence, although there was the danger of encouraging her acting out. I could sense the tenuousness of the therapeutic alliance, and the ease with which it could be disrupted were prohibitions and restrictions to enter my attitude. A countertransference-based regressive identification was giving impetus to my empathic responsiveness, which was then exposed to more advanced secondary process functions. The end result was translated into interpretive interventions that were meant to diminish the distortions produced by her defensive organization.

During this time much pressure was placed upon me by her family to meet with them. However, the patient herself made it clear that if I spoke with them the therapy would end. The office had become a contained space within which she could find herself, and were her family to come in the door that space would be hopelessly contaminated. I felt she was underlining the necessity of my not being pressured by her into behaving like a pathologically symbiotic figure, lest I be unavailable as an adequate symbiotic partner. On one occasion she announced that her family was in the waiting room. She wanted me to inform them that I would not speak to them. I simply commented that she seemed to be inviting me to make therapy impossible. She smiled and left. Later she referred to this moment as crucial to her. It was, she said, like a breath of fresh air to have what was said be what was done.

Shortly thereafter I received a phone call from another country. She had gotten on a plane, was being held, and refused to explain anything. Her only identification was my bill. She was put on the phone and I laughingly stated, "Well, you are two thirds cured." She giggled as she explained that she had gone to the airport to fly to India, became "invisible," had gotten as far as another country, and was stopped for not having a passport. She had felt totally defeated, wanting to die or to kill herself, and began to fragment in response to the questioning of others. It occurred to her then that if she told the truth they would consider her insane, and if she told a lie they would understand and send her home. She decided at that moment to remain silent. When she heard my voice she anticipated an attack or a condescending reproach, but my laugh gave her an infusion of life and energy; she told the truth, and returned home.

In the succeeding sessions she spoke of her involvement with acting upon a fantasy that she needed to live. She saw how it protected her from forming a deeper attachment to me; how she was searching for a mother in India that she ought instead to find in the therapeutic relationship. It was clear to her now that she had been attempting to heal herself through the body ego experience of an adequate symbiosis, but had run away from the relationship in which that potential existed. Most important was her need to discover that I could allow her the autonomy, independence, and freedom to move. The regression, vulnerability, and lack of differentiation embodied in a symbiotic relationship necessitated her knowing that I understood the particular conditions constituting an adequate symbiosis for her. Her flight was a prelude to entering the relationship with that degree of commitment and trust.

After she returned she could not eat, sleep, or remove her contact lenses. She was unable to sleep because she was terrified of being totally enveloped by the powerful forces within. This expressed her fear of the regression that was now extremely active. She described being awake as a way of staying alive, facing herself, and not escaping. She thought of sleeping as being enveloped, escaping, and running away. I replied that it seemed to me she had it all reversed—that *sleeping* appeared to me to be the equivalent of flying, of entering her internal world without the weight of her defensiveness; and that staying awake appeared to be an escape, reflecting her defensive opposition to regressive infantile experiences. She was also terrified that if she ate she would gorge herself and never be able to stop. The only way to manage was to either not eat or to eat only the barest minimum. She feared even being near food, as she was beginning to experience the effects of her infantile instinctual life. In addition, she refused to take off her contact lenses because she feared going blind. She could see clearly with them on, and was concerned that without them her vision would become blurred and she would be unable to distinguish anything. Once again she had the right idea, but went about it in the wrong way. She did need to see clearly and was frightened that her vision would become undifferentiated. I consistently interpreted her defensive reversal.

The patient began to respond by exposing herself to food, which gave her a sense of regulation and restraint. She selected foods to cook in interesting and imaginative ways, as she became aware of skills and abilities that had always been dormant. In addition, she allowed herself to sleep and found dreams accessible to her. She reported a dream in which she was in the court of a French king, was offered anything she desired, and could not allow herself to have what was available. The recognition that the obstacles were within herself was enormously relieving, and was accompanied by a feeling of containment and of being in charge of her life. Therapy was opening potentials and making her aware of the importance of words. Words could now be used to articulate internal experience, to define boundaries, to contain feelings, and to aid in the process of gaining perspective. This was a marvelous feeling for her, who once felt that she had no skin. She now felt like a whole person with troubles, conflicts, and problems.

A key facet of the therapeutic properties of the relationship centered around the significance of flying. She stated that she had to fly in order to live, and I agreed. To both of us, flying meant being able to move freely. However, to me it signified facilitating a regression in the patient to a therapeutic symbiosis, which would entail a temporary loss of advanced psychic functions. A new integration could then be achieved allowing her to move freely and fly. For her a symbiotic relationship had not been negotiated, and she could only anticipate being enveloped. She feared I would be unable to aid her in the task of self differentiation, and she would lose any ability to fly. Her enactment of a dramatic flight expressed her wish to be separated and differentiated, and to have the experience of knowing whether I truly grasped her conditions of an adequate symbiosis. In this sense the acting out was necessary. She had to have an actual experience in order to gain the mental representational capacity to internalize the symbolic meaning of my interpretations.

There was much to suggest that had I not been able to ally myself with the meaning of this powerful fantasy, she would have been unable to fully engage in a regressive therapeutic attachment. Although her enactment of the fantasy carried her away from the treatment, the connection to me was sustained by my empathic recognition of her need. My acceptance of it, expressed by a laugh, allowed her to return fully prepared to focus her regressive infantile strivings into the relationship. Had I been unwilling to appreciate the significance of her risky behavior, I might well have undermined her sense of trust that I would protect her autonomy in a symbiotic attachment. The interrelationship of countertransference and empathic responsiveness was an important ingredient in maintaining the therapeutic properties of the relationship. Distinguishing one from the other was essential for the task of giving emotional support to the necessary enactment, without encouraging it to the extent that it would degenerate into a destructive form of acting out. This underscored the fine line that existed between empathy and countertransference in the therapist, and between a necessary enactment and destructive acting out in the patient.[9]

---

9. Limentani (1966) referred to the disturbing episodes of acting out that occur even under satisfactory analytic circumstances. In selected patients with a severe tendency toward splitting, denial, and unreality feelings, plus a history of trauma in infancy, there may be violence and excessive acting out related to disturbance in the preverbal phase of development.

Ekstein (1965) identified a form of acting out that is different in nature than what is usually described. It is much more reminiscent of a dream sequence, and he called it *psychotic acting out*. It reveals a thought disorder that has to be understood analytically in order to permit interpretation. The interpretive technique frequently makes use of "the metaphor," or symbolic gratification, and the like.

McDougall (1979) highlighted the reasons why a therapist's subjective responses and a patient's behavioral enactment become a crucial dimension of the treatment situation with primitively organized patients. These are individuals for whom the ineluctable factors that structure human reality have not become meaningful. Otherness with its reward of personal identity and privacy, sexual differences with the reward of sexual desire, the refinding of magic fulfillments in creativity, the acceptance of death as the inevitable end that gives urgent and important significance to life, all may be lacking. For such people, others then tend to be seen only as vehicles for externalizing the pain of living, and a system of survival is thereby created.

5

Leaps and Acting Out

Acting Out as a Form of Communication

Action-discharge modes of interacting and communicating are more familiar to a therapist who has had extended contact with children in a treatment situation.[1] Although the significance of this form of adaptation has uniquely different conscious, preconscious, and unconscious meaning, it is generally indicative of a defensive and regressive retreat from an anxiety-arousing internal or external situation. This has proven to be the case even in those younger children for whom action-discharge phenomena, play activity, playacting, and various other behavioral expressions are relatively consonant with their developmental level of intrapsychic functioning. Action and behavior serve well as a means of avoiding the experience of powerful affective states. Remembering, fantasizing, symbolizing, and containing the mental representational linkages to the underlying unconscious motives is thereby bypassed. Thus action and behavior provide a potential pathway to understanding unconscious forces that might otherwise be unavailable.[2]

---

1. Ekstein (1965) has pointed out that the older a patient gets, the more difficult it seems to be for a therapist to cope with acting-out language. The language, whether it consists of free association, dialogue, playing, or acting out, is not in itself what cures. It is the question of what is communicated that is decisive. If it is a successful form of communication, and if for stretches it is the only form of communication, we should use it to understand the patient.

2. Ekstein (1965) described acting out as a special form of either reenacting past conflicts or of reenacting future conflicts within the context of the transference. A therapist must react in a truly democratic way and stop the segregation of

When intrapsychic events are expressed in behavior it can have a multiplicity of meanings. It can be (1) a sublimatory activity as a logical extension of instinctual integration on a solid background of healthy psychic structuralization, (2) a compromise effected by the ego for expressing disguised instinctual drives under the controlled regression involved in play, (3) a transformation of unconscious instinctual impulses and conflicts into symbolically determined actions designed to avoid remembering and experiencing inordinate anxiety, (4) a breakdown in symbolic functions leading to the need for discharge so as to gain some measure of tension relief from intolerable affects, or (5) a deficiency in psychic structuralization that leaves behavior as the only avenue open for expressing a powerful unconscious demand. An individual's actions are thereby accompanied by either a plethora of instinctual derivatives, vivid fantasies, intense ill-defined affective states, or a complete dearth of mental activity, depending upon the particular substrate of mental structuralization from which the behavior is derived.

The Significance of Action and Behavior in the More Primitively Structured Personality

For those individuals who are incapable of consistently exercising symbolic functions, the conditions of the treatment have to be adapted somewhat in order for the interaction to be internalized and represented.[3] In these situations the management of the thera-

---

acting-out behavior from other forms of a patient's communication devices without denying its differences.

Limentani (1966) denoted how acting-out patients often have a belief in the magic of action, and exhibit a disturbance in the relation between action and speech verbalized thought. These behaviors are a form of remembering, though they may not always be so; faulty verbalizations and remembering are not always responsible for acting out. Acting out can imply both memory and efforts to rectify early feelings of helplessness, and to recollect and work through a pathogenic early relationship primarily with the mother.

3. Winnicott (1963) was most explicit in outlining the therapeutic need for caretaking types of interventions in certain individuals whose pathology was

peutic framework becomes primary. Until a firmer structural foundation can be established to make it possible for symbolic processes to be operative, interpretations are not effective. Behavioral expressions of intrapsychic needs and demands are then a predominant feature of the therapeutic interaction. This makes it essential to distinguish between those behaviors that are the end result of defensive constellations, and those that are motivated by a need to carry inarticulable experiences into the relationship in order for progress to be realized. The treatment problem, when action represents the only vehicle for attaining access to therapeutic influence, is further complicated if there is an intermingling of defensive and progressive movements. A therapist's acceptance and implicit encouragement may be essential before the unconscious meaning of the behavior can be exposed and unraveled. The fine line between fostering a destructive form of acting out and a constructive form of reaching infantile and preverbal traumas can be difficult to negotiate.

---

formed in the earliest periods of development. He valued the role of interpretation highly, but called attention to the incongruity when they were applied to those who are incapable of grasping their meaning and could only experience them as evidence of a lack of empathic resonance re-creating the traumas of early development.

Bott-Spillius (1983) on the other hand stressed the way in which Kleinian technique embodies a rigorous maintenance of the psychoanalytic setting with emphasis on the transference, and the use of interpretation, especially of the transference, as the agent of therapeutic change. In general Kleinian analysts disagree with the idea of encouraging regression and reliving infantile experiences through non-interpretive means.

Gedo (1984) underscored the significance of identifying the primitive mode of organization that is characteristic of some individuals, which implies a whole array of adaptive deficits involving multiple lines of development. It necessitates that we go far in adapting treatment techniques to the individual requirements of given patients.

Kinston and Coen (1986) illustrated the manifestations of trauma associated with primal repression, and showed how they created a situation in treatment wherein interpretation must give way to recognition and action if understanding is to develop. They saw three overlapping phases: First, the transformation of neurotic conflicts and object narcissistic armor into awareness of deficit and need. Second, explicit awareness and assertion of primary relatedness with the therapist. Third, the reemergence and working through of unmet needs and traumatic states, so as to establish new understanding.

Some dimension of transforming unconscious strivings into behavior is probably inevitable in every individual under the sway of regressive forces. Consequently, a therapist must exert every effort to help contain the behavior within the therapeutic interaction, thereby making unconscious drives more accessible to a therapist's understanding of their nature and diminishing the tendency toward acting out. Whenever unconscious mental activity is expressed directly through behavior, important psychic functions are bypassed, creating the potential for serious lapses in judgment and leading to inaccurate assessments of external reality with sometimes dangerous consequences. At times this may place a patient's safety in jeopardy, which was behind the oft given injunction to desist from significant decision making and actions while in the throes of a regression. However, this type of intervention can in and of itself either intensify the danger, reenforce a pathological defense, or work in opposition to the conditions of safety required for a benign regression to unfold.[4]

An Empathic Lapse that Evokes Dangerous Acting Out and Forces a Leap

In many instances the appearance of behavioral acting out, within or outside of the confines of the therapeutic relationship, is indicative of a lapse in a therapist's empathic responsiveness to an unconscious communication. This may occur as a result of an

---

4. Limentani (1966) noted how some therapists advocated prohibitions of acting out, although such direct interventions may make analysis impossible and limit further understanding. Acting out contains a signal that help is required, and it asks for a response from the therapist who is often inappropriately tempted to abandon interpretive technique.

Anna Freud (1968) commented on the dilemma posed by patients exhibiting a tendency to behave in destructive ways, observing how as a general rule this must stop short of motor action, leaving the therapeutic alliance intact. However, there are situations in which the strength of repressed strivings sweeps beyond the imposed limits and into action, rupturing the alliance, and may lead to an abrupt termination. Such patients generally direct their impulses into the motor sphere, and relive what emerges in their lives. In all, acting out does play an important constructive role in analysis, at the same time that it may create specific dangers.

incorrect interpretation, an inappropriate silence, or perhaps by unwittingly encouraging this form of expression. A therapist's ideal attitude is supportive of autonomy, integration, growth, and independence, and though behavior is accepted as material to be understood it is not viewed as the most effective pathway toward increasing self-knowledge. For this reason introducing a leap, which often extends interventions into the behavioral realm, carries with it the possibility of a therapist's acting out. This must always be taken into account, because such interventions have embodied in them the potential for encouraging a patient to do likewise. Yet to avoid actions or behavior when they are called for can be equally as risky, though often not as dramatically apparent. A therapist's silence can also be a stimulus for a patient to act out, particularly when an interpretation is required to help in containing a transference experience; its absence is perceived as an implicit message to engage in such behavior.

Clinical Example

This point was demonstrated in the treatment of a 7-year-old girl. A life-threatening incident with profound transference significance forced me into abandoning an interpretive posture and engaging in a leap, with no time or opportunity for careful consideration. The immediate reason for her needing therapeutic help was her great difficulty in going to school. When she was confronted with leaving home she either feigned a somatic illness or broke down in severe episodes of crying. In addition, she was described as controlling, demanding of parental attention, having wide and labile mood swings, and erupting in temper tantrums at the slightest provocation. For her first four years she was the only child of doting middle-aged parents. Her every wish was granted, and she appeared delightful and charming to them in every way. When she was 4 years old a sister was born, followed in rapid succession by two younger brothers. There was a drastic change in her entire bearing and attitude. She became whiny, clinging, and demanding. In addition, she was openly hostile to her siblings and to her parents whenever they devoted any attention to them. This behavior continued to escalate, with her parents feeling increasingly helpless about being able to comfort or reason with her. Her difficulty in regard to school finally led to their seeking help.

In the initial session she was extremely warm and friendly; she had looked forward to coming, and enjoyed talking about her resentment over her siblings' having replaced her from a special position in the family. Periodically she became somewhat tearful, remembering what it was like before they were born. Her whole life had seemed to fall apart from that point on. Her mother, to whom she had been very close, had become harassed and unavailable to her. The child's entire demeanor changed as soon as she mentioned her mother. She noted the anger in her voice, became worried, and repetitively asserted how much she loved her mother. My comment on the guilt she seemed to feel about being angry with her mother was not responded to directly, but it elicited a flurry of thoughts and feelings about the specialness of her father. Her face lit up as she described his taking her on trips. She was animated and excited while she elaborated on what a wonderful man he was and how well he understood her. She went on to describe their relationship, implying that she could care for him much better than her mother.

During this phase of the treatment she appeared to be experiencing the relationship with me in much the same way; the sessions were like the special times she had spent with her father—she was excited about coming, and the only difficult moments were at the beginning and the end. She was anxious and guilt-ridden when faced with leaving her mother to enter the office, became excited once in the session, and her anxiety returned when it was time to leave. I referred to this phenomenon and commented on how guilty she looked at these times. She paused, looking very uneasy, and then stated that she just loved to make pictures and wanted to draw. Her sessions were then occupied with highly symbolized portrayals of her thinly disguised sexual preoccupations.

She drew figures patterned after Barbie and Ken dolls, hinting at their hidden, secretive sexual activities. Vague references were made to their sexual organs, accompanied by her giggling and embarrassment. As she drew, she displayed more regressive behavior for the first time. When I verbalized what her drawings and associated comments implied, her initial reaction was to get more animated and expand upon her drawings and fantasies. I finally remarked that the feelings and fantasies she was expressing in her play might very well be a reflection of what she was experiencing toward me deep inside, which might explain why she felt so guilty as she left her mother and when she returned to her. It looked as though she felt the relationship with me was terribly forbidden. Her reaction to this interpretation was immediate. She looked embarrassed and anxious, and softly spoke of having something to talk about but of being unable to tolerate the idea of looking at me or of me looking at her.

She looked for a comfortable position, crawling under a desk all curled up, squeezing under a chair, but none of these felt right. She continued to search, and when she saw the couch her face brightened. She directed me to sit in a chair behind her while she lay on the couch, setting up a classical psychoanalytic position. At first slowly and then with mounting intensity she unveiled her deep involvement with masturbatory activities. The genital instinctual arousal was exciting, frightening, and infused with vague hard-to-articulate fantasies involving a large, ominous, guilt-producing presence in the back of her mind. I likened the feeling to her experience at the start and end of the sessions. She nodded vigorously in agreement, and burst forth with a flood of thoughts about how betrayed she had felt with the birth of each sibling. She had felt so special to her father, but the births seemed to emphatically demonstrate his primary attachment to her mother, destroying her own sense of specialness. She then paused and remarked on how different she felt toward her youngest brother. She took care of him and realized that she treated him in her fantasies much as though he were her own. Then she jumped up from the couch, saying she wanted to draw, and began to draw pictures of herself as the mother of a new baby.

I was silently listening, absorbing the impact of this powerful oedipal drama and the ways it had affected all corners of her life. Suddenly she threw down the pencil, ripped up the paper, and cried out how badly she felt. Her mother could never love her, it was all just so awful, and she hated herself. She bolted out of the room in obvious distress, and after a brief moment of hesitation I followed. She had run to a window in the hallway and opened it and was climbing up to throw herself out onto the pavement many stories below. I grabbed her and held her close while she sobbed deeply. She nestled in my arms, her head buried in my shoulder, and continued to cry. Interspersed with her tears were anguished statements about my hating her for feeling this way as much as she hated herself and her mother hated her. She was gradually comforted, and talked quietly of how clear her troubles were becoming to her. She had always denied that there was anything wrong with her, blaming all of her difficulties on others around her. For the first time she could see what her treatment was all about.

In subsequent sessions she was eager to explore her internal world, and did so in a penetrating fashion. She revealed her feelings, fantasies, earliest memories, and transference experiences. The ebb and flow of regressive and progressive movements all took place on the solid background of a strong therapeutic alliance. She often made reference to that dramatic incident as a turning point in her life. Later it was explored in some depth. She remembered experiencing my silence, while she was drawing her picture, as a subtle encouragement of her wish to replace her mother. She linked it to similar sensations she now recognized were present in her attachment to her father. With great relief she could see how overstimulating his preferential treatment of her had been. It was now apparent to her why she had such an exaggerated feeling of guilt, and was spending her life trying to avoid this internal constellation by clinging to her mother or provoking her into angry attacks.

The patient had experienced a regressive breakdown in those ego functions involved with fantasy formation and symbolization, which resulted in an eruption into action of guilt-producing infantile prohibitions, leading to a life-threatening form of acting out.[5] The feelings aroused in the transference relationship, rather than eliciting psychic content that was suitable for interpretive work, were discharged in her impulsive self-destructive action. In reacting with human compassion

---

5. Milner (1952) described the position of play as halfway between daydreaming and purposeful, expedient action. Play links the worlds of subjective unreality and objective reality, harmoniously fusing the edges but not confusing them. There is a need for a medium between self-created and external realities, for these states are a necessary phase in the development of object relations. The medium is an intervening substance, through which impressions are conveyed to the senses, and is the pliable stuff out of which fantasies are made. Both the therapist and the setting can serve as this intervening pliable substance.

Rexford (1966) traced the developmental aspects of a variety of factors that may come into play when acting out is manifested. The psychic institutions have to be sufficiently developed to produce the particular form of motor activity, and the acting out may appear as a phase specific phenomenon with well-defined defensive and adaptive functions. Specific events may clarify what situations predispose a patient to acting out and which counter-forces mitigate against it. The role of parent–child relationships in encouraging or curbing a tendency toward acting out is a significant factor.

Boesky (1982) elaborated upon the pain of the transference, as the tension between the actuality of the experience of affects and the futility, danger or both of ever fully realizing or actualizing transference wishes. Actions at this point facilitate a compromise, which is required because of the defensive imbalance. With the neurotic the ego is generally able to tolerate the imbalance, though for most it is defensively necessary at one time or another to supplement defenses by shifting to the realm of action and behavior. When that which has been actual in the past converges with that which inappropriately becomes actual, by virtue of the therapist's inadvertent complicity in the present, the potential for acting out is much increased. The shift to action is not necessarily inevitable, and the inadvertent compliance of the therapist on some occasions may give rise to a dream instead of, or in addition to, acting out.

and concern for the patient's welfare I had had to momentarily abandon an exclusively verbal interpretive posture. The concrete act of physically stopping and holding her had a positive influence, suggesting that some early preoedipal factors were involved in her pathology. I had been operating on the principle that what could be symbolically represented, fantasized, and communicated could also be interpreted, but the sudden eruption of a regressive form of action brought the validity of this premise into question. The patient later revealed, however, that it was my silence, not an interpretation, that had precipitated the event. Furthermore, the silence itself was resonating with a powerful unconscious fantasy, and its impact could no longer be contained in the absence of interpretive help.

Whenever the therapeutic properties of the treatment are compromised, the timing and content of interpretive interventions, the appropriateness of silences, and the effective management of the framework should be carefully examined to determine whether they are correctly addressing what is required to promote constructive growth.[6] In the incident with this 7-year-old girl an exploration could take place only in retrospect, due to the demand for immediate action. A benign regression had been induced by the conditions of the treatment, and the defensive opposition had been mobilized to guard against an underlying, inordinately conflicted positive oedipal attachment and was in the process of gradually being reduced. The exposure of the derivatives of her genital oedipal fantasies was then unfolding within what appeared to be a secure framework. My management of the ground rules and boundaries, interpretations, and silences were allowing this to transpire in an orderly fashion, utilizing a verbally symbolic mode of communication. Periodically she turned to play activities, and this regression in the service of the

---

6. Wolf (1983a) believed it was vital to examine the therapist's role in creating an empathic failure when any obstruction to therapeutic progress was exhibited. He considered the analytic ambience, in combination with analysis of resistance, to be a crucial feature of an environment of relative safety. The balance between need and fear then shifts; hope is encouraged, the expectation of needs being heard and understood mobilizes a revival of archaic repressed and disavowed needs. However, an inevitable failure to maintain total empathic intuneness with the patient disrupts the relationship, causing a temporary return to archaic modes. The therapist ideally can recognize the legitimate self-object needs underlying the archaic, distorted manifestations, and explain and interpret the sequence of events and correct the previous misunderstanding. The patient again feels understood, the empathic flow is restored, and archaic merger is changed into empathic resonance.

ego seemed consonant with her developmental age. Although it did possess some of the characteristics of a behavioral acting out, the continuation of her symbolic productions was furthering the emergence of new material. There was then a transition from lying on the couch where she verbalized her masturbatory experiences, to engaging in play by drawing enabling oedipal fantasies to be elaborated further, to an abrupt escalation of archaic prohibitions resulting in a regressive breakdown of ego functions, and finally to a self-destructive acting out.

The initial consequence of her impulsive action was to rupture the contained conditions of the therapeutic framework, but it resulted in a concrete experience of comfort and protection through physical contact. It was certainly clear that were such an intervention to have been offered earlier it would readily have been experienced as seductive or invasive. Even though it might have prevented her potentially dangerous action, at best it would have reenforced a pathological defense. The rapidity of the shift from talking and playing to an uncontrolled act raised questions as to whether that act could have been averted with a more sensitive handling of the transference. Ultimately, it emerged that it was the timing of an interpretation that was remiss. However, my actual involvement had an enormously favorable impact upon the subsequent relationship. The therapeutic alliance was strengthened and through its effects a deeper self-awareness was promoted. These factors fostered a positive identification, and eventually led to her achieving a resolution of intense instinctual conflicts.

Upon reflection I realized that my preconscious sense of the patient's susceptibility to being overstimulated had led to an overconcern with maintaining a firm and secure therapeutic framework. It produced a subtle rigidity, motivated by a countertransference-based reluctance to be perceived as seductive or overstimulating. This was reflected in the way I went about defining the ground rules and in an inflexible insistence on holding to an exclusively interpretive posture. Consequently there was not room enough for a limited degree of acting out, and this attitude may have contributed to the extreme form it took.[7] This treatment situation

---

7. Racker (1957) divided countertransference into countertransference thoughts and positions, with the difference involving the degree to which the ego was included. In the former, reactions are experienced as free associations with no great emotional intensity and as somewhat foreign to the ego. In the latter, the therapist's ego is involved, which is felt with great intensity as a true reality. The therapist then has two ways of responding. He may either perceive his reactions or he may act them out.

LEAPS AND ACTING OUT

called attention to the fact that there are some circumstances in which some form of acting out may be the only route to attaining effective therapeutic influence. If the relationship does not allow sufficient latitude for acting-out behavior to take place, such behavior may then have to escalate in intensity.

Engaging in a Leap by Participating in a Form of Acting Out

Unconscious forces often make use of behavior to gain access to expression, even in the more structured personality. One inherent danger in encouraging this form of communication resides in its lack of clarity, since the connections required to elicit derivatives have been bypassed. A therapist's receptive attitude is essential for the meaning of the behavior to be fully revealed. An absence of flexibility may be received as a repetition of an infantile trauma, rather than a helpful constructive adjunct to a secure and contained treatment framework. Frequently, an admixture of healthy and pathological factors compounds the difficulty, for it brings confusion as to specifically which ground rules, boundaries, and conditions must be rigorously maintained to constitute the proper framework for the relationship.

Clinical Example

This feature of acting out was evident in the treatment of a young adult woman, who originally sought treatment because of her concern about moving from one conflicted love affair to another. She felt driven to enter into intense relationships that ended in rejection, and knew she incited the trouble.

In the beginning sessions she was constantly worried as to whether she would be seen as sexually provocative, and anticipated being humiliated. She recalled previous therapeutic contacts in which she had been totally offended and frightened by interpretive comments concerning her "seductive" behavior. She fled from these encounters, since this had been mentioned during them without her having felt seductive. This had meant to her that there was something in the other person that was either frightened of her, or that would be seductive, and she reacted by leaving, never to return. She thus indicated how vital it would be for me to create a secure framework, and suggested that any departure from clearly defined ground rules and boundaries would be perceived as overstimulating. Also suggested was how important it would be to enlist her participation in establishing the conditions of the treatment, and to carefully examine her responses to the various ground rules.

She was knowledgeable about psychoanalytic treatment, and knew she would need to be seen often. She sensed that for treatment to be successful she would have to face powerful and inaccessible childhood experiences. However, she was inordinately anxious about the couch, and especially concerned that I might insist upon it as a condition of the treatment. Whether it was in her best interests or not, she was too frightened to consider it. While we discussed all of this in face-to-face contact she couldn't help but notice how drawn she was to searching for my reactions in order to appease an inner feeling of insecurity. It was not until she saw how this prevented her from observing what was occurring deeper inside herself, that she decided to use the couch. In this manner the ground rules and boundaries were gradually constructed, with the patient discovering some evidence of their importance in facilitating growth at each step. She was constantly afraid that the conditions of the treatment would be rigidly fixed, making her feel trapped and immobilized. The experience of having her associations listened to and taken into account was reassuring.

This approach became a matter for special attention when I noted a peculiar pattern in the way she handled the payment of the bill. After the first few months of regular payment, the bill began to build up to a specific amount every month with the patient explaining it on the basis of some external reality. She would make a payment, always reducing the remaining amount to that exact figure. She was concerned that I would expect her to pay in full, which she felt was impossible to do. Therefore she was relieved when I said the decision about the payment could be made jointly when its unconscious meaning was more apparent. It was clearly vital to her to manage the fee in this fashion, and I became a participant in what appeared to be a subtle form of acting out. In a quiet way I had engaged in a leap having the potential of resonating with some as yet unknown unconscious fantasy, possibly reenforcing a pathological defense, or even re-creating a presently inaccessible developmental experience. Although she gave many indications that a secure framework was an essential factor for enabling a benign regression, and that any deviation had the potential of becoming so overstimulating it would be a detriment to therapeutic progress, she had also underscored the fact that too rigid an approach to this task would have traumatic, as yet unseen implications. Furthermore, she had already indicated that if someone else's agenda was imposed upon her it could easily precipitate a flight from the treatment.

Shortly afterward the patient entered the office in a revealing tee-shirt and without a bra, seemingly unaware that her body movements exposed her breasts. I silently recalled how offended and frightened she had been by interpretive comments about her "seductive" behavior. I therefore simply registered and watched silently what appeared to be a seductive scene. She then began to talk about people who saw something, said nothing about it, and as a consequence were untrustable. She went on to express her uneasiness and irritability, along with a concern that her words could be heard in the waiting room and a question as to whether my office was properly soundproofed. The patient seemed to be reenacting a sexual encounter, with the unconscious motives rendered defensively inaccessible. In addition I had disengaged myself from the impact of her exhibitionistic behavior by defensively assuming a distantly observing stance. I was concerned about calling attention to the transference meaning of this behavioral enactment before the associative linkages had become available, for I could sense, hovering in the background, her readiness to invoke humiliating prohibitions. Although my silence was facilitating, it also evoked distrust, probably due to its defensive component.

The patient's uneasiness about the room being soundproofed was apparently a derivative expressing her unconscious perception of my distant attitude. It vividly illustrated her sensitivity to even the slightest erosion of the containing influences of a secure therapeutic framework, and immediately made me aware of the source of my defensiveness. This led to my stating that when I had said nothing about what she was showing me with her body, I caused her to distrust my motives. She reacted by becoming totally humiliated, feeling out on a limb and overwhelmed. She explained that she had awakened late, dressed in a rush giving no thought to her appearance, and had not realized what she had done. Now she felt like there was no place to hide. She then fell silent and with mounting anxiety spoke of being aware of my breathing. With great difficulty she expressed a fantasy that I was sexually aroused and masturbating. After a pause she was flooded with memories of her father when she was 7 or 8 years old. He was a schoolteacher who was out of work after having been fired for child molestation, and was home while her mother worked. One day, when the patient came home from school, her father was on the couch and he held her, became sexually aroused, and masturbated. A clearer picture of the unconscious meaning of her anxiety about using the couch was now emerging. It added a further dimension of understanding to the vital importance she attached to having the therapeutic boundaries clearly defined, and clarified why even the slightest lapse in empathy was arousing extremely high levels of anxiety.

When I was defensive and not functioning with the combined attributes of a good object, the fixed attitudes of her character pathology were in readiness to be invoked as a defense. At that moment I was infantilizing her, and in addition behaving like the absent mother. My interpretation of her distrust made her acutely aware of her poorly regulated phallic exhibitionism, and elicited a fantasy of my sexual arousal. This led to the return of childhood memories that were at the foundation of her fixed character defenses. She did not experience herself as seductive because the reaction-formation of humiliation was so predominant. When her unconscious perception of my defensiveness was addressed, the empathic lapse was rectified and her need for this defense was diminished. Validation was provided in a dream the following night: She was alone in a beach house, teenagers having a party threatened to invade it, a man corralled and talked to them, and she felt safe.

A short time later when making out a check to pay her bill she noticed the balance. She was tempted once again to reduce it to the same figure, but instead decided she could afford to pay it all. While she was talking about her hesitancy, the amount suddenly reminded her of some money left to her by her grandfather to further her education. This elicited memories of her attachment to him, which had represented a haven of safety in the sea of overstimulation and the lack of protection surrounding her relationship to her parents. My willingness to accept her need to allow the bill to accumulate was resonating with this inarticulable containing influence, making it possible for the extremely disruptive experiences of instinctual overstimulation to enter the transference relationship. It was certainly essential to this patient for the ground rules, boundaries, and conditions of the treatment to be clearly defined and secure, for any modification carried with it the unconscious meaning of being overstimulating. However, it was also important for there to be enough flexibility to allow this element of acting out to be given room for behavioral expression. Similarly, her exhibitionistic behavior was acting out an unconsciously determined sexual scene, which could be expressed only in this form. It was the only available pathway to her traumatic childhood memories.

The patient had been acting out the unconscious experience of being securely held through accumulating a specific unpaid balance on her bill.

This served as a background of safety upon which a traumatic childhood scene could be reenacted. In spite of my awareness that any modification in the ground rules or boundaries of the treatment had serious implications for eroding the containment required for an unfolding of the transference, and my awareness of the potential danger involved in reenforcing a pathological defense—or worse, in repeating an infantile trauma—I allowed the bill to accumulate without any knowledge of its unconscious meaning. I had introduced a leap, encouraging a form of acting out that in this instance was essential for promoting constructive growth. I was guided by my best reading of the patient's unconscious perception of what was required in the relationship. Then, with the emergence of the traumatic sexual scene, I began to have second thoughts about the advisability of this decision. The return of her childhood memories, however, enabled the patient to integrate an aspect of her character functioning that had previously remained obscure. The effectiveness of this therapeutic work, in conjunction with the validation provided by the dream, gave me reason to wait until this other facet of her acting-out behavior could gain access to expression. Once the connection to the containing influence of her grandfather surfaced she no longer had to act out, and her unconscious instinctual life was expressed exclusively in the transference relationship.

Introducing a Leap through Implicitly Encouraging the Expression of Acting-Out Behavior

While the entire thrust of psychoanalytic psychotherapy is aimed toward enabling, supporting, and encouraging a verbal mode of communication, an important facet of a therapist's attitude must include the receptivity to and acceptance of an acting out through behavior.[8] For some individuals acting out may be the only means through which unconscious forces can be expressed. This is not

---

8. Stein (1973) distinguished between the impulsive forms of acting out that emerge specifically as a consequence of the changing conditions induced by psychoanalytic treatment, and the tendency to act out that can be regarded as a character trait. This implies that the patient has been acting out for much of his or her life, and further that the acting out in the transference that occurs during analysis is a secondary development and a crucial one for the success of the analytic method.

true of all behavioral forms of acting out, and for some it may represent a pathological means of avoiding verbal communication. In such situations a therapist's acceptance of the behavior may reflect a collusion with pathological defenses antithetical to growth. It is thereby vital to make the distinction, and the difference is not always dependent upon the degree of psychic structuralization in the patient's personality. Behavioral forms of expression may serve an important communicative function in individuals with more advanced levels of psychic organization, although a therapist's encouraging attitude under those circumstances would be a departure from an exclusively interpretive stance. In that sense it would possess the attributes of a leap.

Clinical Example

This became a significant part of the treatment of an 8-year-old girl, originally referred because of her underachievement in school. She was eager to come to her sessions and wanted to talk about her internal troubles. She felt constantly frustrated, bored, and suffered from what she called "growing pains." These were pains everywhere in her body, which felt as if something was trapped within and trying to grow.

In the early months she complained of her pains, becoming extremely irritable and upset in doing so. She was convinced that I did not believe her and was laughing inside. Nothing I did or said could alter this conviction, and it was terribly disturbing to her. The tenacity of this fixed defensive attitude made her certain that she both could not and would not be understood. In this context she was identifying me as a bad object, making it vital to locate the source of this impression. My first consideration was that I might have been functioning in a depriving, overstimulating, or impinging manner, or that I was defensive in some fashion. After exploring the patient's material and my subjective reactions this did not appear to be the case. In addition, although the patient was responding to me as a bad object, she did not indicate that I possessed any of these qualities. She put emphasis on the fact that it made no difference what I did, thereby suggesting it was a product of her defensive attitude. However, a therapist can also be perceived in this way when an important communication has not been understood.

She was preoccupied with disturbing body sensations, accompanied by a constant anticipation of being humiliated. By implication this seemed to express how much opposition there was to any instinctual activity. Her greatest concern was that I couldn't understand. In a sense this was accurate, since the only way her instinctual activity could be expressed was through the language of her body. Out of these considerations I told her she had the right idea in thinking I did not believe her. I told her that I was aware of a hidden message in her body's communications, but that it looked as though she did not believe I could hear how her body talked, and if I couldn't translate this language she would remain trapped. Her response was immediate and filled with excitement, as she talked about exploring caves, forests, and jungles. She placed particular emphasis on the thrill and danger associated with the exploration.

When she had focused so much attention on her body sensations and referred to them as "growing pains," it alerted me to the intense internal conflict between her instinctual drives and prohibitive responses. Her irritability suggested that she anticipated the underlying instinctual demands would be exposed. I had been reluctant to address this instinctual conflict directly lest it intensify her defensive posture and further entrap her. The interpretation I finally made was directed to her unconscious perception of my reluctance, and her implied appeal for help was openly acknowledged. The result was a lessening of her need for defense, and elicitation of her thinly disguised masturbatory wishes.

I then said that I thought her involvement with exploring these spaces reflected her search for help in talking about the exploration of her body and its inner parts. Her reaction was striking. She lay down on the couch, became very subdued, and openly rubbed her genitals. She talked softly about my words giving her permission to do what she had wanted to do ever since she first began treatment. She felt blocked when she tried to talk, and had always known that the only way to relieve the block was to masturbate. When she did, the words came easily. She went on to talk about a wild young cousin and their sexual games, and she recalled seeing a guard at a toll booth who had frightened her because he reminded her of this cousin. She thought of being overly attached to her mother, and of wanting to be free but feeling unable to survive without her. Her parents had been divorced when she was 2 years of age, and she had periodic visits with her father that were exciting and frightening. She now began to remember that when she was with her father she always felt pulled to return to her mother, and when she was with her mother she felt an excited wish to return to her father.

My interpretation of her masturbatory wish, which had been so actively defended against, led to her openly masturbating and describing what it accomplished for her. Accentuating these genital body ego experiences overcame her resistance; prohibitive responses subsided, and instinctual derivatives entered the perceptual field of her preconscious and conscious systems. She received my interpretation as granting her permission, and this was implicit in my overall attitude. My presence had been so resonant with her infantile prohibitions that she could not engage in a regressive pathway toward instinctual integration, and hence felt trapped. The strength of these archaic obstacles could be bypassed only by the acting out of her masturbatory wish. My recognition of her dilemma, communicated through an interpretation in combination with an attitude receptive to her behavior, enabled her to modify the intensity of the prohibition. She then perceived me as an ally in finding her way through the inhibitions, strengthening the therapeutic alliance. Were I to have seen this form of behavior simply as a resistance, or to have conveyed an attitude that insisted upon her talking without acting, I would only have amplified the pathological defenses at the foundation of her "growing pains."

The patient had also indicated that the pressing need to masturbate was present within her from the outset of therapeutic contact. Thus the actual seeking of a treatment relationship contained within it an element of acting out, which in this instance was hidden from me. Had I engaged in a leap by encouraging this form of expression prior to establishing a secure framework, it is doubtful that it would have had the same outcome. Under those circumstances it would probably have emanated from a countertransference-based regressive identification; it would in all likelihood have been unconsciously perceived by the patient and been overstimulating, and her internal prohibitions would then have been intensified rather than alleviated.

Distinguishing between Destructive and Constructive Expressions of Acting Out

When the movement toward therapeutic contact is an expression of acting out, and this is apparent to the therapist, the entire focus of the treatment centers around the unconscious significance of the act. This usually happens when the patient's personal knowledge of the therapist has been the primary determinant for entering the relationship. There are occasions where just the acceptance of the referral may be resonant with a powerful unconscious fantasy, or represent a collusion with a tenacious pathological defense. In that case effective therapeutic influence is obviated by virtue of carrying on the relationship. Continuing the treatment then represents a serious rupture in the conditions required to support a benign regression, and it would be destructive to do anything other than refuse to participate or make another referral.

Most therapists have experienced being contacted for therapeutic help by people who are significant others either to themselves or to their patients. The potential for unhelpful and detrimental consequences to all parties is usually immediately recognized. The powerful unconscious forces motivating these subtle and blatant expressions of acting out are best dealt with in a relationship wherein the proper conditions for effective treatment can be established. Once again, however, to deal with it by invoking a rigid set of rules may also close a door to making a proper assessment. This particular choice by a patient, even though it represents a form of acting out, may be motivated by an unconscious perception that the relationship possesses the unique features essential for realizing constructive psychological growth. A therapist's willingness to consider it as a possibility can then lead to a much better referral if it turns out to be a product of a destructive form of acting out. Of course if it were perpetuated it would work against the goals of treatment. Conversely, it could provide an otherwise unavailable opportunity were it to be a feasible undertaking.

Clinical Example

I was faced with a vivid example of this kind of situation when I was contacted by telephone from a distant city by a 20-year-old male who I had known intimately when he was a young child. He was the youngest of four boys in a family that had been extremely close to me during my formative years, and I still maintained close ties with his parents. I had known him quite well from the time of his birth until he was 5 years of age, but then had little direct contact with him. He was now calling because he was desperate and had nowhere to turn. His voice trembled as he spoke of his despair, of having no life for himself, and of feeling depressed and hopeless. Seemingly anticipating my question he described having been in treatment on several occasions with different therapists. They had all turned out to be unsuccessful, and with great emphasis he stated he was not calling for another referral. He went into detail about his previous contacts in order to underscore the fact that he had absolutely no interest in going through this process again. On each occasion he had either ended up getting so angry that he stormed out and never went back, or did something to get into trouble so he was unable to return. He said that I was his last hope, implying but not explicitly stating that he was considering suicide. When I asked if this is what he had in mind he softly remarked that it was, yet he felt he should make one last try. He thought of me as the only one he would be able to talk to. I said I would be open to meeting with him to discuss his options for obtaining help, but in all likelihood it could not come from me. The ongoing relationship with his family might prevent me from functioning adequately on his behalf, and therapy could be further complicated by whatever meanings that relationship held for him. He sounded relieved, and an appointment was scheduled.

I was deeply affected by this appeal for help, and recognized that he was probably acting on the basis of some powerful unconscious fantasy. Even though I had made no specific commitment to treatment, I was worried about the possibility of colluding with forces antithetical to his growth simply by agreeing to see him. I had to consider whether my motive grew out of an as yet unseen regressive identification mobilizing a rescue fantasy, or whether it was a straightforward response to the threat of his suicide and some concern that a total refusal would inexorably push him in that direction. There were so many unknowns, and the stakes were so high, that I felt at least I could try and determine if there were other alternatives.

In the interim period before his initial appointment I looked for any evidence of potential blind spots that could interfere with my ability to make an accurate assessment. I wanted to be able to listen to him without distortions created by my personal history. This young man's father had been an important figure in my life, particularly during adolescence, and he continued to occupy a special place as a loved and respected source of positive identifications. I was acutely aware of the father's character flaws, especially in relation to his children. I had come to grips with them long ago, through confrontations and challenges, and had found a loving, sensitive, tender man who possessed many admirable qualities underneath his protective armoring. The patient's mother was a very warm, outgoing, and giving woman, who had tried very hard to intercede with the harshness of the father, particularly with this child. He was the baby of the family, and she tended to both infantilize him and cater to his every whim. I remembered that as a child he was sometimes clinging and fearful, drawing his mother closer to him; and at other times aggressively controlling, demanding and grandiose, a caricature of his father's worst characteristics. I realized that my prior knowledge of this family, and my continuing involvement with them, contained within it the potential for obstructing a necessary listening attitude in therapy. I approached the initial contact with a pre-formed idea of trying to assist him in finding an appropriate therapist.

The first moment of contact was filled with emotion for both of us. In spite of my preparation I felt a surge of warmth upon seeing and greeting him. He had been sitting stiffly in the waiting room with a characteristic aura of arrogance, but when he saw me he became tearful. His whole manner softened as his protective facade seemed to fall away. A firm handshake was exchanged wordlessly. I could feel the intensity of an as yet unarticulated message in the handshake that would later be clearly understood. At the moment my doubts and reservations receded into the background, and I felt open to receiving him as a person needing to be understood. I was taking a leap not only in declaring myself to be a participant in a prospective patient's acting out behavior, but I was also doing so by engaging in a somewhat subtle form of acting out myself.

I spent the entire first session listening silently to an uninterrupted stream of associations, as I slowly moved toward the realization that I had intuitively decided to become his therapist at the first moment of contact unless there was evidence to contradict it. He began by describing his reaction to the telephone call. It had made him think deeply about his reasons for turning to me and for scheduling the appointment. The call itself had seemingly been an impulsive act born out of his desperation, but he could sense there was much more to it than that. It had something to do with his character traits, which he knew were obnoxious to others as well as to himself. They protected him from being vulnerable and humiliated, and though he hated these traits they were so firmly entrenched there was nothing he could do to change them. He constantly behaved as though he knew everything. He had to always be in charge, and showed off by trying to be a "big shot." All of this was at the expense of feeling any warmth or closeness in any of his relationships.

His mother had initiated his previous therapeutic contacts. She was worried about his lack of direction and probably sensed the depths of his despair. He had feigned resistance to the idea, because he did not want to admit weakness in any form. This was an issue in regard to psychiatric help, since in the eyes of his father such help was a crutch for which he had great contempt. The son had put on his usual act of arrogance with previous therapists while actively fighting any attempts they made to establish an empathic bond. At the same time he hoped that someone would be able to see through and penetrate his unyielding facade. On each occasion he had left treatment abruptly. He recalled feeling contempt if he thought a therapist was soft or tender, and erupted in anger if he met with what he thought of as an authoritarian attitude. Speaking to me now, his voice became subdued, for he noticed how much his words reflected his own attitudes and the way in which he experienced his parents.

With the previous therapists, however, he was overwhelmed by the strength of his reactions, and felt defeated in being unable to gain the help he needed. They had tried to explain these reactions to him, telling him pretty much what he had just recognized. Looking back it seemed as if they were talking *at* rather than to him. He experienced their words as designed to overpower him and force him into submission, so he could only fight against them. It was precisely for this reason that he had selected me. He somehow knew, even before coming, that he would not feel compelled to present himself to me in this fashion. This is what seemed to offer a ray of hope. Although he knew that he was driven to engage in all relationships in this way, and that its surfacing in treatment brought his troubles right out in the open, he did not feel capable of doing anything else but running away. Now he felt relief in being able to talk about it without the associated compulsion to get embroiled in a struggle for control. He hoped that I would be open to working with him and not see fit to refer him elsewhere. At the end of the session I was not yet fully cognizant of having already made the decision to see him, but I indicated that I was considering it as a possibility. I expressed uncertainty on the basis of our relationship in the past, and my involvement with his family in the present. I was afraid it might interfere with the conditions he needed for his treatment to be effective.

The initial contact was clearly an expression of his acting something out in his behavior, though the unconscious significance of why he had selected me was at this point obscure. I did not know the specific determinants behind my conscious hesitation, but the critical factor in making a decision was whether there was evidence of it being a constructive pursuit. In spite of the potential obstacles he had shown some strikingly positive features during this first session. He had been introspective, leading to a useful recognition of his propensity to run away from the possible emergence of deeply buried, unseen, unconscious strivings. He suffered greatly from the consequences of his fixed defensive character attitudes, and was able to report disturbing transference experiences. There also seemed to be a readiness to allow a benign regression without his losing the capacity for observing psychic contents. Earlier treatment efforts had all ended badly, but he exhibited an emerging ability to begin to understand the part he played in their failure. Perhaps most importantly, this was the first time he had sought help entirely on his own.

Meanwhile I discovered that in the course of the session I was able to listen without being noticeably influenced by the meaning of my involvement with his family. I could not identify any barriers to being able to function effectively. It was likely that countertransference-based conflicts would arise at some point, but I had no internal sense of their being unworkable. I realized that in treating this patient I might have to end all future contact with his family, and though this was difficult I found myself willing to do so. Taking all of these matters into consideration, I finally agreed to embark upon a therapeutic journey with him, despite the likelihood that I was facilitating his behavior in living out an unconscious fantasy.

The therapeutic relationship was launched on this somewhat uncertain ground, and he proceeded to form an intense transference attachment. Repressed instinctual strivings were elicited, frequently triggering his impulse to create a hostile confrontation and leave. The difference in this case was his increasing ability to recognize the source of what he was running from, the inescapable discrepancy between his transference distortions and his personal knowledge of me, and a growing commitment to face and integrate the regressive experiences that so dominated his internal life. Childhood memories returned and reflected his extreme hunger for closeness and intimacy with his father, along with a feeling of being enveloped, suffocated, and depreciated by his mother. He had also been preoccupied with instinctually overstimulating experiences from a very young age. A negative oedipal constellation dominated the early phases of the transference, and he attained a deeper appreciation of his underlying passive homosexual longings. These were actively warded off by his aggressive, hostile, controlling attitudes, which he could see as a caricature of his father mirrored within himself. Slowly he recognized and integrated more threatening positive oedipal yearnings. The accompanying castration anxiety, which was of enormous proportions, had stood as an obstacle to his developing any attachment to a woman. There were minor episodes of acting-out behavior centering around his attempts to establish personal contact with me outside of the sessions. Usually this came up when conflicted unconscious instinctual impulses were surfacing. He was able to quickly recognize the connection, and maintain his involvement within the context of the therapeutic interaction.

Therapeutic progress was reflected in the gradual dissolution of his arrogant, defiant, argumentative attitude. A delightful sense of humor became evident, and he began to form significant relationships in his external life. The changes he was making were also apparent in his dreams. Initially they had a nightmare quality involving scenes of violence and destruction. Gradually they shifted to symbolic images of whatever therapeutic work he was occupied with at the moment. On one occasion he dreamt of a squirrel gathering nuts together to have them all in one place, and laughingly commented that it reminded him of uncovering his sexual wishes through a series of "crazy" memories scattered throughout his life.

In the closing phases of the treatment he was able to articulate the reason he had specifically chosen me to be his therapist. Early in his life he had noted that I had somehow managed to get through his father's intimidating qualities and find a loving connection to him. This meant to the patient that I might be able to help him find a pathway through these same qualities in himself to his softer, more loving side, and thus get closer to his father. Previous therapists had seemed to have a negative reaction to his hostile, controlling behavior, while taking the extent of his negative feelings toward his father at face value. As he saw it they could not show him how to love his father. It is conceivable that if I had been knowledgeable about this internal motive, and been able to bring it to the surface, he might have been amenable to accepting an appropriate referral. This did demonstrate, however, that the patient's acting out of an unconscious wish to reach his father was in fact an avenue for exposing the meaning of the wish, and my participation was an essential component in accomplishing that goal. The treatment continued for a period of three and a half years, during which time he completed his schooling and felt ready to move on with his life. The outcome was successful, as he ultimately went on to attain a meaningful occupation and to marry, have children, and realize a life that had seemed unobtainable to him. Some years later, on the occasion of his father's death, he wrote me a moving letter expressing gratitude for having given him the tools to make peace with his father before he died.

Acting out can certainly be a means to avoid remembering, but it also can be a way of expressing what needs to be recalled. There may be times where a therapist has to participate in order to

LEAPS AND ACTING OUT

gain access to psychic content making the transformation possible. The critical factor is whether the acting out serves the purpose of reenforcing a pathological defense, or whether it is in the interest of developmental progression. When both factors are intermeshed it may be a therapist's willingness to engage in a leap that is decisive for a successful outcome. Even in the more structured personality, where acting out behavior is clearly a defense against experiencing the powerful affects associated with remembering, a therapist's involvement may be required for the underlying unconscious experiences to be revealed and integrated. It is only if the therapist's involvement is a product of acting out that the resulting collusion obviates against therapeutic progress.

Consequently, a therapist must have a usable grasp of personal motivations, be alert to indicators of a loss of ideal functioning, and be prepared to rectify any mistake. The therapeutic environment must have room within it for unconscious experiences to find expression through the transference relationship, and the invoking of authoritarian rules only closes off avenues of potential growth. When a leap into the unknown is called for it has to be launched from the solid foundation of a strong therapeutic alliance; otherwise there will be deleterious results. The ultimate goal is to enable the unspeakable to reach the realm of verbalization, where it can be exposed to the constructive influence of unconsciously empathic interpretations.

6

Leaps and Reenacting Preverbal Traumas

The Fate of Preverbal Experiences

Preverbal experiences are registered and represented to form the foundation of an evolving representational world, and though they cannot be articulated they exert an ongoing influence. When mental structuralization advances sufficiently for the body ego experiences, comprising a self system of representations, to be united with and differentiated from their object impression counterparts, the effects of preverbal experiences may go unrecognized as such since they do not pose a serious hindrance to ongoing self-expansion. The impact of preverbal experiences is then primarily manifested in the symbolic configurations of fantasy, in various body sensations reflective of the specific impressions they have made, in the makeup of defensive constellations, and in the background presence of a containing or disruptive influence depending upon the nature of the experience.

With this degree of developmental progression the symbolic processes are functional, object constancy and continuity of experience are established and relatively stable, and an open pathway is available for unconscious mental activity to gain access to expression. Under these circumstances preverbal experiences, even those that have been traumatic, adhere to higher order mental configurations that enable them to be incorporated within their realm of functioning. The existence of an inordinate degree of intrapsychic conflict, however—due to the intensity of unconscious drives, the relative weakness of integrative ego functions, the archaic nature of defensive opposition, or some combination of all these factors—may block the pathway to their full integration. Nevertheless there is resonance throughout the personality so that at least some element of these preverbal difficulties continues to retain access to representation and expression. Whenever behavior is utilized as a vehicle for managing instinctual drives, the resulting actions contain some symbolic features that are reflective of the impulses being defended against. They can be identified through a verbal interchange and hence are amenable to interpretive influence. Therefore, the most effective means of enabling unconscious wishes to be directed into the transference relationship is by maintaining a secure therapeutic framework, within the context of which their encoded unconscious meanings, including those involving preverbal experiences, can be unraveled with the aid of empathic interpretive interventions.[1]

In the more primitively structured personality, preverbal experiences are often associated with trauma of such proportions that their impact has either been incapable of mental representation, or rendered inaccessible by the effects of splitting mechanisms. These preverbal experiences continue to have a disruptive effect, usually only noticeable in body sensations or behavioral enactments. The absence of available psychic content, the impairment of symbolic functions, and the predominance of primitive defenses all combine to prevent or interfere with the integration of these early traumas. At times it may require the concrete experience of contact with an external object, under circumstances paralleling the original event, in order to gain the mental representations necessary to register its effects. Yet for the actual expe-

---

1. Bleger (1967) described certain patients who bring their own framework, which is characterized by the institution of primitive symbiotic relationships. When the therapist breaks this frame with inevitable time changes, vacations, and the like, this allows reality to enter, which appears catastrophic to the patient. Thus any variation in the frame brings the non-ego to a crisis and contradicts the fusion, challenges the ego, and generates defenses against the psychotic part of the personality. It is a reflection of traumatic preverbal experiences that have adhered to more advanced structural positions, and they are thereby accessible within an interpretive process. Therapist and patient bring different anticipations regarding the framework, the patient attempts to have the therapist modify this frame, and when the frame is respected this will bring to life the steadiest, most permanent elements of the patient's personality, the "psychotic core."

rience to be internalized it must occur under conditions of safety and containment so as not to be received as another repetition. It is in just this way that preverbal traumatic experiences tend to be enacted in the transference, making it essential that the interaction be carried on under the guidance and protection offered by the basic psychoanalytic principles. What has previously been unthinkable, unimaginable, and unspeakable then has the potential of being included in the ensuing relationship.

In order for these behavioral enactments to emerge in their own unique way, and to be understood, they must be encouraged rather than impeded. In addition, a therapist may have to take an active role in providing what is needed before self-expansion can be furthered. A critical aspect of the treatment may center around creating the proper conditions for enacting an otherwise inexpressable intrapsychic event. These are the most common moments for deciding whether it is advisable to introduce noninterpretive interventions.[2] Some patients can continue to progress, even though traumatic preverbal experiences are left untouched. Others, however, can proceed only when an avenue is discovered for communicating what can be an overwhelming and destructive force. These situations must be as clearly distinguished as possible from those

---

2. Winnicott (1954) believed that failures in adaptation on the part of the environment resulted in the development of a "false self." Under those circumstances treatment is not effective unless a regression can be induced that is sufficiently far reaching so as to include this early level of functioning. At such a point the therapist's caretaking functions become primary, for interpretive words are an intrusive impingement. Through the creation of this specialized environment a belief in the possibility of its correction is invoked, and the unfolding of new forward emotional development is promoted.

Tolpin (1971) presented a developmental background for understanding the principles and processes involved in the formation of new mental structure, centered around the internalization of a transitional object and its evolution into soothing psychic structures. This suggests that mental equipment includes innate factors, which—sufficiently supported by mothering—potentially guarantee development into a self-regulating, separate psychic entity with partial independence from external regulation. In contrast, traumatic disappointments in the mother, as the psychic regulator, leaves a structural deficit.

Weill (1985) noted the impact of early developmental traumas on evolving psychic structuralization, making its manifestations a primary factor in determining therapeutic interventions.

in which the behavioral enactments are motivated by pathological defenses; otherwise the various modifications will work against constructive growth.

The Impact of Preverbal Experience in the Cohesive Personality, in Which a Leap Is Contraindicated

The enactment of preverbal experiences undoubtedly transpires, and is an essential component, in every transference relationship. When these early environmental influences can be symbolized they add depth and richness to the unfolding revelation of regressive wishes.[3] Preverbal experiences serve more as a background presence in individuals whose personality is cohesive, and in whom transferences are stable and object-related. A therapist introducing noninterpretive interventions under these circumstances would in all likelihood disrupt the holding properties of a secure framework. The result would be in activating a patient's unconscious perception of an empathic lapse. An effective therapeutic alliance would be eroded and interfere with the gradual emergence of unconscious transference wishes. In addition it would probably resonate with any preverbal experiences having had a traumatic quality, and thereby obstruct their integration.

---

3. Stern (1984) gave evidence to demonstrate how clear it is now that there are non-language-based recall memory systems operating very early, and for some events recognition memory appears to operate across the birth gap.

Piontelli (1987) used ultrasound techniques to study the behavior of an undisturbed fetus in its natural environment in order to show the persistence of preverbal memories. Each fetus relates differently to its environment and its various components, giving some indications of its future character, since a continuum is shown both before and after birth.

Emde (1988) highlighted a slightly different perspective upon the influence of preverbal experiences. He thought that what was most informative about infancy experience is not that infant behavioral patterns get set in an enduring way, but rather that infant-caregiver relationship patterns get set in an enduring way. What appears to be a lack of continuity from infancy, from the individual's point of view, is now seen as continuity from the point of view of the relationship. The specifically experienced relationship environment is of overriding importance, and temperament and affectivity play a special role for individual differences in early development.

Clinical Example

Within a well-managed treatment framework, surrounded by a relationship empathic to unconscious communications, the symbolic portrayal of preverbal experiences can be readily and fully elaborated. The way in which these inarticulable experiences tend to be symbolized, as an almost incidental feature of a therapeutic interaction, was reflected in the treatment of a 6-year-old boy. He was a bright, cheerful, outgoing child who had sought help because of concern over periodic episodes of extreme fearfulness and clinging. He had told his parents that he had many questions inside that were too heavy to carry, and wanted to see someone who would be strong enough to help him lighten the load.

He spent the early months of treatment eagerly exploring his thoughts, feelings, and fantasies, which he consistently brought to me in the form of questions. He perceived me as somebody who thought about his questions, and returned them to him with a statement about their meaning. He, in turn, took these statements in and the questions were then lighter. That is, they were easier to think and talk about. The questions focused upon his feeling of being too close to his mother. He wanted to find the ability to be more separate and not need her so much, for his considerable talents and skills were encroached upon by this fear of separation. He often looked to male figures to help him develop a different attitude, because he wanted to feel closeness without it being so debilitating.

Gradually his questions turned to the jealousies and rivalries associated with his budding genital sexuality. However, he would immediately become defensive or retreat to the more familiar preoccupation with his infantile attachment. There were moments when he joked about me being a somewhat provocative, seductive figure holding him too closely. This transference fantasy furthered the insight he was developing into his internal world, and my interpretations strengthened the alliance between us. He was a child whose level of personality organization was quite advanced, well into forming an intense oedipal conflict that was interfering with his progress. He had negotiated the early phases of separation and individuation, had established cohesiveness and object constancy, and was in the midst of forming the object-related perspective associated with a genital orientation. The residual effects of his early attachment to his mother had colored each succeeding developmental step, continuing to exert a regressive pull whenever new conflicts were encountered.

His mother then became pregnant, stirring many questions as to the source of her pregnancy and the potentially dangerous consequences of a growing fetus. The birth of the new infant was a powerful stimulus for him. When he entered the first session following the infant's return home, he was uncharacteristically silent. He made rooting mouth movements against the couch before talking about how the baby's cries affected him. It was as though he heard the cries within himself, for he could feel the pull toward wanting to be enveloped, and he recognized his own cry to be close to his mother. These were the feelings he worked so hard to keep at a distance. He elaborated a fantasy of tunneling into a deep pile of snow, hollowing out a space, and crawling inside into a fetal position. Once inside he could not leave the space because the tunnel had become frozen over. The only avenue to freedom was to burst out through the top by thrusting himself against the roof with all his force.

The pregnancy and birth had reawakened his experience with separation and individuation, and he felt drawn to an infantile relationship with his mother. He had been the product of a Caesarean birth, and the impressions of that body ego experience apparently had an effect in shaping at least some aspects of his fantasy life. The fantasy of the pile of snow with the tunnel frozen over, from which he could emerge only by forcing himself through the top, captured the essence of that inarticulable preverbal experience. This movement of forcing himself to escape from an enclosed space also reflected his characteristic manner of responding to infantile longings.

My interventions were almost exclusively interpretive in nature; this was required in order to foster growth by supporting his advanced psychic functions and facilitating a benign regression. His primary pathology was embodied in conflicted unconscious instinctual wishes and the defensive, prohibitive responses they instigated. The resulting distortions, experienced in the transference relationship, were the vehicle through which integration was achieved, with the aid of unconsciously empathic interpretations. Symbolic processes were actively functional, and on any occasion when I introduced either minor empathic lapses or noninterpretive modes of communicating, I elicited derivatives expressing his unconscious perception of their impinging or overstimulating qualities. The effect of these moments was to impede therapeutic progress by reenforcing a pathological defense. Preverbal experiences were incorporated within more advanced psychic productions, and hence could be integrated along with the conflicted instinctual wishes to which they adhered. Therefore there was not only no need to alter or modify the framework to reach the influence of early experiences, but also to do so in

The Regressive Reenactment of a Preverbal Trauma Requiring the Introduction of a Leap

Individuals manifesting unstable narcissistic transferences usually exhibit evidence of preverbal experiences that have had a continuously traumatic effect. This in turn has played a significant role in the structural organization of their personality. A narcissistic orientation to internal and external stimuli is a predominant feature of a therapeutic interaction, with more primitive levels of psychic organization going hand in hand with the presence of developmental deficits and arrests. When the subsequent impairment involves symbolic functions a serious obstacle to the internalization of verbally interpretive communications is created. The management of the treatment framework rises to the forefront as the most crucial factor in providing the necessary conditions for a benign regression to unfold. The impact of preverbal traumas will tend to be expressed through behavior, generally accompanied by an urgent demand for an immediate response. There may be moments wherein the established conditions of the treatment, in conjunction with a therapist's interpretive interventions, may simply not be enough to meet what is needed for gaining access to inarticulable but powerful infantile experiences. The inability of verbally communicative forms of interchange to elicit the necessary body ego experiences may thereby leave a gap in the patient's internal world. A therapist's posture then appears either distant and uninvolved, or unwittingly takes on the characteristics of a repetition of the as yet unrecognized preverbal trauma.[4]

---

4. Balint (1969) postulated that trauma had a three-phasic structure. First, the child is dependent on the adult, and though frustrations may occur the relationship is mainly trusting. Second, the adult, contrary to the child's expectations, does something highly exciting, frightening, or painful. This phase, though appearing very impressive, does not always impact traumatically. The real completion of the trauma sets in with the third phase. The child either approaches the

Some individuals have been relatively successful in compensating for developmental deficits growing out of early trauma. Thus the effects may not become evident until a therapeutic regression has been induced, at which point they can dominate an archaic transference. Their appearance in the treatment relationship offers a potential opportunity for discovering a means of bringing positive therapeutic influence to psychic forces that have been unrepresentable. If successful, the traumatic impact can be symbolized and eventually integrated. In order to accomplish this aim a therapist may be called upon to participate in the interaction in a way that alters the ground rules, boundaries, and conditions of the treatment. It may even involve those that had initially been established to create enough safety for the regression to take place, but that now have become too limiting and narrow in scope.

Clinical Example

This was exemplified in the treatment of a 6-year-old boy who had been referred in response to his school's concern over his isolated and withdrawn behavior. His parents saw him as an extremely independent child, though they were at times worried about his intense determination to accomplish tasks beyond his abilities, and they were surprised at the depth of the school's concern. When he came to his first session he was fearful, embarrassed, and clung to his mother. She was somewhat taken aback, as he had never exhibited this behavior before. He stated that he could not talk but his body could, and after I remarked that I would try

---

partner with a wish to continue, or, still in pain about being unrecognized and misunderstood, tries again to get understanding, recognition, or comfort. However, what happens is a completely unexpected refusal. This changes the basis of the theory of trauma from a one-person psychology to a study of object relationships. Within that context transference is irresistible, so that the forgotten past is acted out in the relationship with the therapist. The therapist must not participate as the original object did in phase two, but equally must not respond by a nonparticipating, passive objectivity if this would amount to a repetition of phase three. The therapist must diagnose what may have occurred originally, and then choose behavior deliberately so it is different from the original object. The question of this new role, and what would make it safely therapeutic, opens new avenues for analytic technique. The techniques involve the creation of a therapeutic relationship that goes beyond interpretation.

to understand his body's messages he immediately left his mother and came into the office. He drew a picture, calling it his fort. There were no windows or doors, and inside it he was perfectly safe where no one could hurt him. I reflected upon the great expense he paid for his safety, since nothing could come in and he was limited in not being able to get out. He matter-of-factly commented that he could find a way out if he wanted to. Later in the session he agreed that it would be a good idea to meet regularly and explore whether he would want to find a way out.

Even in this early session the patient was hinting at the existence of traumatic preverbal experiences that could not be articulated, yet could be expressed by his body movements. By implication he was showing how effectively he had both compensated for them and successfully covered them up. He appeared to be probing for my style of responding to regressive behavior when he expressed an awareness of unspeakable internal experiences. I indicated my willingness to be open to this mode of expression, and he responded by entering the relationship and symbolically portraying the compensatory, protective measures with which he had surrounded himself.

His parents were warm, sensitive, psychologically naive people, who had adopted him when he was 6 months of age. They had very little information about his earlier life, knowing only that he had come from a single parent and that his mother was an extremely disturbed woman who had taken her life after putting the child up for adoption. They had been told by the adoption agency that he had suffered some physical abuse at her hands; she had subsequently become severely distraught, and had left a crying baby at their doorstep before taking her own life. From the parents' point of view, after an initial period of appearing somewhat withdrawn, he had been receptive and responsive to their care and they had been extremely pleased with how he had developed. I suspected that the child's statement about not being able to talk, though his body could, was a reference to these early experiences. However, at this point there was no way of knowing how these experiences would be manifested, or whether anything beyond an interpretive posture within a well-managed framework would be required. He seemed responsive to my words, while indicating with his drawing of the fort that his symbolic processes were functional. There was an aura of concreteness in his attitude, however, and he was either unwilling or unable to elaborate fantasies about it. In addition, his comment about finding a way out if he wanted to had implicit in it a powerful defensive need to hold on to his autonomy. Thus I was alerted to the possibility of the conditions of the treatment offering an arena that the patient might very likely use to challenge and push against. I hoped I would get a clearer picture of whether he needed to experience the containment provided by a secure framework, or whether he would require room to express some preverbal trauma in his behavior.

During the early months he vacillated between laboriously working on some project he brought in, and being teasing and provocative. He gradually revealed how tightly controlled his emotions were, and how frightened he was of "letting go." Someone, including himself, would get hurt. He cautiously tested me to determine if it was safe. On a few occasions he brought ropes to tie me up so I couldn't intervene. He fantasied being in total control, having the freedom to ravage the office. The idea was extremely exciting to him. He then "inadvertently" knocked over various objects in the room, as he talked about people who were weak and helpless and for whom he felt contempt. I commented that he seemed to be coming out of his fort, and looked afraid that I would be helpless in containing him, especially when he could so easily knock over my belongings. This comment was extremely facilitating, for he laughed, drew a picture of his fort, and pointed out that construction work was being done on the doors and windows. He continued to draw, referring briefly to his biological mother for the first time. He imagined himself in a distant city where he heard her frantic cries. She was on top of a high building in total despair, was trying to kill herself by jumping out of a window, and he rescued her by stopping her at the very last moment.

The fantasy was reminiscent of the known facts about his first six months. It suggested that he was carrying the experience of this preverbal period into the transference relationship. Up to this point I was able to maintain clearly defined ground rules and boundaries, with verbal interpretations being the predominant mode of communication. Concomitantly, there was a consistent background aura of his testing the strength of the relationship in providing holding and containment, with small glimpses of a readiness to erupt into out-of-control behavior. He had verbalized his conflict over the extent of his aggression, either fearing that he would be overwhelmed by its intensity or that he would destroy a need-supplying object. In addition, I sensed an underlying experience of object loss. It looked as though he needed to thrust himself aggressively against me and have the actual experience of my not being destroyed or driven away, while at the same time maintaining his autonomy.

This evolving internal impression was realized dramatically in a subsequent session. He entered the office appearing wild and uncontrolled; he yelled, raced around the room, and in an overexcited fashion grabbed an object and threw it across the room. He protested as I held him gently, and while crying screamed out in rage, "Don't trap me, you're hurting my feelings!" I released him only to have him once again become wild and excited in a similar manner. This time when I held him I stated that he had the key to get free, simply identifying the key as telling me to let go. He continued to get wild, I held him, he indicated that he wanted to be released, and he was freed. This behavior continued uninterrupted for a considerable time until with great surprise he exclaimed, "I'm playing!" He went on to describe his inability to pretend. He could imagine things, but he could never play. It seemed that whenever he put into action what was happening in his mind, everything built up until it reached a point where he felt driven by some unseen force. He lost all sense of what was happening or why, and didn't know how to stop what were now explosive outbursts.

In this description he was beginning to bring what had been unthinkable into a communicative modality. In so doing he was giving evidence of a viable mental capacity that had previously either been deficient or nonfunctional. It appeared to represent an intrapsychic event that could be expressed only in behavior, accompanied by rage alternating with a fear of envelopment. The out-of-control attack was directed against me, but interpretive interventions had no influence whatsoever and the framework of the treatment had to be extended to include concrete physical contact. A vital aspect of my response to this enactment involved the search for a means by which control of my actions could remain in the patient's hands. This particular feature was repeated until it could be internalized, at which point it became possible for him to articulate what was happening inside of him. It suggested that an intrapsychic gap was being bridged by his representing the experience, enabling a pathway toward symbolizing and verbalizing what had previously been inaccessible.[5]

---

5. Frosch (1967), in considering the nature and significance of severe regressive states, indicated the importance of determining the purpose they serve. Are these phenomena inherent in the analysis of certain cases and to be experienced as a precondition for ultimate improvement, or are they unwelcome intruders and disrupters of the analytic procedures and therapeutic alliance and to be negated and removed as soon as possible? Ultimately the therapist must present himself as an indestructible object, which encourages the patient not to fear destructive drives. The indestructible qualities of the therapist are conveyed by attitude, appropriate encouragement to face destructive fantasies, carefully

Had I adhered to a firmer stance, insisting upon talk rather than action, in all likelihood there would have been a different outcome. The intensity of his rage and the extent of his fear of engulfment were not susceptible to any interpretive influence. It could only have ended in either a chaotic destruction of the office or in eliciting counteraggressive, defensive responses on my part. Were he to have been only physically controlled, his autonomy would have been eroded, and no avenue toward achieving perspective would have been made available. The helplessness of his preverbal state would probably have been repeated. In this situation a leap had been introduced because physical restraint was needed for the protection of both of us, yet I had to be willing to place control in the patient's hands in spite of my awareness that it would continue. It was also important to enter into this interchange repetitively until its underlying meaning could be discovered. The reverberation of his preverbal trauma with a very disturbed, enveloping mother seemed to be clearly reflected in the therapeutic interaction, though on this occasion it had a different result. Consequently, he was able to include the experience within the realm of his self-observational capacities, suggesting that his symbolic processes were more broadly functional.

In earlier sessions his ability to symbolize had been operative to only a limited extent, and easily broke down under conditions of overstimulation, impingement, or deprivation. With this in mind I turned my attention to reestablishing firm ground rules and boundaries. I began by attempting to foster his ability to communicate in a verbally symbolic mode. I did so by wondering if anything came into his mind that could show more clearly what it was that he was now playing. He became thoughtful before telling me he wanted to use my furniture to play a game. He then constructed a den, into which he crawled through a small opening. Once inside he started to coo like a baby. It was warm and comfortable, but the opening was so small he felt like he might suffocate in trying to crawl out.

---

timed interpretations, and so on. In the interest of restoring and preserving the therapeutic relationship it may be necessary to introduce many modifications. However, the impact of these modifications may be subject to analysis, and it is important to be aware that a patient who has a proclivity for developing severe regressive states is manifesting a significant facet of the internal world rather than something distinct and apart from the rest of the treatment. If the climate, mood, and thinking is analytic from the beginning, the subtle shifting over into a more classic technique will be a natural one, and these regressive states will have continuity with the treatment as a whole.

The patient's newfound ability to symbolize and communicate regressive experiences was now more fully in evidence.[6] Continuity with the preverbal dimensions of his internal life was available, providing an avenue for incorporating its effects. It was no longer necessary to introduce unusual measures to facilitate the integration of his early trauma, since the treatment could progress with my maintaining an interpretive posture. On the rare occasions when I unwittingly deviated it was in fact disruptive, eliciting derivatives expressing the patient's unconscious perception of an empathic failure. Thus the patient would at times request that I move out of my chair so he could have room to draw. If I complied without exploring or interpreting the meaning of his request he became anxious and distrustful. In rectifying this stance there would be a mutual recognition of his no longer having to be in control of my behavior, and of his feeling more secure in engaging in a process of internal exploration.

Utilizing a Leap to Gain Access to What is Otherwise Uncommunicable

Traumatic experiences during the earliest phases of development have an extremely debilitating effect on psychic structuralization.[7]

---

6. Blum (1977) has pointed out the vital significance of preoedipal reconstructions, and noted how Freud's historical reconstructions were preoedipal in nature. They involved not simple actual events but the meanings attached to the experience. The ego state and developmental impact become more important than a consideration of actual history, although the historical reconstruction of real experience and real traumatic episodes remains significant in enabling a patient to reorder the infant's misinterpretation of internal and external reality.

7. Freedman (1981) approached the impact of continuous preverbal traumas developmentally, observing how it seems to be that we inherit psychological *potentialities* rather than actualities. How the new potential will be expressed in behavioral and affective terms is a function of the ambience in which it is actuated. This amounts to an extension of the concept of the undifferentiated phase from its limited application to the differentiation of psychic structure so as to include all aspects of psychic functioning; affects, drives, and object relations. Good and bad experiences anticipate in development good and bad selves and objects. With the increasing ability to differentiate self from object these will be experienced as unitary wholes with good and bad aspects. Because these wholes are synthetic they are vulnerable to splitting into their component parts. When splitting occurs on this basis it cannot be considered a defense, but must reflect a failure of adaptation that leads to a disruption of psychic structure.

If these early traumas were continuous they could not be well compensated for or even covered up in any significant way. Therefore, they occupy the center of attention in a therapeutic interaction right from the onset of contact.

Adapting the basic psychoanalytic principles to be in accordance with the structural organization of a patient's personality presents the combined qualities of a good object, and elicits whatever containing forces are existent. A context is thereby provided, giving an opportunity for new body ego experiences and their object impression counterparts to be represented. This is an essential component for early splits in the self and ego to be healed, and for building a psychic foundation capable of supporting self differentiation. However, a therapist has to be receptive to a patient's directions as to what specific conditions are required. This means making an accurate assessment as to when the directions are distorted and defensive and when they emanate from the patient's unconscious perceptions of what is necessary to promote growth.

The various elements embodied in the construction of an unconsciously empathic and secure therapeutic environment may have to fluctuate, in order to be consonant with the changes taking place within the patient. The way in which well-defined ground rules and boundaries are maintained also may have to be flexibly altered. Within this contained psychological space the reenactment of preverbal traumas may then lead to an integration rather than a splitting off of psychic content.

Clinical Example

The importance of a therapist's receptivity to being guided by a patient's directions was illustrated in the treatment of a 4-year-old autistic boy. He was referred to me after having been evaluated on three separate occasions, at ages 2, 3, and 4, and being diagnosed as retarded and autistic. Intelligence testing had resulted in an I.Q. score that was consistently extremely low; the parents had been told there was no help for him, and they were seeking another opinion. He did not speak, and would remain in one position for hours. It seemed as if he had no needs, as he would never give any sign of being hungry, thirsty, or in pain.

From the first moment that he crossed the threshold into my office he became very active and vocal. His vocalizations were unintelligible, and his actions were limited to relatively constant pacing unless I did anything other than listen. Even a questioning look had the effect of triggering a fit of rage. When I simply sat back and listened he paced the room restlessly and vocalized, sometimes to himself and sometimes obviously to me. At the end of a session this mode of functioning ended abruptly, which was strikingly shown on one occasion when he tripped over the door sill as he left. He fell face down on a hard tile floor, got up and assumed a rigidly controlled posture, and slowly walked on as though nothing had happened.

Thus this autistic child almost immediately relinquished his primitive defense of withdrawal within the therapeutic setting. Tacitly, the conditions he seemed to need in order to feel safe and contained involved absolutely no demands or impingements. He was obviously communicating in his own unique fashion, and it was important to him that I be a receptive listener who offered nothing other than a framework within which he could be in charge of the interaction. The relationship continued like this for several months. Finally, one day I understood the word *train* among his verbal productions, and remarked that he seemed to be trying to tell me about a train. His reaction was remarkable. He got excited, hugged me, and from this moment on the entire interaction changed. All of my attention was now focused upon understanding his communications. I became more adept at grasping his idiosyncratic language, as he in turn made his words more comprehensible. It was a gradual process that escalated as more was understood. Along with it his behavior became provocative, controlling, and on occasion irritably out of control. He was no longer passive and compliant in the external world, and he took on the appearance of an exceptionally hyperactive child. His communications consistently made indirect reference to wanting to get close to me, but the associated threat of annihilation motivated his uncontrollable, frantic behavior.

He continued to struggle with the internal demand to effect an infantile attachment. However, the anxiety it mobilized was of life-threatening proportions and it pushed him into out-of-control behavior, preventing the relationship he so desperately needed. The initial conditions of the treatment that had enabled this intrapsychic movement to surface were no longer sufficiently facilitating, and a change seemed imperative. Interpretations were felt to be intrusive, intensifying his aggressive attacks on either me or my belongings. There was also the implication that any attempt to control his destructiveness evoked a fear of his being destroyed. I was placed in the position of being experienced as an annihilative object, or of being totally helpless and at the mercy of his hostile, invasive attacks. Through his behavior he seemed to be forcefully showing the internal consequences of traumatic events from his early development. I thought he might be re-creating a parallel interaction, which brought with it the potential for representing a different outcome. He was unable to verbally communicate this aspect of his internal world, and I did not know specifically what he would require from me to accomplish this goal.

At this juncture I was operating almost entirely on the basis of subjective, intuitive responses, and was waiting for some guidance that could point out a direction. At last he said, "I have to show you how to hold me." I was now in the position of deciding whether to follow his lead and leap into the darkness to find the light. I had to keep in mind the potential danger of repeating an early trauma or of reenforcing a pathological defense. There did appear to be some solid footing in the therapeutic alliance, so I indicated my willingness to go ahead. He placed himself on the floor, while directing me how to hold him so he was contained without being hurt. He felt in charge, was not restrained, and in that position stated, "That's just right." He was sufficiently secure to allow what was in his mind to be expressed without creating havoc, and he then proceeded to describe his internal world. He was most preoccupied with an image he labeled as bad. This image was a weak, ineffective, intimidated, incompetent, and submissive figure. This bad internal imago tried very hard to be accepted, but no one had any interest in him other than to destroy him. There were many other figures labeled as smart, wild, and so on, all of which reflected various facets of himself. He also described a family raised amid violence and destruction, with the mother constantly trying to kill the other members who would escape after sustaining severe injuries.

It was significant that the patient was trying to communicate even in the midst of his aggressive attacks. Although the direction he gave was not subject to validation, I opted to follow it and remain alert for any signs of a collusion with pathological forces. Whenever conscious directions are given by an individual who has attained continuity of experience, they are listened to as derivatives. In these situations a therapist's interpretations are all that is desirable or required, as the transference relationship unfolds. However, this child was clearly expressing a need for some concrete experience with me, and could do nothing but be driven into aggressive attacks until he could be properly contained. His psychic functioning was dominated by splits in the self; he knew his internal world with much more clarity than I did, and the directions he gave could only be presented consciously. The enactment of his early preverbal traumas were responded to in a way that offered a new solution, and he began to display the ability to symbolize their effects.

Engaging in a Leap that Reenforces a Pathological Defense, in Order to Reach Deeply Buried Strivings for Growth

The most difficult, confused, and confusing therapeutic dilemmas concern those individuals in whom the impact of preverbal traumas has produced a defect in psychic structuralization that is compensated for by a defensive organization operating to re-create destructive, pathologically dependent interactions. Early development has been dominated by invasive, enveloping attacks, in which appropriate self boundaries have been indiscriminately violated. This makes it essential for the therapeutic environment to consist of firm, clearly defined ground rules, boundaries, and conditions. However, since self-experience has not consolidated and the capacity to differentiate the influences of an object is defective, the containment associated with a secure framework takes on the meaning of being entrapped. Thus the very experiences required to fill in gaps in mental structure are prevented from being internalized. The transference relationship is readily distorted to invoke an image of a therapist as either too close and enveloping or too distant and abandoning. These distortions are taken advantage of to be used in the service of warding off a fundamental inability to face intolerably painful separations. Individuation is so threatening it must be avoided at all costs. Yet it is only in achieving the capacity to experience the vulnerability and helplessness associated with being separate that growth can evolve.[8]

---

8. Tustin (1980), referring to those individuals who have not successfully been able to negotiate early developmental tasks, observed how they continue to live by expressing feelings through bodily processes with their mental life massively restricted. Such individuals have not developed the capacity for experiencing the delay between anticipation and realization, which, as long as the

These preverbal scenarios are reenacted in intense transference struggles. Interpretations can only be received as impossible demands emanating from a need-supplying object at too great a distance to be internalized. Concomitantly, the experience of the therapeutic interaction is registered as potentially enveloping rather than liberating.[9] Once it has become patently apparent that every conceivable avenue for undoing distortions has been explored and been doomed to failure, and that the admixture of pathological defenses and developmental deficits is so intertwined and enmeshed as to be indistinguishable from each other, the need for participating in reenforcing a regressive pathological craving may

---

suspense can be tolerated, leads to such symbolic activities as memories, fantasies, and thoughts. Subsequently the individual is unable to use and develop genuine means of protection, preventing the possibility of getting in touch with caring human beings who could help modify terrors. These severe disturbances arise when a particularly vulnerable child experiences a series of shocks before the neural mental apparatus is sufficiently developed to stand the strain. Disillusionment occurs too suddenly or too soon, and they have had to cope with the fact of body separateness before the neuralmental organization is integrated enough.

Gaddini (1982) portrayed the overwhelming nature of integrative processes when the recognition of separateness is unbearable. To the extent that the anxiety of loss of the self is bearable, it is an intense stimulus for the formation of further defenses that are useful to start an organization of the self. However, when separation has been traumatic, integrative processes greatly increase the anxiety of self loss. The role of splitting emerges in cases where integrative processes promote unbearable anxiety over self loss, and the attempt is made to reduce such anxiety by disintegration, through establishing the most fragmentary functioning. In treatment the reintegration of that which is split provokes anxiety, the same anxiety originally producing the split and now making reintegration difficult. This anxiety then must be reached and faced. After a pathological separation, any thrust toward a change is experienced as a threat to survival. Integration appears as a fatal step beyond return; the obstacles encountered may seem and sometimes are insurmountable. The object then becomes the limit and definition of the fragmentary self, and it is behind the essential importance of contact.

9. Balint (1968) believed that in every analytic treatment attaining regression beyond a certain point, there are three types of object relationships. First, the most primitive, harmonious, interpenetrating "mix-up," an expression of primary love. Second, the ocnophilic clinging to objects, in which the object is felt as a vitally important support and any threat of separation creates intense anxiety. Third, the philobatic preference for objectless expanses, in which objects are considered as indifferent or as deceitful and untrustworthy hazards to be avoided.

have to be taken into consideration in order to reach and amplify deeply buried strivings for a growth-promoting experience.[10]

There is always the possibility, and even the likelihood, that a therapist's countertransference-based regressive identifications, infantile conflicts, or narcissistic needs are coloring this perception of the relationship and the obstacles encountered. This certainly must be the first area to be examined. When such an internal exploration does not lead to any additional insight, or alter what is transpiring within the therapeutic interaction, a question still remains as to whether the search has been long or penetrating enough to thoroughly encompass what has to be seen. On the other hand it is equally conceivable that even though all visible, sound therapeutic principles have been carried out and maintained, something vital is lacking from the therapist. The deficiency may then perpetuate a patient's position of being hopelessly locked into a destructive intrapsychic and interpersonal struggle. The omission may be preventing the full enactment of crucial preverbal or traumatic experiences, since they cannot take place within the limited confines of the relationship as it has been constructed.

It may gradually become evident that a patient's demand for regressive cravings to be gratified has embedded in it the very conditions required to achieve the mental representational background for enabling developmental progression. The therapist, in

---

10. Lipin (1963) thought that deficiencies of essential experiences in early development led to discharge-blocking of normal maturational drive patterns, and to complex distortions of structured functioning. The resultant defensive, adaptive stress structures are based upon a profound intrasystemic reorganization, wherein instinctual discharge-subserving tension regulation is predominant and any movement subserving maturation is inhibited and distorted. The implications for treatment are immense, for there is little to engage in a relationship that is not seeking to reenforce these underlying pathological structures.

Khan (1963) elaborated upon the effects of the nurturing figure's ongoing maladaptation to the infant's anaclitic needs, which creates breaches in an evolving protective shield. Subsequently, pathogenic reactions and relationships are established, which operate as a basis for pathological defenses, and exist as the only available way of reacting and responding to impingements. Thus the pathway to reaching any forces that are viable and striving for growth is always connected to, and surrounded by, a search for a pathological form of interaction.

altering the treatment framework, at one and the same time reenforces a pathological defense and actively supports the weak and vulnerable forces striving for growth. Because of this dual function in the patient's mode of interacting, gratifying a regressive craving may be the only means of effecting therapeutic influence. Such an intervention represents a leap in the most extreme form, and as such is the essence of a dangerous opportunity.

Embarking on a journey with this magnitude of risk makes it essential that the powerful forces undermining growth be consistently identified and diminished. The validity of the undertaking will be determined by the emergence of functional capacities associated with higher levels of psychic organization, and the treatment will have to shift once again to be in accord with this more advanced psychic state. Unfortunately, the nature of the overall relationship may then have an effect on the transference, creating limitations on the extent to which evolving unconscious instinctual conflicts can be fully resolved.

Clinical Example

This complex problem was encountered during the course of an eight-year period of treatment with a 31-year-old woman, who was initially referred as a suicidal emergency. The first appointment was scheduled after she was intercepted by a relative at the airport just prior to her leaving for a distant city, where she had planned to kill herself. She was tearful and distraught, saw no reason to live, and had finally decided to quietly end her life in a faraway place where her identity would probably not be discovered. She then proceeded to outline the reasons for her despair, emphasizing her constant internal sense of being totally dependent on others in a clinging, helpless, vulnerable fashion, unable to fend or function for herself. She knew it had a great deal to do with the events that shaped her developmental years, but that knowledge did absolutely nothing to change the way she felt and she saw no way out.

She had been in treatment on numerous occasions beginning at the age of 13. Although her therapists all seemed competent, their efforts to help only made her feel more despairing. The numerous medications she had received did little but make her feel numb and sleepy. In addition, she had been hospitalized on several occasions for suicide attempts, which she recognized were desperate appeals for help. She no longer wanted to travel that route. She felt no hope for herself, and ending her life appeared to be the only answer that made sense. After her last period of hospitalization she had been sent to a residential treatment center in order to remove her from the invasive presence of her mother. She felt totally incapable of extricating herself from the enveloping symbiotic atmosphere that pervaded her home environment. The treatment center was in an isolated rural area, and the milieu was devoted to encouraging each individual to actively participate both in helping the others and in managing the various tasks of daily living. Following an initial period of extreme anxiety she had adapted to the setting extremely well, until she was offered a job as a supervising counselor. She couldn't tolerate the idea of accepting the responsibility, became panic-stricken, and regressed precipitously. Psychiatric consultation was sought, and she was once again placed on medication.

In the midst of this disruptive period she had her first sexual experience with another patient. She became pregnant, had an abortion, no longer felt safe in that environment, and returned home feeling completely humiliated. It was at this point that she decided to take her life, planning a trip so that no one who knew her would find out. At the airport she ran into the relative, who noted how upset she was and talked her into calling me. In a very defeated tone of voice she wondered if there was any point in our meeting. I noted that the session was drawing to a close, but in spite of the life-threatening urgency I thought it would be important to end on time. I was concerned about the effect that extending her time would have upon her pathological dependency. I decided it would be best to establish clearly defined ground rules and boundaries right from the outset. I stated that so far, from what I could see, she experienced closeness as suffocating, distance as abandoning, and expectations that were beyond her capacities as enormously anxiety-arousing and intolerable. I went on to say that I thought it would be important to meet further and see if more light could be shed on why she experienced things this way, and maybe then we could determine whether there was anything that offered hope. She was silent for a moment, indicated her agreement, but underscored her inability to wait too long and suggested daily meetings until an answer could be found one way or another. I remarked that this didn't feel quite right to me, although I wasn't sure if it was for my reasons or hers. She smiled warmly and appointments were arranged on alternate days. The other elements of the treatment framework were left unsettled until their meaning could be explored in subsequent sessions.

The severity of the patient's pathology and the potential for self-destructiveness was abundantly evident from the beginning. My most immediate concern was to discover the proper conditions to provide a contained and safe interpersonal environment. She had emphatically indicated that the protective walls of a hospital were out of the question, making it essential for me to listen carefully for any derivatives that would give guidance in creating a workable framework. There were already suggestions of a primitively organized intrapsychic world, with insufficient mental structuralization for the pain and vulnerability associated with separateness to be bearable. At the same time she could not stand the regressive loss of differentiation associated with an attachment. On the one side she seemed to be fragmented by the demands of independent functioning, and on the other side was immobilized by the loss of her functional capacities when drawn toward a relationship. My initial task was to gain a grasp of the structural composition of her personality and the makeup of her pathological defenses. I could not yet see how to apply the basic principles of psychoanalysis in such a manner that there would be enough safety to allow a benign regression, while at the same time encouraging the use of her potential and latent resources. Her description of previous therapeutic contacts implied that interpretive interventions were not able to be usefully internalized, so that the management of the framework would most likely take precedence before some as-yet-unidentified means of effecting positive therapeutic influence could be determined.

There were hints that her experience at the residential treatment center had at least in some measure been in the right direction. It seemed not to have gone astray until expectations were imposed in place of acceptance of what she was capable of accomplishing. Preverbal traumas that had enveloping, invasive qualities appeared to be at the root of her crippling dependencies, and the interweaving of pathological defenses with weak and vulnerable movements toward growth had kept her fixated in an impossible dilemma. Her attempts to seek help were repetitively doomed to failure, and her opting for a way out through suicide carried with it a suggestion of how highly she valued her autonomous decision-making power. Even at this early stage in the relationship I was anticipating that I would be confronted with the question of engaging in a leap. Whatever would happen, however, had to begin with establishing a solid and effective therapeutic alliance, and my major focus of attention was in this shadowy area. She had already underscored the critical necessity of gaining her cooperation in constructing the conditions of the secure framework she would require; but if I was guided by her pathological defenses in this venture, the experiences she needed in order to negotiate separation and individuation would be prevented. I heard her request for daily sessions as carrying this mixed message. I had only my intuitive response to go on, and I took full responsibility for the decision to meet less often. At the same time I indicated a willingness to be receptive to her input, with the implication that it could subsequently change.

The early sessions were occupied with deciding upon the appropriate conditions of the treatment, by discerning as clearly as possible their unconscious meaning. I was searching for whatever emerged as a growth-promoting feature of the relationship to guide my conduct. The idea of her parents paying for the treatment aroused the patient's memories of their controlling her every move, making her feel helplessly enraged, ineffective, and weak. On this basis I said that it sounded as if it would be important for her to pay for the sessions herself. Her response was first to agree, and then to become panic-stricken when she was faced with finding a job.

She did proceed to find work, but it left her feeling hopelessly trapped in a lonely, isolated existence of demands and expectations that she could not meet. A lifelong pattern of anticipating total abandonment when confronted with the need for independent functioning was now being repeated in the therapeutic relationship. This instigated an upsurge of regressive cravings, accompanied by a deep sense of anguish over her neediness and helplessness. Interspersed were her tearful demands for medication to help her sleep or ease her pain. When I wondered what it would mean to her for me to prescribe them, she was reminded of having been followed to school by her mother and of her mother's hovering presence, which made her constantly feel self-conscious, incapable, and inept. Her efforts to achieve independence had become increasingly more feeble until at the age of 13 she dropped out of school, spending the ensuing years, with the exception of one short interval, being taken care of by others. The one exception took place in her early twenties when she had tried to move out of the parental home and live with a younger sister. However, she had felt so distraught that she made her first suicide attempt at that time.

Initially my interpretations focused on the transference relationship. I called attention to her apparent belief that I wanted her to be helpless and dependent, and would punish her with total abandonment were she to utilize her resources in achieving some measure of autonomy. She reacted to these words as if they were concrete expressions of intent. They served only to deepen her feeling of despair and led to an escalation of her demands for some form of relief. She tried in every conceivable way to alter the conditions of the treatment, which up to this point had made her feel safe enough to allow it to become the most significant part of her life. At the same time she felt trapped, experienced the conditions as too confining, and was filled with despair. She finally felt totally unable to work, quit her job, and was without a means of paying for her sessions. Her demands for medication, extra appointments, extending the time, and using the telephone, as well as for concrete expressions of caring and concern, were all dealt with by interpreting their defensive meaning. I especially emphasized how frightened she was of the symbiotic attachment she seemed to be crying out for. Furthermore, in quitting her job she appeared to be re-creating a pattern in her life, in which she would have to be cared for by me if the relationship were to continue. Once again she responded as though my words were statements of intent, for she felt attacked, criticized, or invited to be infantilized. The symbolic meaning of my interpretations was simply not received by her.

The regressive transference relationship that was evolving totally dominated her existence. I continued to see her without a fee, and she became increasingly depressed. Suicidal preoccupations surfaced in a very active manner. The temptation to kill herself loomed so large that she became extremely frightened lest she act on it impulsively. She brought in her suicide kit for me to hold, thereby ensuring that the impulse would be brought into the relationship before she would be able to act. In doing so she stressed how much it was based on a deep sense of trust. It represented a token of security that she had never shared with anyone before and had never allowed to leave her hands. This initiated a period of several months in which she was continuously preoccupied with feelings about her parents and what it was like to live with them. She expressed rage at her mother's intrusiveness. The mother insisted upon hovering over her to anticipate and fulfill every conceivable need without regard for her separateness or autonomy, and made her feel terrible by declaring extreme hurt whenever she angrily retaliated. She also described for the first time her father's blind, sadistic demands for subservience and conformity. His explosive outbursts, for no discernible reason, created impossible arguments from which she could only retreat in exhaustion.

It became increasingly apparent to her that she had to leave this destructive environment, yet she felt too paralyzed to do so. She had a deep conviction that if she could only find a way to take the initial step, her ability to function independently would surface. It was puzzling to her, but the first move seemed overwhelming—she didn't know how to go about it and was immobilized with panic. What appeared to be lacking was a way to make the transition. She was able to imagine being on her own, but was totally incapable of picturing how to accomplish it. She felt enveloped, smothered, and immersed in rage in the environment in which she lived, but the idea of breaking loose from it left her feeling abandoned, lost, and panic-stricken. She felt as if some crucial element was missing internally that prevented her from taking action on her own behalf. She began to make tentative, indirect references to needing something from me that would enable her to negotiate the movement from her current environment to her own separate space. I had interpreted the feelings she expressed about parental figures as reflective of her experience in the therapeutic relationship, so I now remarked upon how much she seemed to need my active support of her autonomous movements. Her response was to become uncharacteristically silent, looking deeply troubled as she left the session. Shortly afterward I received an emergency phone call from her. She stated that she needed to have her suicide kit since she no longer wanted to live, and insisted upon arranging an immediate time to have it returned. I simply said that it belonged to her, I had been holding it in safekeeping, and if she wanted it I would give it to her in our next session.

She entered the following session appearing disheveled and distraught, glancing briefly at the suicide kit in plain view on my desk. With her head bowed she cried softly as she talked. My words had touched her deeply, making her realize the sincerity of my wish to see her grow. A ray of hope entered her life, for she suddenly knew that if it was in her best interests I might even help her move. Instantly she felt completely ashamed. She had kept a well-guarded secret from me and the only escape she could think of was to retrieve her suicide kit and once and for all end her life. She had called expecting resistance to the whole idea. She had anticipated arguing with me, demanding that it be returned, and either finally getting it or, if not, using some other means to kill herself. My statement that it belonged to her and she could have it at any time reaffirmed her earlier realization that I was not trying to control her but wanted to help her grow. The swirl of lies and deception with which she had conducted her life raced through her mind. She decided to reveal her secret, and to conduct her therapy and her life in as honest a way as she possibly could.

Her secret involved a significant amount of money that she had saved over the years. She had been holding it in reserve where it had been collecting interest, while it could have been used to support her treatment. She had been testing me to see if I really cared, but had also been terrified to use this money because it represented the only source of strength she possessed. The idea of it being depleted made her feel as if her life would be draining away. She now saw it in a different light. It was a means of supporting the help she needed, and of giving her a start toward building an independent existence. She threw the suicide kit into the wastebasket, and presented a plan for redressing the fee during the time she was out of a job. She paused and wondered if her perception that I might aid her in the move was accurate.

I had been concerned for some time about the sense of something missing in the treatment. The concrete way in which she responded to interpretive words, and the build-up toward another failure, this time probably leading to her self-destruction, worried me a great deal. The impact of preverbal traumas had left some marked impairments in her personality. Symbolic functions were severely limited, and her ability to achieve advancing levels of self differentiation was hampered by the absence of mental representations reflective of the rapprochement phase. The need for a concrete experience capable of providing the wherewithal for effecting this transition did appear to be essential. The question of how to offer it, within the context of a secure framework with well-defined boundaries and ground rules, had been a consistent but as yet unanswered question in my mind. It was not yet clear whether the breakthrough that was being manifested was a product of my having maintained an unyielding interpretive attitude, or whether it involved the prospect of finding the concrete experience she required in order to negotiate separation and individuation. The ray of hope that had shifted the balance emanated from the idea of my being an active participant in the move away from enveloping and crippling dependencies. Consistent with her whole manner of functioning it involved an actual rather than a symbolic experience.

I was confronted with the possibility of providing a missing experience that, if successful, could enable the symbolization of preverbal traumas and also make it possible for the influence of interpretive interventions to further her developmental progression. Her description of the money she held in reserve captured the essence of her lifelong dilemma. She had managed to preserve latent resources, but they had to be kept secret, for their use represented depletion, rather than a means of enhancing or constructing a richer life. The need for a leap had been in the back of my mind from the beginning of the treatment, although until this moment there had been no direction as to how it might be introduced. Although it might act in opposition to the secure framework already established, it might also present a much needed opportunity to foster her growth. Her focus on this aspect of my interpretive words seemed to be in the service of her striving to reach a position of separateness. It contrasted markedly with the clinging dependency accompanying her earlier regressive cravings. I was aware that the concrete meaning of my interpretive statement, about actively supporting her independence, certainly carried the implication expressed in her question. Thus I had acknowledged being open to considering this form of involvement, but needed to gain a more penetrating view of its unconscious significance.

During the next several sessions she tried very hard to articulate just why my participation was important to her. However, all she could think about was how lost she had been when attempting to grasp various abstract concepts at school and at work, and how there seemed to be something missing inside her that made these meanings elusive. She also reported a sequence of dreams that were strikingly different from any she had ever had before. Earlier dreams had always been vague, leaving only the impression of intense affect. In these dreams the images were of construction work being done that had to be held up due to a missing item. While the exploration of these dreams proceeded she found employment, and became extremely interested in picking out a puppy to express the love she felt welling up inside. Her desire to move intensified, as did the feeling of immobilization in regard to being able to take the first step. Taking all of these factors into account I thought they reflected the existence of a gap in her mental structuralization, which might possibly be bridged by the experience of my joining her in achieving independence. I therefore agreed to participate in a direct and active manner. She was extremely excited at the prospect, and the next several weeks were spent in locating her new place and helping her to transfer her belongings.

Subsequent sessions were occupied with exploring her internal reactions to my involvement, which mainly centered around her deep feeling of gratitude. She felt hope and optimism about her ability to construct an independent life, and was exhibiting an increasing capacity for symbolization and abstract thinking. This was reflected in her receiving job promotions, in seeking out new relationships and discovering friendships for the first time. It was becoming apparent that although my participation with her in the move had served to facilitate ongoing developmental progression, it also had obviated against my being the focus of regressive transference experiences. Her positive feelings about my willingness to be engaged with her in this way, and what it communicated about the depth of my commitment to her welfare and growth, made it impossible for her to allow the intensity of her primitive rage at being enveloped to enter the transference relationship. In addition a newly emerging genital organization, with its inherent infantile instinctual wishes and conflicts, could only be deflected and displaced onto figures outside of the therapeutic relationship. She rejected any interpretations that related these feelings to me, and in a very important sense she was correct.

Her rage over being enveloped was too discordant with the distinct impression of my involvement with her thrust for independence. Thus it could only be perceived as emanating from the past. Otherwise the new and tenuous mental representations she had established as a foundation for ongoing progression would be disrupted. Her evolving genital attitude did not belong to the past, because it represented the manifestation of a whole new level of psychic organization. She could not allow the unconscious component to enter the relationship, as it would undermine the stability of the foundation she now depended upon for retaining a position of separateness. There was then mutual agreement that she had reached a point where her development could continue, but that it was time for this treatment relationship to end. She accepted a referral to another therapist to gain a further understanding both of her internal life and of the meaning I held for her in the deeper reaches of her mind.

This patient had endlessly reenacted preverbal traumas, centering around the process of individuation. She was unable to clearly articulate or symbolize their effects, but rather was compelled to live them out with no avenue for their integration. Consequently, she experienced any movement toward separateness as associated with abandonment and fragmentation, while any regressive movement was associated with the frightening loss of her functional capacities. The idea of moving out of her home gave expression to this internal state in a concrete form, and my actual participation in the move represented a new solution to the original trauma. The representation of the experience, which had been so necessary to foster her growth, now stood as an essential building block within her internal world. Therapeutic work around emerging infantile instinctual conflicts was still indicated, but I could no longer serve as a transference figure for their resolution.

The question as to whether the same result could have been accomplished by maintaining a consistent interpretive attitude, without modifying the framework of the treatment, remained unanswered. There was much to suggest that if I had desisted it might have been a serious error of omission. In this situation it might have accentuated the patient's deep-seated feelings of hopelessness, and perhaps have led to a suicidal outcome. I chose the path of being directed by her request, since it seemed to emanate from her search for a growth-promoting experience, and in fact therapeutic progress was manifested. There were elements of an error of commission, in that defensive structures were reenforced. My attempt to rectify this aspect through reestablishing a secure framework, and engaging in an interpretive exploration of its effects, was only partially successful. The eventual therapeutic result was positive, though referral to another therapist was still required. It underscored one of the problems in working with some primitively organized patients—no matter what avenue is selected to offer therapeutic help, there may be some dimension of an error in technique that a therapist may not be able to completely rectify.

The purpose of a secure treatment framework is to support a benign regression, and to enable verbal interpretations to be the primary therapeutic input. This is achieved by following the guidelines of the basic psychoanalytic principles, with their application being consonant with a patient's requirements for constructive growth. There must be room for preverbal experiences to be enacted, even though it occurs primarily through behavior. If the need arises for a therapist to engage in a leap it should only be introduced after careful consideration and when all indications in both parties point to this move being warranted and appropriate. A therapist must maintain constant vigilance for any signs of an empathic lapse.

In general, errors of commission are more openly disruptive, hence recognizable, and thereby more accessible to corrective measures. Errors of omission tend to be more silent and insidious, less easily recognized, more susceptible to being rationalized, and thus harder to identify and correct. This is not to suggest that given such a crossroad errors of commission are necessarily a preferable choice, for these too can be destructive and at times not able to be rectified. There is a lot yet to be learned about addressing the treatment needs of primitively organized, structurally deficient patients. The willingness to enter this unknown territory with a thoughtful, carefully considered therapeutic attitude, and an awareness of the inherent dangers, is an essential ingredient. Preverbal traumatic experiences may be capable of expression only through enactments. This may make it necessary for a therapist to participate with concrete behavioral interventions before the effects of the trauma can be included within the realm of symbolization, and ultimately be exposed to therapeutic influence.

7

Leaps and Errors of Commission

The Risks Accompanying an Inappropriate Leap

The errors of commission that are a part and parcel of every therapeutic interaction refer to inaccurate interpretations, inadvertent alterations in the conditions of a secure framework, or any unempathic intervention resulting from a therapist's defensive response to the impact of a patient's input. During any period of treatment, if a therapist's subjective responses are dominated by unrecognized narcissistic needs, infantile conflicts, or regressive identifications, interventions will tend to be unempathic, and thus introduce an error of commission. Therapeutic progress will be halted until the empathic failure is noticed, acknowledged, rectified, and its effects interpreted. An unconsciously empathic stance can then be reestablished.

The circumstances are somewhat different with the decision to engage in a leap. A therapist is modifying the framework of the treatment with a full awareness of the risk involved, and a high level of uncertainty and alertedness to the potential for error. In situations apparently calling for these unusual measures, if a therapist's position is not empathic with what the patient needs to facilitate growth, an ensuing error of commission can have more serious consequences and be more difficult to rectify. When a leap constitutes an empathic failure it tends to re-create infantile traumas in a more extreme fashion, because the move has been carefully considered, a deliberate alteration has been made in the containing conditions of a secure treatment framework, and a therapist's conscious intent is included.

A leap is designed to further a patient's healthy strivings by offering an experience that would otherwise be unavailable if the conditions of the treatment were adhered to rigidly. It is a creative intervention that is well thought out and examined closely over time for any evidence of detrimental qualities. On the surface the leap might appear to go against sound therapeutic principles, but a therapist has been as definitive as possible in identifying his motive for the leap as emanating from an empathic appreciation of the patient's unconscious communication of what is needed to progress. Subjective responses have been explored in depth, in a search for any signs of inappropriate countertransference-based reactions. A conscious decision has been made to move into the darkness with the purpose of finding the light by introducing a seemingly unconventional method or procedure. In addition each step is accompanied by a continuous process of self-examination, along with a careful assessment of the patient's productions so as to be consistently attuned to any indication that the leap is a mistake. Errors of commission are thus of a different order than those a therapist has been accustomed to dealing with, in that there are serious consequences if the therapeutic need of a leap is not taken into account.

It is always essential for a firm therapeutic alliance to have developed before the idea of a leap can be considered. This usually takes a fairly extensive period of time, during which a therapist gains a deeper grasp of the makeup of a patient's internal world and of the subjective responses that either enhance or hinder an understanding of the unconscious meaning of a patient's productions. Gradually, enough safety and containment is provided for a benign regression to unfold, which may continue to a point where there is a distinct impression of some vital ingredient being missing. The patient may give a direction outlining a path that must be traversed before therapeutic progress can continue, but what is entailed may violate the secure framework already established. It is mandatory to explore the underlying motive, for if it comes from highly vulnerable healthy strivings rather than a pathological force, the question of engaging in a leap is raised. Following a patient's lead into this unknown territory may be essential in order to discover a heretofore inarticulable experience.

Upon entering into this risky venture it may emerge that the therapist has been misled. The result may be in the therapist's collusion with the reenforcement of a pathological defense, the living out of an unconscious fantasy, or the re-creation of an infantile trauma. Evidence of these detrimental attributes will then begin to surface, and the task of fully understanding how the therapist was drawn into this error of commission becomes paramount. Only then is it at all possible to acknowledge the mistake in a meaningful way. The inappropriate stance must be corrected before its effects can be interpreted, out of which the part the patient has played can come to light.

There are many inherent risks whenever the clear-cut guidelines of a secure treatment framework are abandoned. Even though a therapist may be relatively convinced that a thorough evaluation of all observable factors has been made and some unusual step must be undertaken, the intervention may still represent an error of commission. In spite of a vigilant attitude toward the appearance of any adverse signs, the mistake may not be immediately apparent. It is quite possible for serious ruptures of a contained framework to seem helpful for a short period of time. Eventually, the detrimental influence will become overtly evident, but by then it may have assumed such large proportions that it is either extremely difficult or impossible to rectify. The unempathic intervention and the associated emotional atmosphere may turn out to have been feeding an unconscious fantasy, momentarily creating the impression of having a positive effect from the initial glow of an inappropriate gratification. Meanwhile, the destructive forces in the personality are gradually and often silently intensifying and undermining the therapeutic alliance.

A relationship given impetus by the union of a therapist's empathic responses and a patient's reenactment of an infantile trauma has a very different quality than one involving conflicted countertransference and acting out. In the former situation the therapist is providing a much needed experience, while in the latter the therapist is acting out. Empathic responsiveness is accompanied by an attitude of quiet contemplation with the consistent accessibility of suspended advanced psychic functions, whereas conflicted countertransference is accompanied by a defensive attitude with a sense of urgency or compulsion.

Engaging in a Leap that Reenforces a Pathological Defense

When the movement toward introducing a leap elicits signs of reenforcing a pathological defense, it is crucial that a therapist take responsibility for the error. Unearthing the unconscious reasons for its occurrence will solidify the framework of the treatment, strengthen the therapeutic alliance, and be a spur to ongoing progress.

Clinical Example

This was an important part of the treatment of a 35-year-old man who had initially contacted me to discuss a problem he and his wife were having in dealing with the loss of a foster child.

The child was 5 years of age, and had been living with them for two years when they made plans for her adoption. Just before it was to take place she was returned to her natural mother. He had an intense reaction to the circumstances surrounding her leaving, and was concerned about doing what was best for the child. The courts had apparently acted solely on the basis of the mother's rights, had ignored the long history of abuse and the likelihood of its continuing, and had disrupted the meaningful attachment the child had made. He had become enraged at the injustice. He wrote angry letters to a variety of state agencies and officials, which had given them the impression that he was too emotionally disturbed to even be considered as a potential parent. Consequently, any slight chance of having the child returned to them was completely undermined by the way in which he had responded to the situation.

I listened to their story, and commented on how sad it was that his outrage only placed bigger obstacles in the way of sustaining their attachment to the child. I suggested that if in fact they were her emotional parents the best thing they could do was to continue to respond to her from that position. Even though they could not parent her in a direct and immediate way, she might sense from the way they continued to interact with her that the relationship was still alive and intact. They left, and two months later he called me to talk about the possibility of beginning treatment.

He began by describing his resistance to the whole idea of psychotherapeutic help. He knew there were a lot of things wrong inside of him, but so distrusted the therapists he had come to know in a variety of situations that he had decided he would have to live his life as he was. He was unwilling to place himself in a relationship where his inner world would be misperceived, and where he would most likely become the object of someone else's projections or need for control. He anticipated that all therapists would tend to behave much in the manner of the state officials. Weekly sessions were arranged to explore whether we could work together. At first he used humor and sarcasm to devalue all the visible evidence of things I held in high esteem, seemingly probing for any signs of defensiveness. He caricatured the couch and analytic concepts, attacking analysis for being distant from human experience. He saw therapists as having smug attitudes as if they knew the dark and hidden recesses of a person's inner life. Mockingly he referred to their giving appropriately timed dosages of oracular insight, while demeaning and depreciating a patient's input. In all of these semi-humorous tirades he appeared to be tacitly challenging me to prove that he was wrong. I sensed that this was his way of expressing how vital it was for him to have access to my emotional responses, and of how sensitive he was to when their absence was a product of defensiveness. In an unspoken manner he was revealing the qualities he required for a therapeutic relationship to promote growth. At the same time, he was probably showing the destructive impact of having been the target of a need-supplying object's projections during his developmental years.

He also teased a great deal about watching the clock, laughingly commenting that he was taking over this function for me. I thought he was calling attention to the importance of my maintaining an awareness of time, and, by implication, indicating the need for clearly defined ground rules and boundaries. This was subsequently borne out on one occasion when I did not note the passage of time. He suddenly became inordinately anxious and worried about his words being heard by others outside of the office, and his concern made me aware that it was several minutes past the time. When I linked his anxiety to this lapse in the safe conditions of a secure framework it was extremely facilitating. Memories were elicited that shed light on why these conditions were so important. He had grown up in an environment where his feelings were either not recognized or were subjugated to the narcissistic needs of parental figures, especially his mother. Any defensive withdrawal of emotional responsiveness on my part became very threatening. He perceived it as a prelude to having an attacking projection directed against him. My failure to notice the time was seen by him as ignoring the clear direction he had already given. It suggested that I was gratifying some narcissistic need at his expense.

The conditions of the treatment were gradually established over a long period of time, allowing an atmosphere of safety to strengthen the bond of trust in the evolving therapeutic alliance. Through the careful attention that was given to the details of time, spacing, fee, manner of payment, and position of the patient, positive memories of an early relationship with his father were evoked. This was surprising to him, for he had thought of his father as weak, ineffective, dominated by his mother, and totally uninvolved with him. He now recalled a time when he had enjoyed a very warm attachment to his father, who was then sensitively in tune with him. However, when the patient was 5 years old, his father had a heart attack and became totally self-absorbed, ignoring the patient. The father died ten years later and the patient had had no noticeable reaction. Recovery of these memories opened up a period of mourning for the loss, which helped him understand his extreme reaction to the loss of the foster child. It was intolerably painful to him to be in the position of a father abandoning a child to a destructive mother, and of being totally helpless to do anything about it. The institutional authorities who wielded such power over his life were, in his mind, connected to the emotional dominance of his mother. He was once again a victim, losing a close and intimate relationship.

Following the emergence of this material the therapeutic relationship slowly became somewhat stagnant. The same themes were reviewed in a repetitive manner, with a vague but consistent sense of a lack of vitality to his productions. He started to put pressure on me to take a more active role in talking, interpreting, and revealing personal responses. One helpful interpretation, in the midst of what was becoming a barrage of demands, was my remark that I was beginning to feel what I imagined the patient had experienced with his mother. The sensation was of my every move being controlled, and I wondered if he was showing me how he had identified with her. He lapsed into silence for the remainder of the session. In the following session he reported a dream in which he was watching a group of people rob a bank and take a bank teller hostage. He suddenly became aware that he was a member of the gang, and had to escape to avoid being captured. The rest of the dream was spent trying to get away, with the conviction that he would eventually succeed. My words concerning his identification with his mother had apparently exposed his efforts to control me. He was devoting all of his energy to escape detection, and was convinced that his pathological defenses would ultimately assert themselves. The interpretation had apparently made an inroad upon a hidden defensive aspect of his personality, but what it was designed to protect remained obscure.

Shortly thereafter he complained about a lifelong problem of lower back pain. It was extremely severe, occurred episodically, and had been treated in a variety of ways since his childhood. He had discovered that certain medications either did not help or altered his sensorium in an uncomfortable manner, but there was one in particular that was perfect. It alleviated the pain, and did not affect his thought processes. Although he could get a prescription from another doctor he felt strongly about getting it from me. Most important of all was his need for me to accept the request by having faith in his judgment. He went to great lengths trying to convince me that his knowledge of the medication and its effects came from a trustable, reliable part of himself. He believed that if he could have an experience in a relationship in which he was trusted it would serve as an antidote to the poisonous interactions he had with his mother during his formative years. She had always discounted the validity of his needs when they were presented to her, either ignoring them, belittling them, or insisting that she alone knew best. He wanted me to write the prescription because it would offer concrete evidence of being trusted, and in the process give him the wherewithal to fully explore the relationship with her. It appeared to him that this relationship was a powerful force inside him, and that I was behaving much like his mother in refusing to write the prescription. My insistence on seeing his demand as an expression of her influence upon him, and of avoiding the underlying feelings that would give a deeper perspective on its meaning, was making him increasingly enraged. Whenever he imagined me giving him the prescription he felt connected in a way that revived his early empathic relationship with his father. This is why he was so strongly convinced that I was denying him an opportunity to reach the very things he had always kept hidden. It seemed to him as though he could face the destructiveness of his mother only with this in the background.

I began to waver, and the possibility of yielding to his demand entered my thoughts. The pressure he was exerting did carry the earmarks of his seeking to reenforce a pathological defense. It looked as if he was fighting to avoid the painful experiences that were starting to surface in the transference. I also had a nagging sense of doubt about the advisability of introducing such a leap. Subjectively, it did not feel "right," yet my interpretive words seemed defensive and distancing. I could easily justify my reasons for not complying. A secure framework had been important in reaching this point in the treatment, and would most likely be necessary for the underlying forces pushing for expression to come more fully into view. I was vacillating between holding a firm interpretive posture and considering the idea of following the patient's direction. My uncertainty must have shown in my attitude, for he commented briefly on how I seemed to be giving his demand careful thought. Almost immediately afterward, however, he got up to leave and in a coldly hostile way announced that since I had not given him the prescription he did not know if he would return.

This helped me become aware that in wavering I had probably frightened him, and might even have instigated a flight from treatment. The vacillation may have been helpful to a certain extent, in that it indicated my willingness to take his productions seriously. However, the possibility of my abandoning what had been a helpful stance must have echoed with his anticipation that it was serving some narcissistic interest, and aroused the dangers linked to his mother. My experiences in introducing a leap with other patients had played a role in this situation, more so than was warranted by the patient's input. There was probably some desire on my part to prove the validity of the concept, utilizing it now in the service of avoiding the impact of his regressive transference. The narcissistic element was especially noxious for this patient.

He returned to the following session teasingly asking if I was surprised to see him. I said that I was surprised because I thought he had sensed I was thinking of writing the prescription for all of the wrong reasons. Thus he probably couldn't be sure whether I was trustable, and finally could not be certain that I would recognize this message in the way he left. The effect was both immediate and striking, as his entire demeanor visibly softened. He lay on the couch looking very sad, and his uninterrupted stream of associations expressed an expanding realization of the extent of his addictions. He was noticeably moved while he spoke of how he had been successfully masking his destructive involvement with alcohol, food, drugs, and relationships.

His food addiction was easiest to hide for he ate only the best foods, but in enormous quantities and compulsively. The alcohol addiction could readily be denied since he drank only at appropriate times, but again in massive quantities. His addiction to relationships centered around the repetitive re-creation of pathologically dependent interactions, mirroring the relationship to his mother. His recognition of this connection was most startling to him as he spoke. He was exquisitely sensitive to vulnerabilities in others, exploited them to the point where he became a desperately needed partner, and exerted complete domination and control over what had now become a helpless individual. His addiction to drugs was covered over by relating their use to his back pain. The particular drug he had selected was just right because it evoked a feeling of elation that successfully covered over the pain he was feeling of separation and loss. He could see clearly how he was bringing these powerful regressive cravings into the transference relationship around the question of the prescription, and how my vacillation had made him feel frightened and distrustful. The entire tenor of the treatment changed, and in subsequent sessions a benign regression unfolded without any serious interruption. Occasional empathic lapses were quickly identified, and whenever a question arose that touched upon the framework of the treatment he would laughingly refer to what he had learned from this experience.

I had established ground rules and boundaries that seemed to fit the patient's need for safety and containment, and I adapted the conditions of the treatment to enable the unfolding of a benign regression. Out of this groundwork an effective therapeutic alliance was gradually evolving. However, a countertransference-based defensive response to an emerging regressive maternal transference made me vulnerable to being enticed into an error of commission. The lure of being experienced as an empathic father, rather than an overcontrolling and destructive mother, misled me into considering the possibility of participating in a form of acting out, rationalized as a necessary leap.[1] Fortunately, the patient's emphatic statement, indicative of anxiety and distrust, called the error to my attention. This eventually led to a deeper understanding of the unconscious forces at work in both parties. The mistake could then be corrected, its effects were interpreted, and the conditions of safety were restored.

---

1. Bird (1957) described the acting-out patient as primarily externalizing conflict, involving others, and being highly susceptible to outside influence. There is a failure to establish the internal structure necessary to enable the struggle to remain within, based upon a developmental defect wherein the differentiation between the child and maternal ego is impaired. Such individuals are uncannily able to sense the hidden impulses of others including the therapist. They attempt to get the therapist to act out with them, and invariably succeed to some degree. If they succeed to a considerable extent the analysis will fail. Thus they detect acting out tendencies in the therapist and exploit it. Bird believed that it was important to develop an infantile, narcissistic symbiotic relationship, and that from this transference state, through steady interpretation, there can be a gradual shift to object-relatedness. He also emphasized how personal remarks about the therapist may not be a projection, but an actual observation, and these perceptions must be recognized.

It is certainly vital to take a patient's demands seriously, looking at their meaning from all possible angles instead of simply invoking a rigid adherence to the framework of the treatment. In doing so a therapist can be open to the possibility of there being value in them. This is not tantamount to acting impulsively, nor does it mean that the unconscious significance of the demands is ignored or overlooked. It emphasizes the importance of being willing to entertain the idea of a leap, while at the same time not moving too quickly before a careful assessment of its meaning to both parties is made. In this situation, my actual participation in the acting out would clearly have been detrimental. Although my wavering was not desirable, the insight it provided was ultimately put to good therapeutic use. It illustrated how difficult it is to be truly receptive to the idea of a patient's demands having in them a search for a potential growth-promoting experience, without being equally vulnerable to countertransference-based mistakes.

Engaging in a Leap that Re-creates an Infantile Trauma

There are occasions when a patient in relinquishing a defensive stance feels the impact of inarticulable intrapsychic events, and as a consequence re-creates circumstances paralleling an infantile trauma. The internal sense of becoming more open repeats an infantile situation in the transference. Thus if a therapist is not empathically responsive at that precise moment the resulting error of omission can be so resonant with the original trauma as to be intolerable. The experience of being open in a relationship and of not being heard may be identical with what was an overwhelming trauma, and if an empathic response is not forthcoming the chance may never recur again. For this reason the possibility of utilizing unusual measures in a creative manner, still being guided by sound therapeutic principles, must be consistently available to a therapist who is going to work with more primitively organized patients. It is not always possible to immediately distinguish these rare situations, and it is in this area that a therapist's abilities are most stringently tested. The differences between subjective responses that are a product of countertransference-based infantile conflicts, narcissistic needs, and regressive identifications must be clearly discerned, and the differences between the manifestations of acting out and reenacting infantile experiences in the patient's mode of interacting must be understood in depth. These distinctions are crucial to make in every treatment endeavor, but they are highlighted when the success or failure of the treatment depends upon their being almost instantly available.

A therapist's free-floating attention allows subjective reactions to become more noticeable, thereby enlarging the capacity for understanding the unconscious significance of the relationship to both parties. However, the advanced functions that have been suspended to achieve this internal state must be periodically invoked, so as to monitor the way a patient's input is being received. The information is then used in determining an appropriate intervention. One of the functions of a secure framework is to provide a background of safety within which this transference–countertransference interchange can take place. It gives the therapist a dependable safeguard for maintaining the therapeutic properties of the relationship, while undergoing the controlled regression required to gain full access to empathic and countertransference responses.

When a patient's demands are directed toward modifying the conditions of the treatment, a vigilant attitude must be in operation. Otherwise a therapist may become a participant in rupturing the necessary containing influences of an intact framework. It may be so reminiscent to a patient of an intolerable infantile trauma that once it occurs there is no other alternative than to flee.

Clinical Example

This was illustrated in the treatment of a 17-year-old boy, whose father made the initial contact. The father had been trying for years to find help for his son with no success, although the boy had gone to many different therapists, attending one or two sessions each time before quitting. He was now refusing to go at all, having told his father he could not tolerate being with people who were bound to conventions and followed established values. The father had heard I was open to new ideas and thus wanted to make an appointment for his son. This was all stated in a commanding tone of voice. I said simply that I would be glad to talk to his son about it if he wanted to call. Several days later the son called asking for help, referred to an awareness of his father's call, and made an appointment.

He arrived late to his first session, which turned out to be a repetitive pattern. Without the slightest hesitation he proceeded to talk at a rapid pace, hardly pausing for breath. He was tall, athletic, and handsome, adopted an exaggeratedly self-assured posture, and his presence filled the room. He had a deep resonating voice, and appeared much older than his years. His attitude exuded a sense of dominance and control. He began by remarking on his having so much to say that there didn't seem to be enough time to get it all out. He was very concerned about himself, and just could not understand why he had so much trouble relating to other people. He was attracted to girls but after a short time they would have nothing to do with him; he had male friends he enjoyed but no one ever called him; and people in general tended to shy away from him. As a result he felt alone, isolated, and cut off from experiences that people around him seemed to enjoy.

He thought of himself as very bright, capable, and talented, although he was doing badly in school. This was the reason his father was pushing him to get help. He was in his last year of high school and the school officials were threatening to prevent him from graduating on the basis of his refusal to turn in assignments that he considered unimportant. He was unwilling either to do homework or to follow directions that he thought of as authoritarian. He did extremely well on tests, felt he knew enough to meet anyone's qualifications for graduation, and was steadfast in not bending to anyone else's rules. His father was worried because he was failing. However, the patient was concerned because he couldn't decide whether to fail while standing up for his principles, or to give in and go on to college in the way that was expected of him. Above all he was very confused about what he wanted to do with his life. He paused to ask what I thought he should do. I commented on his question, which seemed to be searching for some indication of what this relationship would be like. Perhaps he was trying to discover what rules or conditions he would come up against here, and he had certainly indicated how upsetting it was to him to be in a position of following other people's rules. I added that I didn't understand as yet what this all meant to him. He became thoughtful, and proceeded to talk about the intensity of his reactions to rules. He first related it to his father's dominance over the household, which led him to review his background for me during the session.

My impression was of a child desperately searching for limits, hinting that well-defined ground rules and boundaries would be an essential component of the therapeutic relationship before he would feel safe enough to regress. I thought he was probing to see whether the

LEAPS AND ERRORS OF COMMISSION

conditions he required would be imposed upon him. It would thus be extremely important to listen carefully and interpret the derivatives of his unconscious perceptions of what was required to promote growth, rather than for me to present conditions he had to follow. The various ground rules, including fees, manner of payment, spacing and frequency of appointments, position, and so on, could all be discussed and his responses hopefully would point out a direction as to how these rules might best be established. My interpretation was a beginning attempt to introduce the conditions of the treatment, by emphasizing that the focus of attention would be on understanding his internal world. His response in revealing his life history seemed to indicate this approach was on the right track.

He was the only child of middle-aged parents. His father was a very successful and influential man who had totally controlled everyone throughout his remembered years. His words were law, and anyone he came in contact with had to yield to his commands. The patient's mother was much younger, and was recalled as a soft, gentle, loving person who gratified his every whim. Anything he wanted was immediately provided; she was always available to comfort him, and to buffer him against the father's explosive attacks and demands for excellence. He never felt intimidated by his father while in his mother's presence, and in fact welcomed his outbursts then because they were always followed by special favors from his mother to make up for it. Both parents delighted in his performance from the time when he was very young. He could read at an early age, he played the piano, memorized poems, and was physically adept. His parents showed off his talents to others, and stood together in pride at his accomplishments. He was enormously gratified, taking every opportunity to occupy the center of this stage. This heavenly and blissful world, as he saw it, was traumatically ended with the mother's death when he was 5 years of age.

His mother had been debilitated for about a year from the effects of a fulminating cancer, which had left her bedridden and in great pain. The father reacted to her death by becoming profoundly depressed, and the patient was left for a time with a succession of caretakers until he was old enough to care for himself. The patient emphasized that although he knew that his relationship with his mother, and the loss of it, had a profound effect upon him, he doubted whether it had much relevance for his current life. The only thing he recalled about it was the change in the circumstances of his surrounding environment. He was no longer the focus of attention in his household, and he even missed his father's explosive outbursts. The father seemed too depressed to care very much.

The patient missed being a shining star, and he was totally defeated in his efforts to assume that place on the playground, in school, or with his father. He felt isolated and alone, feelings that persisted to the present time and were the reason he sought help. My comment about his reaction to fixed rules had struck a responsive chord in him. I made him feel understood, and fueled a wish to know his internal world in greater depth. He had been pleased to know I was an analyst, because he had spent several years reading Freud and attempting to achieve that kind of understanding. He was intrigued by the whole idea of an unconscious world, over which he had no control, exerting control over his life. He wanted to gain total mastery over that part of himself.

He went on to underscore how he wanted to demonstrate to me the strength of his commitment to this venture, and stressed how willing and eager he was to meet every day for as long as it took even if that meant several hours a day. I remarked that I wanted to listen long enough to learn what would further his growth, and to be directed by that, but I didn't feel that was available as yet. He took this as a challenge to be resisted, overpowered, and depreciated, side by side with proclamations of his respect for the unconscious and its importance. He gave emphatic statements about the vast extent of his knowledge of himself and awareness of what was best. He added that he knew beyond the shadow of a doubt what he needed, and I was either unable or unwilling to provide it. I said that he was correct in sensing I was unable and unwilling to respond in this way, but I also wasn't sure what he was seeking in the deeper, more hidden parts of himself. He had certainly shown me how vital it was for him to be the center of the stage, which hinted that it was traumatic to have lost that position and he might be attempting to recapture it in this relationship. He was intrigued by the idea, but treated it much like he did everything else in his life. First he expressed the feeling of my understanding him in an important way, saying that as a consequence I must know how valid it was to meet his request. All of my interpretations were reacted to as declarations of my intent to gratify his every wish, rather than as efforts to encourage a process of internal exploration.

It soon became evident that interpretive words were of very little value. I was confronted with the task of trying to reach him in the deeper layers of his personality through the management of the ground rules, boundaries, and conditions of the treatment, though it was not clear as to how it could be accomplished. Initially it was approached around establishing the time and frequency of appointments. I stated that at this point all I could go on was what felt comfortable to me and I would listen to how well this matched his therapeutic needs. Sessions were then arranged on alternate days, in order to assess how he was responding both to the evolving relationship and to the intervening space. He was consistently late. Any attempt to address this behavior as meaningful was short-circuited by some comment he made about the lateness and his anticipation that I would consider it to be meaningful, along with a terse declaration that it was simply a product of his busy life making it impossible to pay attention to time. He would then go on to complain about the time being much too short, for he could never express all that was on his mind. He suggested that I increase the time rather than looking at his being late. He continuously protested about the shortness of each session and about the lack of sufficient time over the course of a week. He felt there was too much happening inside, too much to say, and too much to understand for it all to take place in such a limited time frame. By contrast, I felt he was saying very little while repeating the same theme over and over again, and that neither the spacing nor the time constraints were having any noticeable impact on the way he experienced the relationship. The only element of a therapeutic alliance that seemed to be viable involved his hunger for an attachment in which he could have an admiring audience.

The patient appeared to be living out in his behavior the previously lost position of being the center of his parents' universe. Interpretations did nothing to alter this posture, nor did the management of the time aspect of the framework. This posture was also addressed in discussing the payment of the fee, with the same result. In questioning what it meant for him to be asking for large segments of time, I wondered how he thought about the fee. His response was to refer to his father's telling him he would pay for whatever was decided. When I asked about the significance to him of the manner of payment, he simply stated that he would use his own trust fund if that was important. He also spontaneously brought up the idea of using the couch, adding that from his reading he guessed I must consider him too sick or otherwise unable to utilize it. In order to demonstrate the incorrectness of that idea he proceeded to place himself in a supine position. Partly in exasperation I remarked that I did consider him unable to use either the couch or the relationship to further his self-knowledge, and that I had not been able to find either the proper conditions or the right words to help him do that. This was the first intervention that had an observable effect. He became very thoughtful and expressed his realization that he would have to find a way to bring more thoughts, feelings, and internal experiences into the therapy than he had thus far been able to do. Although he had become momentarily introspective it did not appreciably change anything that subsequently transpired, for he quickly recovered his previous arrogant attitude. It looked as though my words were experienced as a narcissistic insult, and he was loath to admit even to himself that the relationship could be that important.

A consistent theme, however, slowly began to emerge. The ending of a session was becoming more obviously difficult for him and he seemed to be preparing himself for it from the moment he entered. Whenever the end of the time was announced he reacted with surprise, which he tried to cover up with a flurry of thoughts about the shortness of the time. The process of recognizing his discomfort evoked in my mind the image of a lost child searching for his mother and expecting to see her around the next corner. It hinted that the patient was living by the dictates of a fantasy that his mother would appear, and he might experience the ending of the session as a reminder of the reality of her death, which was intolerable. With this in mind I told him I had a feeling that the end of a session was difficult because it reminded him of how suddenly and abruptly a very vital experience can be lost, and I connected it to how he must have reacted to his mother's death. This interpretation had a noticeable influence.

He became tearful and began to recall earlier interactions with his mother. These memories were extremely troubling, for they were contrary to his initial presentation of her as an all-giving, all-loving, comforting and buffering figure. She now emerged as a very frightened, overwhelmed, and depressed woman with whom he had great difficulty establishing contact. She was both fearful of him and intimidated by his demands, and he exploited this vulnerability mercilessly. At the same time he had a constant internal sense of hoping she would stand firm. He also recalled the year prior to her death when she was increasingly sick, and the terrible feeling he had that his tyrannical demands were the cause of her destruction. Poignantly he described several incidents during the time she was bedridden when he would try in vain to make amends. She found his physical presence too painful to bear, pushed him away, and he was then restrained by a nurse. In the midst of this portrayal of being pushed away, the session had come to an end. He looked up at the clock. Rather than maintaining the firm position that up to this point had been held about the ending of the time, I also looked at the clock and by a gesture extended the time. The patient continued, visibly shaken by the return of those very painful memories. He left some fifteen minutes past the allotted time.

He began the following session in a rage about my extending the time. He felt taken advantage of, seduced, and exploited. By virtue of my not holding firm to the clear-cut ground rules he required, and not ending the session precisely on time regardless of the condition he was in, I was behaving so much like the mother he had tyrannized that it was impossible for him to continue. The pain it evoked in him was intolerable. He stormed out, never to return, and did not respond to my efforts to reach him.

I had correctly recognized the patient's need for a firm therapeutic framework, although the underlying reasons were not immediately apparent. After a long period of putting pressure on me in every conceivable manner to alter the ground rules of the treatment, once he saw I could sustain a relatively solid interpretive posture he felt there was enough safety for a benign regression to be initiated. With interpretive help, gleaned from a grasp of the unconscious significance of the ending of a session, the patient had been able to unveil the effects of traumatic experiences associated with his early relationship to his mother. However, in response to the powerful emotions the patient was experiencing, I had lost my perspective. I relented and allowed the time to be extended, thereby repeating an aspect of his relationship with his mother that was most traumatic. The only alternative available to him was to take flight from the therapeutic relationship, for he could not stand the prospect of his sadistic impulses coming to life unless they could be received without destroying my capacity to function. My inability to maintain the firm stance he required, particularly at this crucial moment, was too reminiscent of the painful affects accompanying the early conflicted attachment to and later loss of his mother.[2]

My rationale for extending the treatment framework was based upon the idea of providing the patient with a much needed experience of availability, to counteract the impact of his anticipation that contact would be lost. In fact what had been provided was a repetition of the trauma that was continually active in the deeper reaches of the patient's mind. The error of commission could not be overcome, rectified, or interpreted. I had made a regressive identification with the patient's plight, unwittingly imposed my own meaning upon it, and thereby lost sight of what was most relevant. Looking back, I find that this regressive identification may have been operative from the start. It was at work in enhancing my empathic responses, and probably enabled the therapeutic relationship to progress to the point that was reached. In the face of the

---

2. Segel (1969) pointed out how exposure to early massive stimulation or threat of abandonment is frequently associated with acting out. The acting out is seen as a later repetitive, defensive effort to master or bind the anxiety by repeating aspects that were originally passively imposed in an active role.

patient's arrogant, depreciating, narcissistic attitude I was able to remain open to receiving his input, and could intuitively grasp the vital importance of creating the conditions of safety required to facilitate a benign regression. However, this regressive identification, which initially had been helpful, became an obstacle when the patient's traumatic experiences rose to the surface from behind his narcissistic defenses. Empathy became intertwined with the detrimental aspects of countertransference as I was drawn into offering my own version of a better parent.

I had lost sight of the patient's most pressing anxiety. In attempting to compensate for the developmental trauma, I managed only to recreate it. At this critical juncture it had been vitally important that I sustain an empathic stance by ending the session in the midst of his suffering, thereby remaining connected in a helpful manner. Instead of providing the patient with the missing experience of an attachment to an object capable of containing and integrating his sadistic controlling impulses, I was buffering myself against being experienced as an abandoning figure. The resulting resonance with the predominant feature of his trauma was so intolerable that in spite of my efforts to reengage the patient and rectify the error, it was impossible to do so. I had ruptured the alliance at a time when it was most important to remain firm. The union between the patient's unconscious perception of what he needed to facilitate growth and my unconsciously empathic responsiveness was disrupted. Because it echoed with a specific trauma, mobilizing intolerable affects, it could not be corrected. On the one hand, it illustrated in a very vivid fashion how a regressive identification could further empathic responses, and thereby contribute to the development of a therapeutic alliance; on the other hand, however, when that regressive identification no longer served to broaden my understanding, since it had moved into the realm of a narcissistic countertransference-based reaction, it momentarily produced a loss of perspective. The resulting leap therefore modified the secure framework he desperately required. This error of commission repeated the essence of the original trauma, and the patient had no other option than to leave the relationship.

The Effects of Avoiding Errors of Commission through the Application of Rules in Place of Guiding Principles

A patient's primitive projective identifications have to be received and internalized by a therapist in order to fully understand archaic transferences. However, the degree of openness required to do so may at one and the same time elicit regressive narcissistic needs and identifications that may result in errors of commission. A therapist's subjective responses, in order to contain empathic resonance with the totality of a patient's experience, will include the arousal of regressive states activating rescue fantasies and the remnants of usually dormant narcissistic needs. These countertransference difficulties must be filtered out and distinguished from empathic and intuitive responses, both to gain an accurate understanding of a patient's unconscious communications and to maintain the therapeutic properties of the relationship. If the only answer to this very complex task is to rigidly adhere to the conditions of the treatment as rules to be followed, rather than as principles to be applied, it will close off the only available means of bringing therapeutic influence to some archaic transferences. There has to be enough flexibility to determine when a leap may be necessary to facilitate growth, so that the new roads may be discovered for reaching difficult-to-treat patients.[3]

---

3. Winnicott (1960a) stressed that when the therapist begins to get in contact with the patient's true self, there must be a period of extreme dependence. Often this fails to occur. The patient gives the therapist a chance to take over the false self functions, but if the therapist fails to see what is happening, and in consequence it is others who care for the patient and others on whom the patient becomes dependent, the opportunity is missed.

Anna Freud (1971) reviewed the suggestions for improving analytic efficiency. A starting point was the notion that the ego distortions that hinder analysis are acquired by the individual during the earliest defensive struggle against unpleasure. These considerations carry analysis from the verbal to the preverbal period of development, bringing with it the need for practical and technical innovations many of which are controversial. In these situations the therapist's intuitive and empathic understanding of a patient's signs and signals become the primary modality of the treatment.

Gaddini (1982) elaborated upon the problems in treating certain severely disturbed and difficult to reach patients. These are individuals who have been locked into the dead end of nonintegration, on the one hand by the precariousness of the nonintegration state itself, on the other hand by the tendency toward integration, implying the fearful recognition of a permanent separation. There is then a need to make, by means of contact, a magical repetitive experience out of the integration that is not possible. The fantasy of the repetitive experience of contact belongs to fantasies of the body, and rather than translating itself into images it translates itself into physical behavior. It represents an effort to repro-

A therapist must pay close attention to specifically which conditions are supportive of a secure treatment framework, because it is an essential component of the safety and containment required before a benign regression can be induced. When addressing the treatment needs of primitively organized patients it is all too easy to replace firmness with rigidity, and fail to distinguish between a guiding principle and an inflexible rule. A rigid adherence to rules and an unyielding interpretive posture reflects defensiveness on the part of a therapist, often obscured by the pathological nature of a patient's demands. A truly secure framework serves the differing needs of both parties in the interaction, and on most occasions will operate as a silent background giving steadiness and balance to the transference–countertransference interchange. However, when the conditions of the treatment are misapplied to serve the inappropriate protective needs of the therapist, they characteristically rise to the forefront, making it imperative for the source of the difficulty to be identified. A therapist's training tends to overemphasize the invoking of rules, since it does to a large extent prevent many errors of commission that can be extremely destructive. This approach also makes it impossible for certain patients to attain the experiences they require to be effectively treated. Such patients are often pronounced as either "too sick" or "too resistant," whereas in fact our knowledge may not be advanced enough to conduct the treatment properly.[4] The purpose of

---

duce magically the lost body sensations of self-containment. Analysis favors the natural tendency to develop, entailing the passage from the need to survive to the desire to live, and living appears as an extreme danger. Consequently a therapist has to be open to receiving directions to provide experiences most likely including direct contact that ultimately can enable the shift to occur. This syndrome aroused in early infancy can sometimes disappear in analysis, not so much because of interpretation but because the analytical situation allowed certain natural processes to take place for the first time.

4. Fairbairn (1957) discussed the limitations inherent in followers of classical psychoanalytic technique. The tendency to interpret in regard to internal reality assumes that the form of interpretation will be in relation to fantasy rather than the actual situations that are experienced. It ignores the vital aspect of the true unconscious attitudes of the therapist, which are a factor in determining the efficacy of treatment. There are times when it is essential to offer more than interpretation. Thus the actual interaction assumes greater importance than any particular details of technique.

a leap is to create a means of extending the reliable concepts at the foundation of ideal therapeutic functioning into unknown territory. The range of disorders that can be amenable to constructive therapeutic influence is thereby enlarged.

The concept of a leap can readily be abused, resulting in unwarranted errors of commission. The most effective protection against this happening is through an ever-deepening understanding of the unconscious forces at work in both patient and therapist. There must be room for creative experimentation in every treatment endeavor, but especially for those wherein known methods and procedures are otherwise doomed to failure. In most instances enlarging the horizons of treatability is limited by the capacity of a given therapist to respond appropriately to a therapeutic need, although there are patients whose personality makeup may not be amenable to psychological help as it is presently known and understood.[5]

Blum (1977) referred to the impact of early disturbances upon the therapeutic alliance, noting that the more serious this factor was the more difficult it was to maintain a stable alliance. It is this lack of stability that makes a rigid stance on the part of the therapist intolerable.

Tustin (1980) commented upon the beneficial features of the bearable lack of fit of a "good enough" mother. It provides the space in which chance happenings can occur, for these are the agents of transformation and change. Individuals who have been lacking in this essential experience are constantly confronted with overwhelming distress, panic, rage, and predatory rivalries that need to be addressed before any interpretation about love, aggression, envy, and jealousy can be meaningful.

5. Eissler (1963) thought there were some patients whose intense resistance might be a well-justified measure protecting an ego whose fabric would not be strong enough to withstand the power of id derivatives once they were given access to the preconscious or conscious system. If viewed analytically, treatment would then be considered a failure, whereas maintaining the symptoms may be the only way the individual has to be as fulfilled as possible in adapting to external events.

Anna Freud (1971) discussed the factors that could be recognized as significant for the success or failure of analytic therapy. They included a low threshold of tolerance for the frustration of instinctual wishes, a low threshold of tolerance for anxiety, a low sublimation potential, and a preponderance of regressive over progressive tendencies.

Green (1975) noted an increasing awareness of the therapist's role in creating the psychoanalytic situation, which made it imperative to study the effects of the manner in which the therapist communicated. The therapist influences and is

The level of commitment and degree of responsibility a therapist is willing to assume for a patient's welfare plays a significant role in the treatment of severely disturbed, structurally deficient individuals. This kind of dedication may very well lead a therapist on a path that elicits unresolved remnants of early difficulties, which might not be activated in treating more structured personalities. When they are aroused in response to more primitive productions there may be a lack of familiarity with their manifestations, and consequently the propensity for errors of commission may be increased. Every therapist strives to avoid colluding with an unconscious fantasy, reenforcing a pathological defense, or re-creating an infantile trauma, but hopefully not at the expense of overlooking an opportunity to provide a much needed growth-promoting experience. The problem is compounded when the preverbal traumas that are involved cannot be symbolized or are incapable of being articulated, because they are then reenacted and lived out in the transference. A therapist has to learn how to glean their meaning from subjective responses, which, if infused with inadequately integrated elements, can lead to inappropriate and detrimental interventions.[6]

---

an integral part of the patient's material, suggesting that the limits of analyzability may lie primarily within the therapist.

Gedo (1984) believed there were two sets of constraints that could defeat psychoanalytic efforts. The first was the occurrence of regressive episodes, in the course of which the patient loses the capacity to cope with the exigencies of everyday life, necessitating placement in a sheltered environment. The second was the covert presence of delusional convictions, particularly when these unalterable beliefs concerned the acquisition of valid knowledge. Patients afflicted with this variant of omniscience mistrust any new information they acquire in analysis, even though their unwillingness or inability to change false beliefs may hide behind a screen of verbal assent. In addition, if a patient exhibits a significant propensity to form symbiotic attachments and continues to find outlets in everyday extra-analytic contacts it probably means a poor prognosis. This does not mean that the traditional policy of viewing delinquent enactments as contraindications for psychoanalytic treatment is justified.

6. Emde (1988) underscored the importance of empathic arousal as a prosocial motivator, for a child feels distress at another's discomfort and wants to help. This form of internalization is heavily dependent upon consistent caregiving interactions; it increasingly involves shared intentions, and forms an important scaffolding for later communication involving language. When this process has been impaired in early development its manifestations will be a crucial aspect of an evolving transference relationship, making it mandatory for a therapist to be alert to behavioral expressions of internal experience.

Every step away from a secure therapeutic framework should be considered only after a careful examination of the therapist's internal reactions and the patient's material have indicated there are no destructive or detrimental components at work. Even then it is important to recognize that a therapist can be misled, and a vigilant attitude must be consistently sustained. It is vital for the conduct of the treatment to be guided by clearly defined ground rules and boundaries, and by sound therapeutic principles, but it is equally vital that they not be rigid rules to be followed. Whenever pressure is exerted to alter, modify, or deviate from an established framework, it should be approached with care. The alternative of invoking the conditions of the treatment as rules that cannot vary may protect a therapist against errors of commission, but it simultaneously creates an unempathic emotional climate and may result in equally serious errors of omission.

A patient's demand for a form of participation that means abandoning the conditions of a secure framework requires a response, whether it be an appropriate silence, an unconsciously empathic interpretation, or an exploration of the possibility of introducing a leap. The sense of urgency does not necessarily mean that the moment for a decision is at hand. In fact it often reflects a patient's reaction to a therapist's closure or defensiveness. It is essential for the patient's voice to be adequately heard so that the source of the disturbance can be found. Otherwise the pressure will only escalate in intensity and lead nowhere. The delay and time spent in discovery is what is most essential, rather than an immediate decision to take action. Ideal therapeutic functioning means that the unconscious significance of a patient's communications will be understood, out of which an appropriate intervention will become evident. As long as the therapeutic alliance is viable and effective there is no urgency of time, for the primary consideration is in the uncovering of truth. This growth-promoting experience, even though it may be slow and obstructed by a therapist's blind spots, is enough to sustain the therapeutic alliance and make it stronger. The ultimate revelation of what is true, genuine, and undistorted will be its own reward, because the therapeutic attributes of the relationship are maintained. It may or may not include the necessity of introducing a leap.

In most treatment situations, once an effective alliance has evolved there is enough room in the relationship for errors to be recognized, acknowledged, rectified, and their effects interpreted. This does not mean that their detrimental influence should be underplayed; rather it underscores the extreme importance of a consistent monitoring of the interaction for any evidence of lapses in empathy. Although a therapist's commitment to the treatment is based upon a dedication to the unearthing of truth, personal responses are subject to distortions and must be relentlessly examined for signs of them. Mistakes are unavoidable, but to use rigid rules as a protection against their occurrence can in itself be in error. Hopefully, mistakes can be a spur to further growth, and to an enlargement of our ability to utilize therapeutic principles more effectively.

Whenever we try to reach out to those individuals who have been considered inaccessible to our methods, an opportunity opens up for new learning. It also increases a vulnerability to the introduction of errors of commission. Were this potential to be taken as a reason not to continue in these exploratory efforts, it would close the door to finding avenues for broadening the range of disorders for which help can be offered. The task is to utilize principles that are known to be reliable, and adapt them to the circumstances being confronted. Otherwise they become rules of conduct, which undermines their essential nature. Errors of commission are certainly averted by adhering to fixed ground rules, boundaries, and conditions, but therapeutic progress is not necessarily advanced, and errors of omission may be invoked as a result. These mistakes can in their own way be devastating, especially since they are generally more insidious, subtle, and easily rationalized. A therapist can always find reasons to justify a particular posture, and there is a tendency to point to the possibility of errors of commission as sufficient cause to reject the idea of a leap. There is enough validity in this observation to ignore the opportunities that are then missed. In the process, an error of omission goes unrecognized.

8

Leaps and Errors of Omission

The Function of a Contained Treatment Framework, Its Relationship to the Therapeutic Alliance, and the Need for Flexibility

The basic psychoanalytic principles of free association, abstinence, anonymity, and neutrality guide a therapist's conduct of the therapeutic interaction. The principles are the same regardless of the severity or nature of the individual's pathology. It is the manner in which they are applied that creates differences in the evolving relationship, and this is determined by the patient's level of psychic organization. The success or failure of the treatment is then dependent upon the formation of a meaningful attachment, which can incorporate all aspects of a patient's intrapsychic world within its sphere of influence. A therapist's attitudes and emotions are of tremendous importance, for they can be either helpful, harmful, or a combination of both. It is the therapist's responsibility to filter out those components that are noxious and an obstacle to the patient's growth, while emphasizing those that are helpful and facilitating.

Psychoanalytic treatment relies upon an in-depth understanding of the totality of the personality, placing particular stress on the importance of unconscious forces. Interpretive interventions, which are designed to impart insight, are usually the major instrument for producing constructive intrapsychic change. However, interpretations can be effective only on a background of safety and containment, a function served by sound management of the ground rules, boundaries, and conditions of the treatment. Within that context a benign regression can unfold and enable previously inaccessible infantile experiences to gain access to expression. In addition, a therapist's devotion to uncovering psychological truths, and the associated commitment to the overall welfare of the patient, fosters positive identifications. This interpersonal atmosphere is vital for every patient in order to create an environment receptive to extremely vulnerable, regressive intrapsychic states, and therefore is an essential emotional accompaniment of all transactions. Unresolved infantile conflicts and early developmental deficits and arrests can then be exposed to the healing influence of being handled in a sensitive, unconsciously empathic manner, resulting in an expansion of self-knowledge and self-awareness.

A therapist's dedication to unraveling distortions, so as to identify and provide what is required to facilitate growth, must be carried to its ultimate extreme in addressing the therapeutic needs of individuals whose early developmental experiences have been replete with the impact of unempathic and openly destructive interactions. These are individuals who have gone through their lives trapped within the confines of overwhelming anxieties, evoked by or contributed to by the insensitivities of others. Consequently there is a built-in anticipation that an absence of or failure in empathic resonance possesses destructive intent. Thus a therapist must gain a deeply penetrating understanding of the patient's unconscious communications, often having only subjective empathic and intuitive responses to go on, in order to determine what is uniquely required for that particular individual. Such patients will frequently work hard to destroy that understanding because it might invoke a more dangerous situation than is already present, or because there is a firm conviction that the therapist may very well be motivated by a need to gratify his self-interest at the patient's expense.[1] It is only through a therapist's persistence in

---

1. Bion (1959) made note of the destructive attacks, in the psychotic part of the personality, that a patient makes on anything felt to have the function of linking one object to another. It is a state of mind in which the patient's psyche contains an internal object that is opposed to and destructive of all links whatsoever, from the most primitive to the most sophisticated forms of communication. In this state of mind emotion is hated. It is felt to be too powerful to be contained by the immature psyche; it is felt to link objects, and it gives reality to objects that are inimical to primary narcissism. These attacks on the linking

striving to maintain an unconsciously empathic environment that sufficient trust will eventually develop. With this as a foundation an effective therapeutic alliance can evolve, allowing archaic transferences to be exposed to the light of reason and integration.

Establishing a framework specifically adapted to a given patient's treatment requirements plays a significant role in the gradual building of a firm therapeutic alliance. When pressure is exerted to either alter, modify, or deviate from any of the components it becomes crucial to illuminate the underlying motivation. Primitive transferences are often expressed in this fashion, usually based upon a desperate need to test the firmness and solidity of the relationship and the setting. If this is the case a therapist must sustain a firm but flexible posture, so as to internalize the demands and unravel the unconscious meaning of the primitive projective identifications that are involved. The interchange can then culminate in an interpretation, returning the meaning of the pressure in a more integratable form, while still retaining the conditions of safety necessary for this constructive experience to take place. Under these circumstances it would only be disruptive for a therapist to yield or relinquish the containing properties of a secure framework. Although this may inadvertently occur and subsequently turn out to be correctable or even useful, there are times when the effects are irreparable.[2]

---

function of emotion lead to an overprominence of links that appear to be logical, but never emotionally reasonable. Consequently, the surviving links are perverse, cruel, and sterile.

Wolf (1983a) regarded the goal of a therapeutic process to be a shift from archaic to more mature modes of self-object relationships. He saw treatment as constituting a healing of the injury of the self, in which it must be possible for a therapist to be experienced as performing the needed self-object functions. In order to overcome resistances, the injured self must dare to open itself to the potential of being injured again, and is encouraged by the therapist's commitment and self-revealing attitude. The decisive event is the moment a patient has gained courage from the therapist's self-revelations to know that the therapist does not feed on the patient to achieve cohesion and harmony.

2. Langs (1975a) considered that modifications or deviations from the framework or boundaries of the treatment usually have detrimental consequences of which only a portion are modifiable in the verbal cognitive sphere. When they occur, actual changes in the therapist's stance are essential for the rectification of the harmful effects, and some may be impossible to alter.

There are occasions wherein the very conditions encompassed in establishing a firm therapeutic framework present a special difficulty. If it is automatically assumed that all pressure to alter these conditions stems from a pathological source, a critical facet of a patient's internal world may be overlooked. These situations are encountered when the ground rules, boundaries, or conditions of the treatment, including the use of interpretations as the primary communicative modality, emerge as excessively resonant with unseen infantile traumas or unempathic preverbal experiences. The problem arises because behavioral enactments with the participation of a therapist may be the only means available for bringing these intrapsychic events into a recognizable and workable place. The treatment environment, which was necessary to provide safety and containment at the outset becomes too limiting and restrictive. It now operates to prevent therapeutic progress, and in place of feeling safe there is a persistent sense of something being missing that must be explored from every possible angle. This includes following whatever directions are presented by a patient, preferably with a clear view of how healthy strivings for growth can be fostered.

Such an undertaking requires a willingness to consider the conceivable necessity of interventions that on the surface might appear to be incongruous with sound therapeutic principles. Each step taken must be carefully monitored for any signs of a detrimental influence, and there must be viable evidence of achieving therapeutic progress. There is always the danger of powerful infantile emotions becoming predominant and blurring a therapist's perspective, particularly in any endeavor entered into with this degree of dedication. Any disguised attempt to gratify unconscious needs at the expense of constructive growth creates unnecessary disruptions. An introspective focus of attention, along with a careful assessment of the patient's input, can be of great help in safeguarding against such inappropriate happenings. Together they operate as an antidote to this eventuality. The alternative approach of refusing to even consider the possibility of a leap opens the doors to errors of omission, which in their own way can be equally as destructive as errors of commission. A therapist's refusal, unwillingness, or inability to offer a patient what can be a much needed opportunity for growth, introduces a silent error of withholding. Because the therapeutic stance is in accord with recognized principles, and appears justifiable, the mistake may go unrecognized for extended periods of time. Often the adamancy of this position serves more to protect the therapist, rather than the patient, and is linked to developmental traumas undermining the therapeutic alliance.[3]

Correcting an Error of Omission by Engaging in a Leap

A therapist's reluctance to participate in a leap is understandable to a patient. It is also readily absorbable if based upon an observable effort to unearth the underlying truth that is expressed in a given demand. The insistence upon keeping an unyielding attitude about the conditions of the treatment is what is most troublesome, for if there is a necessity for change it would be impossible to detect. Maintaining an openness to examining the unconscious significance of the treatment framework is conducive to the discovery of an error of omission. The required conditions can then be instituted to provide the experience previously missing, and the resulting leap can be an integral facet of the therapeutic properties of the relationship.

---

[3]. Giovacchini (1974) commented upon the striking sensitivity of some seriously disturbed patients to even the slightest nuances of defensiveness in others. Current culture with its emphasis on the group rather than the individual, on behavior rather than intrapsychic forces, on conformity rather than autonomy is at cross purposes with a therapist's unique viewpoint. The reality sense of severely disturbed and many psychotic patients is not too different from that of many therapists. Such patients highlight the fact that the effects of early trauma are selective; and even though the sense of reality is sufficiently defective that the external world succumbs to delusional distortion, other aspects of the perceptual system, especially those directed to the inner psychic world, can be unusually sensitive and discriminating. The comparative lack of ego structure may lead to a fluidity that enables the patient to be in tune with both his inner psychic elements and some aspects of the external world that would ordinarily be unnoticed. The need to introject rescuing experiences may make the patient particularly sensitive to selective attributes of object relationships, which may be either consonant with or disruptive to his needs.

Clinical Example

This was a meaningful aspect in the treatment of an 8-year-old boy. My adherence to fixed ground rules and boundaries were silently and insidiously reenforcing preverbal experiences that were antithetical to his growth. Instead of providing a safe interpersonal environment, my management of the framework and interpretive interventions were received as further confirmation of his strong conviction that his needs were insignificant. It strengthened his belief that nothing of value would ever be forthcoming in a human relationship. The conditions of the treatment were so parallel to, and resonant with, the unempathic atmosphere of his early development that the transference was impossible for him to discern, much less to perceive as something needing to be understood. The therapeutic framework was reacted to as a repetition of his early traumas. Although in some ways this was visible to me, I did not consider the *patient*'s efforts to alter the treatment framework to be relevant and legitimate. The consequence was in an error of omission, whose effects were consistently present in the background of the relationship until it could be recognized and corrected.

The patient was the only child of the second marriage of both parents, and there were two older teenage half-brothers living in the home. The parents were very wealthy and influential people involved in a whirlwind of activities, with their narcissistic interest the predominant force in the family. During his early years the child was cared for by a succession of maids, who were fired by the mother for a variety of incompetencies. The mother was a very shallow, empty person, tending to her children only when necessary, and always with resentment. From the time the patient was 5 years old he was turned over to the care of his older brothers, who were often chastised for their rough treatment of him. The family originally sought help for him at the behest of his school, because of a concern about his lackadaisical attitude, his frequent episodes of stealing and lack of remorse when caught, his outrageous cheating in class, and a seeming inability to utilize what they saw as vast potential.

Right from the onset he resisted every feature of a contained therapeutic framework; he lingered at the end of a session to extend the time, laughed and made noises whenever I spoke so that my words could not get through, and mocked even the slightest hint of any attempt to understand his internal world. He was very provocative, seemingly testing for the limits that would be imposed upon his behavior. However, any interpretations along these lines only made him act somewhat wild. Yet he was eager to come to his sessions. Although he continually avoided any internal exploration of his feelings or reactions, he appeared hungry for the attachment that the relationship provided. Occasionally he would give a terse, matter-of-fact reply to my words, suggesting that they were nothing more than a subtle command for him to stop making me uneasy and that it was only in my own interest for him to behave well. There was enough truth in his statements to make me pause and consider their accuracy, but acknowledging the truth did nothing more than confirm what he already believed and led to no further associations.

At times he gave the impression of being intensely overstimulated as he told jokes about perverse sexual activities, his joke-telling accompanied by wild and anxious laughter. He would then totally deny that they had any particular meaning, while ridiculing me for taking them seriously. Firm ground rules and boundaries had been carefully established in an attempt to bring safety and order into the relationship, with the intent of making it more possible for him to face whatever internal chaos was behind his behavior. He continually and relentlessly pushed to alter the makeup of these rules, demanding to leave the office and wanting me to accompany him, searching for food and wanting it supplied, or crying out for me to tell him jokes instead of talking. Each session became a replica of the preceding one, with the patient probing for ways to disrupt the ground rules or boundaries of the relationship. It slowly became apparent to me, as an aura of frustration set in, that something was either missing, or was preventing progress. I could find no overt evidence of this push being a product of an insecure framework, and I began to look for some deeper meaning in his behavior.

In listening more carefully I realized that I was being invited to join him in these ventures, not as an adversary but as an accomplice. It seemed as though this was the only way he knew how to effect an attachment. My unwillingness to assume this role appeared to be the overriding obstacle. To comply, however, almost certainly would represent an unhealthy collusion with a pathological defense. I could not see any approach other than to maintain a firm stance guided by sound therapeutic principles. Then one day I received a telephone call from him just prior to a late afternoon appointment. With a tone of false bravado he announced that he had been late in returning from school because he was "goofing around" with friends. His parents had angrily left the house after yelling at him for being at fault in arriving late. They told him that it served him right, and that he would have to fend for himself.

He went into some detail in describing the emptiness in the house, implicitly revealing the anxiety he felt, before hesitantly saying with an unspoken plea in his voice, "I guess there's no way I can see you, but I suppose it won't be too long until my next session." He seemed to be trying to reassure himself, tacitly reflecting the extent of his fear and how the passage of time seemed like an eternity. I was deeply moved by the helplessness and vulnerability he was both experiencing and expressing. At this moment there was an unverbalized but strongly suggested invitation for me to respond with something other than an interpretation. I felt as if I was being given an opportunity to follow his lead and provide an apparently much needed experience. It was reminiscent of the recurring theme during his sessions of wanting me to participate in a way that was outside of the established framework, but this time in a different setting and without the presence of his characteristic defensive armor.

Although my conduct of the treatment had been designed with his welfare in mind, the particular conditions I had established were not experienced by him in this fashion. It struck me that the entire relationship could be understood in this light. A subtle error of omission was being perpetuated by my not following the only directions he could give as to what was needed. Under the pressure of his underlying anxiety he was now bringing it to my attention. I was tempted to limit my response to an interpretation growing out of this realization, but I felt it would be crucial to be prepared to follow through with an appropriate action if this was deemed necessary. I gave thoughtful consideration to the possibly detrimental influence of leaving the office and joining him in what might be a piece of acting-out behavior. However, it occurred to me that on this occasion such behavior would result in his becoming more deeply involved in his treatment, by getting him to his appointment, and so I decided to explore the possibility. It was my last appointment of the day, and there was time to respond to the unspoken suggestion of getting him to the appointment if I determined that it was indicated.

I told him that it sounded as though he felt very frightened at being alone, and that it was the first time he had overtly shown what he experienced inside. I thought he might be wondering if I could help him with it. His voice immediately perked up. As expected, he assumed I would come to his house to see him and he eagerly asked when I would get there. I acknowledged that I did in fact think it was a good idea to meet, but I felt some uncertainty about its taking place in his home and wanted to explore its meaning to him before deciding. He excitedly stated that if I could pick him up and bring him back we could have our session in the office. He would get a message to his parents to let them know. I agreed, and from that point on the whole tenor of the relationship changed.

He began that particular session by showing me a small paper bag he was carrying with him, explaining that his mother had left it for his supper. Without knowing what it contained, he was certain that its contents would say more about his mother than it was possible to say with any words. He opened the bag. It held a few dried-up carrot sticks, two cold, fat-encrusted meatballs, a handful of crushed potato chips, and a stale cookie. His words, "There's my mother," were uttered with a note of sad resignation. The entire session was spent with his speaking at length about the dead, empty emotionless atmosphere that surrounded him in his life, only briefly punctuated by moments of terrorization by his older brothers. It left him feeling helplessly enraged, with a vague sense of longing for comfort and protection. Subsequently, the treatment was no longer deadlocked in the same repetitive pattern. He gained a deeper understanding of the defenses he had erected to protect himself, and continued to exhibit this newfound capacity for self-exploration.

The changes were exemplified in a later session, which began with his presenting me with a Cinderella slipper as a gift. I simply said that before deciding whether I would accept his gift I needed to understand its meaning. He eagerly launched into a description of what he was feeling and of how it had come about. He had been in a store with his mother, saw the slipper, and had the sudden impulse of wanting to give it to me. He didn't know why, or for what purpose; it just felt like the right thing to do. He asked his mother for the money to buy it, but felt embarrassed for fear that she would ask why and consider it babyish or silly. He was relieved when she said no. He then decided to get it on his own, stealthily took it off the shelf, and hid it in his pocket until he came to his session. Although he was glad he had done it on his own, he did feel strange about having stolen it. There just didn't seem to be another alternative. It felt important to give me the gift and he hoped I wouldn't turn it down.

He went on to talk about the slipper. It reminded him of the Cinderella story. He became extremely embarrassed, and hesitantly brought out how much he felt like Cinderella. He remembered the night I had come to pick him up; it was like a combination of finding a fairy godmother and winning the prince. He then alluded to how strange it felt to think of himself as a girl, and he didn't quite know what to make of it.

The transference relationship had become the focus of his unconscious instinctual wishes, expressed derivatively by his gift. In addition, an effective therapeutic alliance was clearly in evidence, so that exploring the underlying nature of these feminine impulses was certainly a direction that could be followed. Although there was a connection to my engaging in a leap, opening the doors to discovering its unconscious significance, and the reasons this was necessary, the fact that the gift was stolen suggested this take precedence before any further therapeutic work could be accomplished.

I remarked that I needed a better understanding of what it would mean to him for me to accept something that had been stolen. With great intensity, and on the verge of tears, he spoke of how he always had to steal to get what he wanted. It didn't feel to him like he was stealing. Instead, such actions reminded him of how he always gave in to what other people needed while having nothing for himself except what he could get in this way. He thought of other times when he had taken things without really knowing why, seemingly just to steal them. In this instance he knew exactly what he wanted, but could find no other way. That was why it meant so much to him when I came to his house. He had seen no way out, had been terribly scared, and it was the only time he could remember that something had been brought to him. When he had seen me for the first time, he felt just as he felt in his home. It was another experience of not being listened to, and he had no way of talking about it. It felt good now to be able to talk, but he had an uncomfortable sense of not being fully understood. I commented that *I* hadn't understood how his stealing was a way of showing me how many things had been taken from him. I would keep the gift as a reminder of our experience together, and especially of how vital it was to not only listen to him, but also to provide what he needed in order to grow. His face lit up as he spoke eagerly of saving his allowance to pay the store for the slipper. He then proudly placed it in a conspicuous place on my bookshelf.

My earlier insistence on adopting an exclusively interpretive stance, while maintaining fixed ground rules and boundaries designed to provide a secure therapeutic framework, had been preventing the specific involvement required by this patient before he could enter into any process of self-exploration. The conditions of the treatment had been too evocative of the unempathic atmosphere of the interpersonal environment that had characterized his developmental years, and that was an ongoing presence in his current life. His provocative behavior, rather than reflecting a need for containment as I had perceived it, was motivated by an inarticulable demand to gain the specific quality of empathic involvement he required to promote constructive growth. This was behind the unyielding, repetitive lack of therapeutic progress. He could express the need for active participation only through behavior based upon character defenses that made it appear detrimental for me to follow his direction. I was unknowingly committing an ongoing error of omission by not providing the degree of involvement he required. Had I followed the patient's lead earlier it most certainly would have reenforced a pathological defense, but in doing so even then I might have discovered a proper pathway to therapeutic progress. The patient's telephone call acquainted me with a more accurate view of what was happening. It enabled the error of omission to be identified and corrected, and eventually led to a deeper understanding of the unconscious significance of both the empathic lapse and the leap that was introduced. In the process an unyielding obstacle to therapeutic movement was removed, and the patient was able to distinguish transference-based distortions.

The Destructive Impact of an Unrecognized Error of Omission

Errors of omission are particularly apt to occur when a therapist is confronted with individuals who give an outward appearance of having achieved considerably advanced levels of psychic structuralization. On closer inspection what emerges is a rigid outer defensive shell, utilizing advanced ego functions to construct a realm of psychological experience based upon conformity and submission to the wishes and expectations of others. This depleted, "false" self has been erected to mask and protect extremely vulnerable regressive instinctual strivings comprising a "true" self. If therapeutic progress is to be realized the true self must be expressed in the transference relationship. The treatment task of adapting sound psychoanalytic principles to the psychic organization of the patient's personality can often be confusing and difficult under these circumstances. If a therapist has the tendency not to distinguish between derivatives expressive of unconscious perceptions, and those expressive of transference fantasy distortions, it may be impossible.[4]

---

4. Winnicott (1960c) reflected upon the way a patient's false self can collaborate indefinitely in the analysis of defenses. In this false-self area more headway can be made by recognition of the patient's nonexistence than by long continuing working on the basis of ego defense mechanisms. This unrewarding task is cut short profitably only when the therapist can point to and specify an absence of some essential feature. These recognitions made clear at the right moment pave the way for communication with the true self.

Attributing all of such a patient's reactions to transference distortions markedly increases the likelihood of activating and fostering a powerful need to conform to a therapist's expectations. A subtle atmosphere of authoritarian dominance may then pervade the therapeutic interaction. The conditions of the treatment become expressions of a therapist's impositions, instead of being directed by a patient's unconscious perceptions, and the entire relationship is affected by a serious error of omission that can be easily rationalized or go unnoticed. Any attempt on the part of the patient to call this to the therapist's attention will be misidentified, and the conditions conducive to a benign regression will not be found. A status quo will be sustained as pathological forces operative in the patient seize the opportunity to present material either expected or implicitly demanded.[5] The treatment may continue over long periods of time, but the interchange will transpire primarily on an intellectual level with no essential change in the basic disturbance.[6] In this sense an error of omission is built into the therapeutic relationship, which may only be discovered, rectified, and its effects understood with a change in therapists.

Clinical Example

This was a significant factor in the treatment of a 41-year-old woman, who initiated therapeutic contact in a state of desperation. She had been in psychotherapy off and on over a span of eighteen years, had seen a number of therapists, and though she was very skeptical about beginning another treatment process, she could think of no other option.

---

5. Eissler (1963) thought patients who became absorbed in the delight of increasing their knowledge of self, even though seeming to be less absorbed in their therapy, had a much better chance of recovering from their psychopathology than those who apparently adhere to what psychoanalysis offers and seemingly are much more interested in their treatment.

6. Bleger (1967) believed the frame of the treatment could become a kind of addiction, particularly if it is not analyzed. As a consequence there will be no internalized ego to give stability, and the whole personality may be a facade. The frame is established with the most psychotic or symbiotic part of the personality, and there is a strong resistance against analyzing it. It is a part of the patient's body image that has not been structured and differentiated, and its analysis disturbs whatever identity has been reached by the patient.

The patient first sought psychiatric help at the age of 22 after ending a turbulent love affair, feeling shattered and lost. The treatment had lasted for ten years. It consisted of daily sessions during which she utilized the couch. A free-associative mode of communication was emphasized. Throughout this period she felt paralyzed in regard to exercising any autonomous decisions, and molded her entire life around the treatment. She idealized her therapist, and described herself as compelled to present an image that would elicit approval. Looking back she could see that the time was spent polishing a "false self." She became extraordinarily adept at formulating psychological explanations for all of her behavior, although this did little to alter the emptiness that dominated her internal life. She was finally declared "cured," and a symptom of uncontrolled eating binges appeared for the first time. The symptom was identified as a reaction to the impending separation, and the treatment was terminated. During the next several years she sought further therapeutic help, but on each occasion it ended when she made a concerted effort to avoid presenting a chameleon-like image of herself and to speak honestly about her internal experiences. She was then seen as either "too sick" or "too resistant" to be able to make use of any insight-directed treatment.

At this time she was making one last effort, feeling she could no longer spend her life this way. Everything looked hopeless, and she was even considering suicide. Her entire existence seemed empty and false, driving her to extreme eating and drinking binges. Weekly sessions were arranged, and that spacing was chosen on the basis of it "feeling right" to her. The idea of meeting more often aroused her fear of a crippling dependency and concern over losing her ability to make autonomous decisions. Meeting less often created too large a gap between sessions, making her feel alone and disconnected. The fee was decided upon after a discussion of what was realistic for both of us, and a sitting-up position seemed best because it allowed her to be aware of my facial expressions. This helped her know if she was being understood. The framework of the treatment was thus determined by my best reading of what she needed to facilitate growth. Impositions, no matter how subtle, clearly had a detrimental influence.

The early sessions were occupied with her feeling of despair as to how being psychologically understood could possibly be of use. She had a strong conviction that unless she could have genuine and actual experiences as a part of her life there was no hope. When she reflected upon her history the only spark of interest she could recall centered around her wish to be an engineer. She loved to create and manipulate objects while observing a concrete result from her efforts. She had started out on this course early in her education but had been diverted by a love relationship. In an attempt to please her partner she had moved into a different career that was very unsatisfying. She identified this time as a crucial turning point, because it seemed like anything real had been totally shattered and she could no longer pick up the pieces. I chose this moment to ask what prevented her from continuing on that earlier career path now, implicitly encouraging this one ray of hope, and not realizing that I was unconsciously reacting to the depths of her desperation. She fell silent, did not know what to say, and looked vaguely upset as she left the session. This represented a nodal point in her treatment. I had created an empathic lapse, which became the focus for identifying the effects of previous errors of omission that had served to so powerfully reenforce her pathological "false self" defense. My remark was not identified by either of us as a failure in empathy when it occurred, but this soon became evident in the following session after she reported a dream from the night before.

In the dream she had applied to Harvard and was taking a test. The idea was to design a building. She was shown a drawing on a screen for a short time, and had to reproduce it. However, when the paper she was to draw on was given to her, it was embossed with the design of a flapper girl. It was bumpy, impossible to draw on, and she was puzzled as to how to go about the task. After describing the dream she was amazed at not having felt frustrated and defeated during the course of it, for that was just the kind of situation that would normally elicit those feelings. Instead she was just puzzled. This led her to the same feeling of puzzlement she had in response to my question about picking up on her earlier interest in engineering. It had felt to her as if I was imposing my agenda upon her, reminding her of how she was always forced into the mold of her parents' expectations. The pervasiveness of this attitude prevented her from realizing herself, a pattern she had continuously repeated in her previous treatment. She had been exquisitely sensitive to even the most subtle indications of her therapist's expectations of her. All of her energy went into producing material that would fit this view, while she totally ignored what it might mean to her. She then became extremely adept at psychologizing about her associations and dreams. Whether her intellectual explanations were accurate or not there was no connection to her internal world of affective experience.

She thought she was probably projecting her feelings from the past onto my question, but the dream and her association to it made me aware of having placed my difficulty onto her. I then told her that I had been affected by her despair in the last session, had not contained it to get a better understanding of its meaning, and had asked the question to avoid feeling helpless. She had apparently unconsciously perceived my attitude, constructed the dream around it, and was trying to provide me with what she thought I wanted. My words made her feel understood and explained why she had been puzzled. A flood of associations followed that reflected upon the numerous occasions on which she had been equally sensitive to others' defensiveness and anxiety. It made her aware of her tendency toward an automatic response that was designed to enhance and idealize any potential need-supplying object.

She gradually developed an increasing ability to distinguish between the derivatives of her unconscious perceptions and those of transference fantasy distortions. She had unconsciously perceived my detrimental input, and the derivative had been incorporated and symbolized in the dream as the day residue. This helped me to see the part I had played, so it could be acknowledged and corrected. In the past, when her unconscious perceptions were treated as fantasy distortions, this so reenforced her "false self" that she had felt completely trapped within its confines.

The Unwillingness to Introduce a Leap, Creating a Serious Error of Omission

There are some rare occasions in which something is demanded from a therapist in an immediate fashion, and the time required to clarify its meaning and assess its appropriateness is beyond a patient's capacity to remain within the relationship. A therapist's ability to gain an accurate reading of whether the pressure stems from forces within the personality striving to attain growth, or whether it reflects the activity of a pathological defense, may be hampered by the absence of a reliable therapeutic alliance. The resulting hesitation may in fact be an error of omission that is intolerable. These are generally emergency situations, probably best suited for evaluation in the safe and protected surroundings of a hospital setting. However, this option may either not be available, or the meaning of such an environment may in and of itself not be conducive to a patient's treatment needs. Some specific action may then be called for from a therapist, which if not forthcoming may precipitate a flight from treatment and from any possibility of constructive influence.

The urgency usually arises out of the need to curb a malignant, out-of-control regression, in an individual having insufficient psychic structuralization for the conditions of the treatment to provide enough of a containing influence until there is the time and opportunity to build an effective therapeutic alliance. This makes it difficult at best to conduct a proper exploration of what specific interventions are indicated. The need for introducing a leap may be pressing, whereas the alliance required for making that determination has not as yet evolved. A preverbal trauma is most likely being enacted, generally in a primitively organized personality manifesting archaic transferences with symbolic processes severely impaired.[7] Consequently, the entire constellation is expressed in behavior that can be extremely obscure and confusing. All of these factors may then be compounded by a therapist's internal reaction to the distorted elements in the material presented, or to the impact of a primitive transference. The myriad of interwoven empathic and conflicted countertransference based responses that are evoked must then be carefully evaluated before any action can be taken.

Clinical Example

An example of this difficult dilemma, resulting in an error of omission that triggered a dangerous flight from treatment, was brought out by the following interaction with a seriously disturbed young adult male. He had just been discharged from a period of hospitalization, and was frantic in his appeal for help. He called me stating that he needed to be seen immediately, since he was terrified lest the voices he heard telling him to kill himself would win out. He had called a number of people who refused to see him unless he entered a hospital again, and he was steadfastly adamant in his refusal to return. An appointment was scheduled

---

7. Grinberg (1979) pointed out that whenever the thinking function fails, for whatever reason, it is replaced by projective identification that tends to free the psychic apparatus from the increase in tension.

for a session, during which he spent the entire time going to great lengths trying to make it clear to me why he could not enter a hospital. He placed particular emphasis on the erosion of his dignity that he had experienced, on his deep concern about being over-medicated to the point of feeling like a zombie, and on an overall terror that was associated with being in an environment over which he had absolutely no control. He felt that he would rather die than go through that experience again, even though he knew he was in great jeopardy when on his own.

The session was ending, and I was extremely uneasy about his potential for self-destructiveness. I felt a need to offer him something to contain the destructive forces running rampant within. There was little material yet available to illuminate how this could be accomplished. Although his protest against a hospital was explicit enough, it may have reflected exactly what was necessary if it could be given in a more growth-inducing form. He appeared to be asking for safety and protection without the accompanying erosion of autonomy and imposition of control, suggesting a setting wherein his feelings could be respected, and the conditions for his treatment gleaned from his unconscious perceptions of what was required to promote growth. I internally agreed with the patient's assessment of the actual hospitals that were available, but was uncertain as to how to proceed. The urgency of the situation did not allow for a proper assessment of his therapeutic needs, and a reliable therapeutic alliance would take time to develop.

I informed him that I thought he did need a hospital, not like the one made of bricks that he had already experienced, but one built out of a relationship that could understand him well enough to grasp and provide what was required. I added that I thought it would be important to meet in order to determine whether we could work together and accomplish this difficult task. He eagerly expressed his willingness to do so, although he was concerned about waiting too long for the next appointment. He felt that as long as it was not more than a day or two away he would be all right. Appointments were scheduled on alternate days, as the process of trying to delineate the conditions necessary for his treatability was begun. At first he talked about the voices, stressing that they were carrying important messages he had tried vainly to get some meaning from over the years. His efforts were frustrated by the power and strength of the voices and his fear of their control over him, and by the refusal to listen of those he had turned to for help. He underscored his sensitivity to other people's reactions to him. He knew he frightened them. Whenever he had tried to talk about the voices, he had been given medication to take them away. In the hospital he had acted as if it worked in order to be released. The medication did soften the impact of the voices, but they remained as a constant presence. He hated the medication because it made him feel numb and helpless, while nothing changed inside. As he was talking in this vein he started to tremble, looking very frightened. He frantically turned to me to ask if there wasn't some medication he could take that could help him be more in control. It felt like he just couldn't stand what was happening to him as he spoke, and he needed something besides words to calm him down. I commented upon his earlier remarks about people being afraid of him, especially when he talked about the voices, and it sounded as though he was questioning whether I could take in the meaning of his internal experiences without being equally as scared. A disappointed look crossed his face. He wondered if that meant I would not give him medicine. He knew it would be important to continue to talk, but he was getting increasingly worried that in doing so he was unleashing forces he just could not control. He went on to state that it wasn't so bad when he was in the session and talking; it was when he left that his internal world became so overwhelming.

He then proceeded to describe what it was like in his external world. He was living with his mother and a sister, tending to keep to himself. He spent his time in his bedroom trying to distract himself primarily by reading, and sensed that the people around him felt extremely uneasy in his presence. He often got lost in his thoughts and fantasies. At those moments he had great difficulty telling whether it was real or a dream. However, it could become so real he had the sensation of not being able to escape. He recalled visualizing a peg-legged man chasing him down a long hall, which reminded him of his early adolescence when he had wanted to be a priest and was living in a seminary. The head of the seminary had a false leg that intimidated and frightened him. He could see there was a connection between his life experiences and what was happening inside, but he hated to talk about it for it made everything come alive. At the end of the session I said that he seemed to be calling attention to how vital it was to be able to carry something with him from me to help him contain his feelings. The idea of medication appeared to be the only way he knew how to express it. He listened silently and left. When he did not return for his next appointment I became concerned and called. I was informed that the patient had been taken to the hospital after making a suicide attempt the previous evening, and I heard nothing more from him.

The patient's appeal for medication had been consistently heard and responded to by me as a plea to be unconsciously understood. Although

LEAPS AND ERRORS OF OMISSION 257

this may have been a correct reading of the essence of his message, in the interim the patient was at the mercy of powerful destructive forces over which he had no control. Looking back, I see that a prescription for medicine might have been the only way it was possible to give him some concrete evidence of my appreciation of this dilemma. In all likelihood, the withholding of it left him feeling alone, abandoned, and having only his own limited resources to turn to. There was much to suggest that the act of giving medication would have been perceived by him as an expression of my unwillingness to face the anxiety aroused by the archaic qualities of his regression. However, this could have been dealt with by participating in a way that encouraged a regression, and interpretively addressing his differing perception. My bias concerning the use of psychotropic drugs to curtail psychotic symptoms, in place of allowing them to be expressed and understood, had in some measure stood as an obstacle to the use of what might have been a valuable adjunct for accomplishing that very task. It exposed the patient unnecessarily to the onslaught of primitive archaic transferences before there was enough trust established in the relationship for an effective therapeutic alliance to develop.

The patient could not encompass the destructive forces unleashed in his personality, which were intensified by the conditions of the treatment. He had clearly indicated that some external support was required, and in addition had suggested a possible avenue through which it could be offered. He even implied that it wasn't necessarily the medication itself so much as the way it was given. Having the experience of participating in the decision as to which worked best for him, monitoring its effects, and adjusting it to what facilitated his treatment could very well have been a focus around which a therapeutic alliance might have evolved. I had been depending upon the influence of a verbally interpretive modality, with a patient whose symbolic functions, though operative, were severely impaired. It seemed to put too much stress on already overburdened psychic structures. In following the patient's direction to prescribe medication I would have been moving into an unknown area, with the potential of either reenforcing a pathological defense or repeating a preverbal traumatic experience. However, such a response on my part also had the potential of finding what he needed, and any noticeable detrimental influences could have been corrected. Prescribing medication with the intent of enabling a regression creates a very different emotional atmosphere than doing so with the purpose of curbing a regression. This was a situation in which a leap was probably indicated; the absence of a firm therapeutic alliance had made me hesitate, however, resulting in what finally appeared to be an error of omission.

The Therapist's Responsibility for Discovering New Avenues of Therapeutic Influence

The therapeutic framework is so important, and so much relevant and deserved attention is directed to examining it for any ruptures, deviations, and modifications, or alterations when disruptive influences emerge in a patient's productions, that it is sometimes possible to overlook the fact that conditions of a treatment may be too rigidly adhered to. In this context errors of omission do not have reference to inappropriate silences or inexact interpretations, or to gaps in the conditions of a secure framework. Instead they refer to those situations in which maintaining the established framework restricts the possibility of discovering what may be an unusual pathway toward facilitating growth.

The process of psychotherapy is an ever-expanding learning experience for both parties in the transaction. Whenever it is halted, obstructed, or cannot move forward, it is incumbent upon a therapist to unearth the underlying reasons for the derailment, or to search for what is missing. Every conceivable dimension of the interaction has to be examined in order to find the source of the difficulty, and in doing so to determine whether a remedy is possible. Therapeutic emergencies, stalemates, impasses, and failures all confront a therapist with either a limitation in the efficacy of the procedures being utilized, or of an as yet unseen breakdown in their growth-promoting properties. This means undertaking a careful assessment of the therapist's mode of functioning, and the makeup of the patient's personality, the specific conditions of the treatment and the manner in which they are applied, and the interrelationship of all of these factors. It is crucial to delineate the part each has played in producing such a disadvantageous outcome.

A therapist's subjective responses must be explored for any evidence of countertransference-based "blind spots," or defensive attitudes. The patient's psychic productions, behavior, and modes of expression must be evaluated for any evidence of missed unconscious communications, pathological distortions, or inability to use the relationship as it is being presented. In addition, a determination must be made as to whether the ground rules, boundaries, and conditions of the treatment are consonant with the personality organization of the patient, with particular emphasis on seeing if they are in some subtle fashion feeding a pathological defense or supporting an unhealthy collusion with destructive forces. Finally, a therapist must be open to at least considering the possibility of following a patient's lead, even if it means temporarily abandoning percepts that have previously proven to be useful. If necessary, an exclusively verbal interpretive mode of communication may have to be held in abeyance.

   A therapist's willingness to receive these directions, with this degree of concern for the ultimate welfare of the patient in spite of their inherent risks and always with a careful search for any signs of a detrimental influence, can in and of itself have a positive effect and alleviate the barrier to therapeutic progress. However, it may also point the way to providing a much needed experience that can correct an ongoing error of omission that has been at the root of the roadblock. In this way the cure may determine the cause. What began as a leap can bring the impact of preverbal and infantile traumas into view, and the therapeutic properties of the relationship can be restored within the guidelines of sound psychoanalytic principles.

9

Out of the Darkness into the Light

P sychodynamic therapy is specifically designed to establish the conditions that are most conducive for the intrapsychic events at the root of the psychopathology to be re-created in the immediacy of the interaction between patient and therapist. Once the source of the difficulty has been determined it is possible to engage in a more definitive search for the factors required to effect a cure. Conversely, curative elements point out with greater clarity the underlying basis of the trouble.

Each treatment venture is a unique experiment, making it essential for a therapist to be open to new learning. The principles and conditions guiding the conduct of the relationship must be flexible enough to allow room for whatever emerges as necessary to promote constructive growth. Particular attention is paid to the effect of unconscious forces, since they are most revealing both of the nature of the pathology and of what is required to foster strivings toward health. The unconscious realm of mental activity is composed not only of unacceptable instinctual drives clamoring for expression, and the archaic prohibitions they mobilize, but also of the representations of developmental experience that are incapable of being retained with consciousness.[1] An important facet

---

1. Segal (1981a) discussed the importance of distinguishing between normal and pathological repression. Repression used by a healthy ego becomes a dynamic layer between the unconscious and conscious in which symbol formation occurs. The unconscious is not cut off from the conscious, but is in a state of constant communication and working through. By contrast, pathological repression is based on an earlier split, in which parts of the self have been split off and never integrated with the rest. The return of the pathologically repressed is a breakthrough of the split-off parts of the ego, objects, and impulses, and is still under the sway of psychotic mechanisms, using psychotic concrete thinking and related to reality in an omnipotent way.

of the unconscious system involves the activity of unconscious perceptions, which are based upon very early representations of good self-experience and reflect a patient's appeals for help in facilitating healthy processes. A therapist on the alert for their manifestations, usually in the form of derivatives, will be less apt to impose an authoritative view as to what constitutes a legitimate therapeutic need.

A treatment situation is concerned with the most sensitive, vulnerable aspects of a patient's internal life, making it mandatory that they are responded to with respect and compassion while communications are presented in a direct, straightforward, and honest fashion. It is always most desirable to shed the light of truth upon a patient's psychic productions under the guidelines offered by the basic psychoanalytic principles. When this is the case, areas of darkness move into the light and there is no need to engage in a leap. Right from the onset of therapeutic contact a great deal of attention is devoted to constructing an interpersonal environment in which an individual can safely reveal what has been carefully guarded in the deeper layers of the personality. The motive for defensive opposition must be gradually alleviated before previously inaccessible psychic content can be experienced and communicated. Unusual measures on the part of a therapist are not only unnecessary, but are also antithetical to therapeutic progress and in all likelihood represent an impinging projection or imposition. Initially, a therapist's task is occupied with listening intently for derivatives of a patient's unconscious perception as to what is required to promote growth, and the ground rules, boundaries, and conditions of the treatment are applied to be in accord with these directions. A therapist slowly learns precisely what circumstances are conducive to fostering a benign regression. In the process, he gains an increasingly in-depth view of the developmental experiences that have shaped the structural organization of the patient's personality.

When the basic psychoanalytic principles are applied as conditions to be followed, a serious problem is posed for those individuals whose early development has been dominated by failures in empathy. The implicit demand that a patient adapt to a therapist's expectations often resonates with inarticulable infantile and preverbal traumas. The resulting anticipation of inflexibility has an intolerable impact, particularly if a therapist remains steadfast in this position. Thus it is the therapist's responsibility to adapt the principles and conditions so as to be consonant with a patient's level of functioning. Each therapeutic journey will then be traversed in a unique and different fashion. If the proper circumstances are created, in most instances there will be safety, containment, and clarity.

There are some patients, however, whose most powerful motivations are invested in misleading and confusing a therapist. They will press hard to establish conditions that instead of invoking safety will re-create the original traumatic events. These maneuvers serve to protect against the threat of change evoked by a therapist's presence and mode of functioning, and it would be disastrous to be guided by such directions. It is essential to identify the differences between communications that are honest, undistorted, and undistorting, and those that are either distorted or designed to produce distortions. Otherwise, abandoning the guidelines offered by proven therapeutic principles can lead into disorganization and chaos, feed pathological forces at the expense of realizing healthy potentials, and be extremely destructive.

A therapist must allow an internal state of free-floating attention so as to expand the range of information that can be received; at the same time he must continuously assess the unconscious significance of a patient's communications, and be attuned to a process of filtering out inappropriate, personal projections. An extended period of self-examination, along with a careful evaluation of a patient's personality structure and treatment needs, is required before any step away from a clearly defined therapeutic framework is considered. It would be antithetical to therapeutic progress to take directions from twisted and distorted mental productions. Even then it is difficult to be certain. Preverbal experiences leave an impression that usually can be expressed only through body sensations or behavior, and unless a way can be found to symbolize their impact they will continue to elicit severe distortions and prevent ongoing self-expansion. Therefore, when a patient's push to alter a secure framework seems to emanate from an attempt to reach this sector of the internal world, which would otherwise be totally inaccessible, the advisability of participating in this way should at least be carefully explored.

The essence of the meaning of a leap is to have a reliable way of entering unknown and unexplored psychological territory, thereby expanding the areas to which therapeutic influence can be carried. Defining a leap as being propelled into the darkness to find the light tends to conjure up images of somewhat irresponsible therapeutic functioning, of taking unnecessary risks without a solid background of safety, and of the absence of sound theoretical constructs to serve as a source of guidance. The question of introducing a leap, however, should arise only after there has been the time and opportunity for a reliable and effective therapeutic alliance to develop, because it is this area of psychic functioning that is devoted to healing and growing. A patient's defensive efforts to sabotage this goal have to be identified. This can be a complex undertaking, especially with individuals who have overdeveloped advanced psychic functions to camouflage very primitive psychic states. They can be adept at exploiting a therapist's weak spots and using them to prevent a regression. There is a dual purpose contained in these attempts to undermine the therapeutic properties of the relationship. The distortions that are produced re-create a pathological attachment as well as test a therapist's ability to undo them. There are moments when this can best be accomplished within the confines of a secure framework, whereas at other moments it may be too limiting and restrictive.[2]

---

2. Heimann (1950) emphasized that the humanness of the therapist can be established without recourse to extra-analytic means, and that mastery of countertransference protects the therapist from joining in the patient's transference enactments or from exploiting them for narcissistic needs.

Weigert (1954) referred to the basic rule of free association and how it could not be enforced. Many patients characteristically deviate from this rule, indicating how vital it is for this attitude to be grist for the analytic mill. Similarly, lying on the couch should be used flexibly, and the patient should be permitted to change positions, since these behaviors may reveal defenses or impulse derivatives that would otherwise not be evident. A rigid adherence to frequency may conceal dependency, separation anxiety, grief or rage reactions; and, in addition, some patients become addicted to analysis on this basis. Furthermore, inflexible rulings can hide unconscious countertransference problems on the part of the therapist.

Fairbairn (1957) felt psychoanalytic technique was idealized and not as pure in practice as in theory, since it was often necessary to offer interventions

A therapist's willingness to ascertain when it is indicated to maintain a firm stance and when this unyielding posture is counterproductive, and his efforts to make the distinction, are essential ingredients of taking responsibility for and expressing a commitment to a patient's welfare. It is accompanied by an acute awareness of the inherent risks involved, for uncertainty concerning the consequences of moving in this direction is ever present. However, an unwillingness or inability to consider it can be equally detrimental.[3] This degree of openness to receiving primitive psychic content is essential, though it must be balanced by a careful reading of what conditions are necessary to foster constructive growth. The alternative, of using the principles of treatment as rules to be followed, introduces an attitude of rigidity that interferes with the free flow of projective identifications fueling the transference.[4]

Primitive forms of pathology are frequently seen as too severe to meet the demands and conditions of psychoanalytic treatment. Other treatment modalities are instituted with no prospect of structural change, and a potential opportunity can pass unnoticed. Thus to always take a "safe" route, following traditional and in

---

that either gave reassurance or safeguarded the patient against danger. Above all, the true unconscious attitudes of the therapist are a factor in determining the efficacy of any interpretation or intervention.

Modell (1976) paid special attention to the therapist's emotional position with narcissistic transferences, wherein interpretations do not seem to get through to the patient. In these situations interpretations tend to be dismissed, not heard, or resented as an intrusion, making it vital to be able to wait with an attitude of acceptance, patience, and empathy.

3. Allen (1956) believed there should be questions about whether maintaining the basic rule would promote too much dependency, whether the analysis would be diminished by a shift to face-to-face interviews, or whether transference phenomena would be detracted from with such changes. The primary consideration should center around the type of psychopathology in the patient, whether changes would favor the lifting of repression, and what the changes would do to the therapist. Ego difficulties may require changes in the basic rule, and failure to modify them can hinder the advancement of the treatment.

4. Stone (1961) commented on how easily the ground rules of the analytic relationship can minimize or omit the human element. It can reach a point where it is incompatible with the human nature of psychoanalysis, for coldness and lifelessness in the therapist interfere with the analytic process.

most situations sound therapeutic principles, can sometimes be silently destructive by eliminating any hope for meaningful change. A patient may be in the position of crying out for help, but in not having words to adequately communicate the nature or source of the distress, he may be able to do so only through the distortions already existent in the personality. A therapist's task is to try to translate what is communicated, and transform it into growth-promoting interventions. If accurate, they facilitate the expression of what has heretofore been unknown.[5]

Each person possesses the unconscious knowledge of what is required to promote growth, even though it may be incapable of being articulated or may be put into words that are misleading. There is almost always an attempt to convey this information in some manner. A therapist has to be attuned toward listening for these directions, ascertain the existence of distortions so as to filter them out, and provide the appropriate conditions for the treatment to be conducted properly. The process of unraveling distortions can be very confusing, and bringing the clarity of insight and understanding into this area of darkness is a difficult matter. For this reason it is of primary importance to create a safe and trustable environment within which new learning can evolve. The basic psychoanalytic principles of free association, abstinence, anonymity, and neutrality offer the best guide for the conduct of the relationship, particularly when they are applied to be in accordance with a patient's level of psychic organization. They ensure clearly defined boundaries between both parties in the interaction, and elicit the necessary containment for a benign regression to unfold. There are some patients, however, who require something either more or different when profoundly regressive internal states are reached, which raises the question of modifying or altering the very conditions that have been so vital up to that point. A greater degree of latitude has to be available to enable a much needed

---

5. Gedo (1984) felt it was vital to be guided in our approach by the realization that the delinquent behavior of a patient represents a primitive channel of communication, leading to a dramatic enactment of a crucial archaic transaction, for which there is no other vocabulary.

experience to be represented, or to allow a patient to communicate more fully through behavior.

The danger of deviating from a secure treatment framework centers around the frequency with which pressure is exerted by a patient to do just that, precisely at a time when it is most important for the framework to remain firm and intact.[6] The threat, often to both parties, of a regression makes it tempting to enter into pathological alliances serving to lessen the likelihood of its occurrence. This is one reason a therapist must be alert to the possibility of being led into modifying the conditions of the treatment by unreliable, defensively distorting forces. When this happens with primitively organized individuals it is an especially serious event, since the foundation of trust embodied in a therapeutic alliance is then left in an untenable position, in that a figure turned to for help has proven to be untrustable and at least for the moment cannot be perceived in any other way. Success in misleading a therapist evokes a variety of intense negative feelings that may remain even if the mistake is recognized and corrected, for the concern lingers that it might happen again. The individual may be left with the feeling that his internal world of experience is so overwhelming and bad that no one can manage an attachment to him without being similarly afflicted. Furthermore, the empathic failure might represent a repetition of an early developmental trauma and with it arouse anxiety of panic proportions. Nevertheless, these detrimental effects do have the potential of confronting both patient and therapist with an opportunity for new learning, depending upon how they are perceived, reacted to, and ultimately handled.

A leap cannot be seriously considered until an effective therapeutic alliance is clearly in evidence. This can evolve only out of

---

6. Winnicott (1960b) noted the change in caretaking functions when merging has come to an end, and the child has become separate from the environment. An important feature is that the infant has to give a signal, which appears in the transference in analytic work. It is important that the therapist shall not know the answers except insofar as the patient gives the clues, unless the patient is regressed and in a state of merging.

the safe conditions of a well-managed framework. The idea of engaging in a leap usually arises with individuals who have been able to reach this point only to have all further therapeutic progress appear to stop. In addition, they give many indications that some unusual measure is required from a therapist if anything is to change. The inherent risks involved in such an undertaking are counterbalanced by the possibility of producing even greater damage by an unyielding adherence to what has already proven to be safe. In this sense a therapist stands at a crossroad, with one path leading toward potential disaster and the other toward potential growth. The crucial factor that indicates a movement toward growth with the introduction of a leap is the emergence of previously inaccessible psychic content, which usually clarifies why a leap was necessary. This is the first step in finding the light.

A leap is thus a metaphorical statement about a particular problem encountered in psychotherapy. In most instances it concerns individuals manifesting pathology derived from disturbances during the earliest phases of development. A therapeutic journey will have been initiated and passed through a variety of a patient's experiences, none of which are necessarily familiar to a therapist, and yet they are close enough to evoke the empathic resonance essential for gaining a grasp of their deeper unconscious meaning. These are followed and explored, and lead to other avenues of understanding; but in a gradual way it becomes increasingly clear that very little is continuing to open up. A strictly verbal interchange does nothing more than emphasize the difficulty, and ongoing movement toward constructive growth does not seem to be coming into fruition. In a slowly evolving manner there is a sense of something missing, with little or no idea as to the source of this impression.

The nature of the ongoing interaction does not possess the features usually associated with a therapeutic stalemate, in that the difficulty is overtly evident. The particular unconscious forces involved may not be identifiable, but there is an obstacle preventing the patient's cooperation. In a stalemate the therapeutic alliance has been seriously eroded, and both parties make a contribution to the lack of movement. The stalemate is created by a pathological defense within the patient making a connection to conflicted areas in the therapist's mode of functioning, and both parties become blocked in being able to proceed. It also does not take on the characteristics of a therapeutic impasse, for in those situations there is a sense of what is taking place. The therapeutic process is held back by a fear of moving forward, which exists in both the patient and the therapist. Were it to exist in the patient alone it would not be enough to prevent ongoing progression. When the therapist can see what is causing the difficulty, and the patient cannot, an impasse does not result. The therapist is then in a position to approach the problem in a variety of ways, and is neither blocked nor stymied; and progress does not come to a halt but veers off in another direction until the impediment is visible. If it is the therapist who is unable to see, the patient is faced with the dilemma of trying in some way to dislodge what has become an uncontrollable barrier. This often leads a patient into abandoning all conscious or unconscious perceptions of what is wrong, and mirroring the trouble in his behavior.

When a leap is being considered, both parties are aware of a missing ingredient in the interaction, and there is a mutual search to discover how it can be provided. Although it could eventually reach the point of taking on the attributes of a stalemate or impasse, as both therapist and patient are increasingly frustrated and despairing of finding an answer, the therapeutic alliance remains basically intact. The conjoint recognition of a missing quality maintains the union of a shared common purpose, making it possible to at least consider every conceivable direction that emerges. Within this context an unusual measure may be called for that on the surface goes against the conditions of a secure framework, or of sound therapeutic principles. This measure is then explored to ascertain whether it possesses detrimental or constructive potential.

Individuals who have sustained severe and continuous failures in empathy during the earliest developmental years have had to go to extreme lengths, under primitive conditions, to protect and preserve healthy processes. They are thus weak, vulnerable, infantile in nature, and able to be expressed in a relationship only if the conditions are precisely empathic and have been proven trustable. When a therapist and patient have worked hard to discern the proper conditions, and have been thwarted for a variety of reasons, both may sense that these underlying life-giving experiences are fading away and losing their vitality from the oppressive impact of unyielding pathological defenses. It may become a matter of life or death to find some avenue for enabling these regressive experiences to gain access to the relationship, before all hope is lost. It is referred to as a leap because it takes nothing else into consideration other than whether it has the potential of facilitating growth. A therapist is entering unknown territory with a large element of risk, since there is no background of prior experience to rely upon. It appears certain that the life-giving forces trapped in the depths of a patient's personality will be destroyed if nothing is done, but whether a leap itself is constructive will depend upon how accurate the therapist has been in the assessment of this therapeutic need. A therapist may be motivated by unseen countertransference-based infantile conflicts, regressive identifications, or narcissistic needs, and thus utilize the concept of a leap to justify acting out. Similarly, a therapist may be misled or seduced into participating as a partner in the acting out of an unconscious fantasy, reenforcement of a pathological defense, or re-creation of an infantile trauma.

Once the introduction of a leap has been deemed advisable, what is decisive in determining the outcome is the manner in which it is handled. A patient may have expressed a strong conviction that unless a therapist can move in a particular direction, something vital that gives meaning to life will die. A therapist in turn may have had a host of questions and doubts about following the direction, but after a long, careful exploration he may have realized that this life-giving force was in the process of dying anyway. At such a juncture a decision to follow a therapist's directions may be made, leading to an intervention that appears to violate the usual percepts embodied in a therapeutic encounter. The most important part of the experience may or may not involve the specific action taken. The openness to finding a way to foster life-giving, healthy strivings, and the willingness to exercise a total commitment to a patient's welfare whether it turns out to be correct or incorrect, may very well be the critical factor. The depth of a therapist's commitment and responsibility to the treatment is communicated in an unmistakable and concrete fashion. It may

represent a quality of experience that has been missing in a patient's attachment to objects. The weak and deficient healthy facets of a patient's personality, which had been seeking to grow and could only be expressed in a distorted manner, may then have gained access to the therapeutic influences of the relationship. The particular intervention may reenforce a pathological defense, which in and of itself is not desirable. However, a therapist's ability to recognize, acknowledge, and correct the part he or she has played in that unwanted aspect eventuates in a clearer discrimination of the functioning of pathological and healthy processes, and the way they are intertwined. Consequently, what was both invisible and inaccessible can now enter the realm of therapeutic work, and be exposed to the light of understanding.

A leap is taken into consideration only when the conditions of the treatment are the limiting factor. It is called a leap because the state of our knowledge is such that the established principles guiding the conduct of the treatment confront some individuals with insufficient space to fully elaborate the essential facets of their internal world. These are most often patients who have been lacking in vital early developmental experiences, and for whom the specific conditions of the treatment resonate with this deficiency. Consequently, the treatment as it is conducted is doomed to failure. No matter how much effort is exerted toward understanding the despair of ever finding what is missing in their lives, it is of no value because the deficit is perpetuated in the treatment. The circumstances of the relationship serve only to re-create an early trauma, which cannot be articulated or, at times, even symbolized. Words are thereby totally incapable of addressing the core difficulty.

The fact that the conditions of the treatment have this kind of impact can be thought of as a tremendous opportunity for accomplishing integrative work, and for most individuals this is the case. The ground rules, boundaries, and conditions of the treatment are a powerful stimulus to the unconscious forces operating in a patient, and they provide a vehicle around which the transference can consolidate. Such patients have relatively intact symbolic processes and can in some way communicate the effects, expressing them either derivatively or in a variety of symbolic actions. But for those patients who possess a gap in intrapsychic functioning, a leap should be considered. Such a gap makes it necessary to first gain the mental representations required before symbolization can occur. The experience of an attachment to an object, with this degree of commitment to the shared purpose of promoting growth, is in many instances the experience that has been missing.

From a therapist's perspective, entertaining the idea of a leap must emanate from an empathic emotional position, after carefully filtering out countertransference-based infantile conflicts, regressive identifications, and narcissistic needs. Ultimately, interpretive words are needed to surround the experience and make the reasons for it explicable. More primitively organized patients commonly put great pressure on a therapist to gratify regressive cravings in the service of reenforcing a pathological defense or destroying therapeutic understanding. An awareness of this potential makes an in-depth exploration for any signs of its presence a primary focus of attention if the possibility of a leap arises. Action is not taken until the underlying motivations have been examined, and it becomes evident that no further progress can be achieved until something missing is provided. A therapist may have to rely upon subjective empathic and intuitive responses, though their unconscious determinants are always involved. Unconscious strivings cannot be a guiding force, due to their infantile character, but a therapist can be familiar enough with their manifestations to utilize them for further understanding.[7] A therapist is constantly monitoring internal reactions, discerning those derivatives representative of unconscious perceptions. The capacity for assessing a patient's input is thereby enhanced. In addition, a long period of therapeutic work will have acquainted a therapist with the ways a patient uses defensive alignments to obscure meaning, and with

---

7. Segal (1981b) underscored the importance of being aware that countertransference is the best of servants but the worst of masters, and that when a disruption in the analytic function occurs the pressure to act out, whether obvious or subtly hidden, is always powerful. Countertransference has been a very abused concept and a lot of sins have been committed in its name. In particular, rationalizations are found for acting under its pressure, rather than using it for a guide to understanding. We will not learn from our failures unless we recognize them as such.

responses that are trustable. All of this information aids in determining an appropriate intervention.

A leap cannot be taken lightly. A connection based upon a reliable sector of personality functioning in both parties must first be firmly established. If a therapist is confronted with a dilemma indicating that a leap may be required before an effective alliance has had time to develop, it is helpful to let the patient know that more information must be gathered and more work accomplished prior to considering such a risky venture. Helping a patient wait can be extremely important, since the delay is spent in gaining a deeper understanding of unconscious processes, and in fostering a stronger therapeutic alliance. If a patient fights against waiting long enough for the alliance to become firm and reliable, it is already an indication that a leap probably should not be taken. In most instances it implicitly communicates that the growth-promoting forces in the patient's personality are not involved in the demand for action, as there would be no safety without a firm alliance. Thus a patient demanding action on the part of a therapist in an urgent manner, and being unable to wait, is most likely pointing out the need to develop an alliance. Trust is based upon experience, and it takes many trustable experiences before the alliance can be strong enough to support a benign regression. It is this particular facet that distinguishes the differences between a therapeutic stalemate or impasse, and a situation wherein a leap is considered. With a stalemate or impasse the alliance is not adequate and firm. The task under those circumstances would be to work on developing an alliance.

The decision to alter or modify what seems to be a sound way of carrying on treatment, because of an impression that something is missing, depends more than usual upon a therapist's subjective responses. Although it is always important for a therapist to both monitor and make use of internal reactions to a patient, in this situation it requires an even more penetrating search. Generally, a therapist tries to achieve a state of free-floating attention, allowing personal emotions, fantasies, sensations, and memories to rise out of the background to shed light on the unconscious meaning of a patient's communications. There is then a constant shifting back and forth, as these more regressive internal experiences are exposed to higher order functions in the service of understanding the patient and formulating interpretations. When the framework of the treatment is under question as being too restrictive, it becomes increasingly essential for a therapist to look more deeply into these regressive experiences as they may be seeking a pathway for discharge into action.

In the process of self-examination a therapist gains a deeper grasp of how the interaction is being unconsciously perceived. When placed in apposition to the patient's input it expands the view of what is emanating from healthy processes and what is a product of pathology. As mentioned earlier, one almost absolute indication for not modifying the framework is the presence of even the slightest hint of a sense of compulsion or urgency in the therapist. There has to be time for assessment, and the inability to delay is pathognomonic of a destructive force. If it is a situation calling for a leap, the healthy part of a patient, aligned with a therapist toward getting well, is even more hesitant than the therapist and in need of assurance that what the therapist is considering is not being done for the wrong reasons. The nature of a patient's demands brings matters into bold relief, adding the necessary input for determining whether an interpretation is required or whether a leap should be considered. It tends to either validate or invalidate a therapist's subjective responses.

The time and effort spent in developing a strong therapeutic alliance comes to a therapist's assistance. Each step has been furthered by trial identifications used to enhance empathic resonance, while other regressive subjective responses have been identified and filtered out. These regressive internal experiences have been exposed to higher order functions throughout, during which time a picture of what advances and what obstructs unconscious perceptiveness has slowly emerged. Sometimes dreams touched off by the experience with a patient may be available, bringing into view more of what has been unconsciously perceived. The symbolic representation of the relationship helps in making the distinction as to whether the motive for a leap is healthy or pathological. If a patient entered a therapist's dreams undisguised, this would suggest that the interaction was occupying a central emotional position, which is a strong indication that inappropriate countertransference-based wishes have been activated. This would be discordant with maintaining the therapeutic properties of the relationship, and would give reason to deem it ill-advised to consider a leap.

A contained and trustable psychological space has to be created before a patient can feel safe enough to reveal psychic contents that were previously inaccessible, and the pressure to alter, modify, or deviate from the existing conditions does not necessarily call for a leap. Although the established framework may offer a dimension of safety, it may also serve to obscure infantile experiences, so that a patient's expressed need to alter the framework should always be taken seriously. The first approach is to ascertain whether the motive stems from healthy strivings. It is important not to make the automatic assumption that because an effort is being exerted to change the therapeutic framework, pathological defenses alone are at work. There are occasions when a modification that later turns out to have been incorrect is less detrimental than doing nothing. These are cases in which errors of omission would be more serious than errors of commission, and may be uncorrectable.

The concern about an error of commission may prevent a therapist from acting in a way that may be the only avenue available toward facilitating growth. Furthermore, at least considering whether it is advisable to move into unknown territory gives expression to the extent of a therapist's commitment to a patient's welfare, and as such may be enough to enable the continuation of integrative work even if an error turns out to have been involved. A patient thus receives a direct concrete experience of a relationship devoted to constructive purposes, rather than one predominantly concerned with protecting self-interests. This situation most often arises with patients who have no other way to communicate the impact of critical early traumas other than through their behavior, and the enactment may require a therapist's participation in order to be fully revealed. It is imperative to recognize these positive translations into action to distinguish them from the sort of acting out that is primarily designed to avoid painful psychic content.

There are noticeable differences between the manifestations of a reenactment and the use of behavior to manage intolerable affects. When a patient engages in a destructive form of acting out, especially if it is persistent, the major motivation usually grows out of a deficiency in the therapeutic properties of the relationship. The behavior calls for an appropriate intervention to aid in containing the impulse toward action, and the specific form it takes points to whether it is an interpretation or more effective management of the treatment framework that is needed. The acting out is often triggered and perpetuated by a reaction to a therapist's blind spots, and reflects the patient's unconscious perception of a therapist's internal difficulties. This is in contrast to behavior that is rooted in a sector of psychic functioning having no other pathway for communication to take place. Interpretive words have little if any positive influence, even when the individual's behavior communicates a message with great clarity. Interpretations are experienced as distancing and rejecting or attacking and critical. A therapist may have a sense of knowing what is being expressed, but words are received in such a concrete fashion that it is as though they have a life of their own rather than representing statements of meaning.

Once it has been determined that introducing a leap is a relevant possibility, a therapist has to evaluate it and decide whether he should simply let a patient know of a willingness to take the necessary steps, or whether some concrete form of actual involvement is essential. A therapist is then moving toward a leap, and in doing so must attain validation from a patient's responses. Most importantly this would include a background feeling of containment associated with an increasing capacity for internal exploration, the emergence of new material that reflects the functional availability of symbolic processes, and evidence making the appropriateness of the intervention explicit. These are all indications that a patient's independence, autonomy, and introspective ability have been enhanced, and are signs of progress toward self integration.[8]

---

8. Stern (1984) defined the experiences available to the infant that are needed to form an organized sense of a core self. These include (1) having volition and expecting consequences of one's actions; (2) self coherence, having a physical whole with boundaries and having a locus of integrated action both while moving

When behavior is a defensive form of acting out, modifying the framework of the treatment contributes a detrimental influence by encouraging a patient's pathology. The relationship is no longer trustable until it is corrected. Under these circumstances a leap could only be disruptive and dangerous. However, if a patient's behavior is motivated by inarticulable infantile experiences that can only be symbolically represented after having direct contact with an object under specific conditions that produce a pathway to their effects, then a leap is called for. A therapist's dedication to discovering the truth, in conjunction with a willingness to explore every conceivable means of enabling constructive growth, gives expression to a degree of responsibility and commitment that can be a new structure-building experience for a patient. In this sense a secure, contained framework, extension of the conditions of treatment to encompass a patient's need for safety and containment, and utilization of a leap to provide the conditions for representing preverbal traumas, are all on a continuum. The delineation of when and how to shift from one position to another has to be guided by a careful monitoring of the interrelationship between empathy and countertransference within a therapist, and between acting out and reenacting infantile and preverbal traumas within a patient. In not distinguishing between behaviors that primarily function as a defense, mirror a therapist's disturbance, or reveal

---

and when still; (3) self affectivity, experiencing inner qualities of feeling that belong with other experiences of self; and (4) self history, having continuity with one's past so that one "goes-on-being" and can even change while remaining the same.

Gedo (1984) described the problem arising when a therapist is faced with the daunting task of dealing with phenomena of the repetition compulsion that create irresponsible actions on the part of the patient. Therapists may be tempted to master their own sense of helplessness by responding in a manner that disavows their actual significance as primitive communications. Among the various avenues of denial, two seem most important. First, regarding the patient's delinquency as a neurotic compromise; and second, misidentifying the patient as unable to face the truth about these transactions without being severely traumatized. Yet the therapist's affective responses may be one of the relevant guides to their meaning. The usual response of persons organized in archaic modes toward the recognition of their trouble is one of gratitude and relief, and of increased commitment to the task of self-inquiry.

otherwise inexpressible internal experience, there can be a tendency to view all behavior as "acting out" in a pejorative sense. In all likelihood the conditions of the treatment will then be invoked somewhat rigidly and restrictively.

Throughout this book I have underscored the importance of the containment and safety offered by a well-managed, psychoanalytically derived treatment framework. The pressure exerted by patients to alter, modify, or deviate from these essential conditions is so frequently motivated by pathological forces, and the temptation is so great for a therapist to yield in an unrecognized attempt to avoid the impact of regressive experiences, that it may obscure those moments when it is appropriate to make changes. Therefore I have tried to illustrate those occasions in which the usual conditions of psychoanalytic treatment can be too limiting, and when the risks and rewards of following a patient's directions into unknown territory are warranted. A therapist's willingness to consider such a move opens the doors to potential errors of commission, whereas a rigid refusal to do so creates potential errors of omission. The idea of a leap grew out of special problems in meeting the treatment needs of primitively organized individuals with preverbal traumas at the root of their disturbance. I have placed emphasis upon the crucial factor of utilizing and adapting sound psychoanalytic principles to guide the conduct of each therapeutic interaction, even those in which unusual measures are employed.

The task of bringing effective therapeutic influence to individuals exhibiting profound and serious psychic disturbances—usually based upon early developmental deficits, arrests, and distortions as a consequence of explicit or cumulative trauma—has been at best an imposing and demanding one. It has been approached from a variety of differing theoretical perspectives, with each utilizing their own distinct language to refer to relatively similar phenomena. A therapist's attitude and posture must possess the duality of transiently sharing a patient's experience, and then placing what is experienced within the context of a larger, more complex and more objective picture of the patient. This has been referred to as *generative empathy* (Schafer), *vicarious introspection* (Kohut), or *emotional knowing* (Greenson). It is essential to grasp the significance of the structurally deficient patient's defensive organization, for its specific composition plays a role in how primitive defenses can be effectively addressed without unduly threatening their necessary protective function. This defensive organization has been variously described as a system of interpersonal relations designed to externalize the painful drama of living by the creation of a system of survival (McDougall); as the presence of persecutory anxiety and the use of projective identification (Kleinians); as the need to use others as containers (Bion); as the urgent necessity to recover the lost parts of oneself (the "selfobjects") (Kohut); as denying the independent existence of others as a defense against pathological forms of object-relating (Kernberg); as "the false self" (Winnicott); and as the use of others as transitional objects (Modell).

In the treatment of primitive disorders, if constructive psychic growth is going to eventuate, conditions must be created that are conducive to allowing a regression sufficiently deep to reach the point at which the disturbance originated. This has been called the *archaic self* (Kohut), the *psychotic core* (Kleinians), the *basic fault* (Balint), the *area of nonintegration* (Gaddini), *breakdown* (Winnicott), and the *transference neurosis* or, more accurately, the *transference psychosis* (classical analysts). The repetition of the origins of the disturbance in the transference relationship provides an opportunity for achieving new solutions to impossible infantile dilemmas, primarily gained through a therapist's sensitive reading of what specific experiences are required to promote growth. A therapist's manner of participating in the interaction is generally modeled after the activities necessary to foster developmental progression; this is variously designated as a *need-satisfying object* (A. Freud), a *primary object* (Balint), the *average expectable environment* (Hartmann), the *container* (Bion), the *facilitating environment utilizing holding functions* (Winnicott), the *basic unit* (Spitz), or as the *extrauterine matrix* (Mahler). One consequence of the resulting interaction will be the representation of the experience, enabling new mental structure to be laid down. Subsequently, a patient is able to utilize processes of symbolization more effectively, which makes transformations possible. Psychoanalytic treatment can then be engaged in without the necessity of any significant modifications.

The need for unusual measures is a frequent happening when confronted with the challenges presented by individuals who manifest the consequences of severe early developmental traumas. These are individuals whose capacity for symbolization is either markedly impaired or lacking, and who are thereby profoundly hampered in their ability to communicate the nature of the disturbance or to internalize and grasp the meaning of interpretive words. Behavioral enactments become the primary means by which infantile experience is expressed, and a therapist's openness to supplying whatever growth-promoting influences are deemed necessary is central to the success of the treatment. A therapist must possess the same attitude toward behavior that is held in understanding the significance of any psychic productions, and must keep in mind that the principles of psychoanalytic treatment are not rigid standards of conduct but a flexible way of facilitating constructive growth. An ideally functioning therapist extends the framework of the treatment to be consonant with the personality organization of a patient, and to be empathic with the unconscious meaning of a given communication. However, there is often a tendency for a therapist to remain distant from the immediacy of the interaction, and although there are patients for whom the distance is desirable, those who have had disturbances in the earliest phases of development may find it intolerable.[9] Contact, emotional involvement, and concreteness are essential for more primitive patients, or early traumas are repeated. The treatment

---

9. Lichtenberg (1981) observed how having a regulatory theory as explanatory for one sector of the personality, and a theory of intrapsychic conflict as explanatory for another, invited the belief that one sector is responded to by a technique tilted toward the experiential and emotional, while the other is balanced between the emotional and cognitive. In fact these are alternating perspectives for organizing different experiential data in the course of analytic treatment. He underscored the existence of differing vantage points for organizing a patient's material. In the traditional natural science vantage point the observer is positioned outside and consequently emphasizes transference based on intrapsychic conflict. The empathic vantage point is one in which the therapist orients a listening stance from within the perspective and state of mind of the patient. Each of these vantage points has advantages and disadvantages as launching points for formulating and communicating interpretations. For psychoanalytic work, however, the empathic vantage point is optimal.

situation acquaints a therapist with the realization that the healing power of the relationship is directly proportional to the extent to which both parties are emotionally involved, and dependent upon the sources of the motivation for that involvement.

From a patient's point of view the motive for the attachment will of necessity be an admixture of healthy and pathological forces. One aspect will be seeking the experiences required to grow and develop, and another will be looking to distort and destroy any potential for growth and change.

From a therapist's point of view, ambivalence in the motive for the attachment cannot be directed into the relationship. A therapist's ambivalence has to operate as a spur to further self-examination, and serve to deepen the unconscious understanding of a patient. It must be contained, filtered out, exposed to higher-order integrative functions, and prevented from entering the attachment. The motivations of an ideally functioning therapist are thereby not ambivalent, and are encompassed within a desire to help a patient achieve ever-widening vistas of self-knowledge and self-awareness. Whenever other regressive motives become a part of the interaction they must be identified, corrected, and their effects interpreted. These mistakes are not desirable but probably inevitable, and can be used to advance therapeutic progress. Certainly no therapist wants to deliberately create an error under any circumstances, but to allow the fear of an error to dampen therapeutic creativity can be equally detrimental as the occurrence of an error, and at times even more so. Within the treatment relationship the depth of a therapist's commitment to uncovering truth, and the extent of the responsibility taken for discovering a healthy outcome, is demonstrated. A therapist's careful, but not overly cautious attitude can allow new areas to be explored.

References

Alexander, F. (1954). Some quantitative aspects of psychoanalytic technique. *Journal of the American Psychoanalytic Association* 2:685–701.
Allen, S. (1956). Reflections on the wish of the analyst to break or change the basic rule. *Bulletin of the Menninger Clinic* 20:192–200.
Arlow, J. A. (1961). Silence and the theory of technique. *Journal of the American Psychoanalytic Association* 9:44–55.
Arvanitakis, K. (1987). The analytic frame in the treatment of schizophrenia and its relation to depression. *International Journal of Psycho-Analysis* 68:525–533.
Balint, M. (1968). *The Basic Fault: Therapeutic Aspects of Regression.* London: Tavistock.
——— (1969). Trauma and object relationships. *International Journal of Psycho-Analysis* 50:429–435.
Basch, M. F. (1983). Empathic understanding: a review of the concept and some theoretical considerations. *Journal of the American Psychoanalytic Association* 31:101–125.
Beres, D., and Arlow, J. A. (1974). Fantasy and identification in empathy. *Psychoanalytic Quarterly* 43:26–50.
Berger, D. (1987). *Clinical Empathy.* New York: Jason Aronson.
Bettelheim, B. (1974). *A Home for the Heart.* New York: Alfred A. Knopf.

Bion, W. R. (1959). Attacks on linking. *International Journal of Psycho-Analysis* 40:308-315.
—— (1961). *Learning from Experience*. London: Heineman. Reprinted in *Seven Servants* (New York: Jason Aronson, 1977).
—— (1967). *Second Thoughts*. New York: Jason Aronson.
Bird, B. (1957). A specific peculiarity of acting out. *Journal of the American Psychoanalytic Association* 5:630-647.
Bleger, J. (1967). Psychoanalysis of the psychoanalytic frame. *International Journal of Psycho-Analysis* 48:511-519.
Blum, H. P. (1977). The prototype of preoedipal reconstruction. *Journal of the American Psychoanalytic Association* 25:757-785.
Boesky, D. (1982). Acting out: a reconsideration of the concept. *International Journal of Psycho-Analysis* 63:39-55.
Bott-Spillius, E. (1983). Some developments from the work of Melanie Klein. *International Journal of Psycho-Analysis* 64:321-332.
Dickes, R. (1967). Severe regressive disruptions of the therapeutic alliance. *Journal of the American Psychoanalytic Association* 15:508-533.
Dorpat, T. L. (1974). Internalization of the patient-analyst relationship in patients with narcissistic disorders. *International Journal of Psycho-Analysis* 55:183-188.
Eissler, K. (1953). The effect of the structure of the ego on psychoanalytic technique. *Journal of the American Psychoanalytic Association* 1:104-143.
—— (1963). Notes on the psychoanalytic concept of cure. *The Psychoanalytic Study of the Child* 18: 424-463. New York: International Universities Press.
Ekstein, R. (1965). A general treatment philosophy concerning acting out. In *Acting Out*, ed. L. E. Abt and S. L. Weissman, pp. 162-171. New York: Grune and Stratton.
Emde, R. N. (1988). Development terminable and interminable. *International Journal of Psycho-Analysis* 69:23-39.
Etchegoyen, H. R. (1982). The relevance of the "here and now." Transference interpretation for the reconstruction of early psychic development. *International Journal of Psycho-Analysis* 63:66-75.
Fairbairn, W. R. D. (1957). Freud, the psychoanalytic method and mental health. *British Journal of Medical Psychology* 30:53-62.
—— (1958). On the nature and aims of psychoanalytic treatment. *International Journal of Psycho-Analysis* 39:374-385.
Freedman, D. A. (1981). The effect of sensory and other deficits in children on their experience with people. *Journal of the American Psychoanalytic Association* 29:831-867.

REFERENCES

Freud, A. (1968). Symposium. Acting out. *International Journal of Psycho-Analysis* 49:165–170.

——— (1971). *The Writings of Anna Freud.* Vol. III, pp. 124–156. New York: International Universities Press.

Frosch, J. (1967). Severe regressive states during analysis. *Journal of the American Psychoanalytic Association* 15:491–507, 606–625.

Gaddini, E. (1982). Early defensive fantasies and the psychoanalytic process. *International Journal of Psycho-Analysis* 63:379–388.

Gedo, J. (1984). *Psychoanalysis and Its Discontents.* New York: Guilford.

Giovacchini, P. L. (1974). Countertransference with primitive mental states. In *Countertransference,* ed. L. Epstein and A. H. Feiner, pp. 235–265. New York: Jason Aronson.

Green, A. (1975). The analyst, symbolization and absence in the analytic setting (on changes in analytic practice and analytic experience). *International Journal of Psycho-Analysis* 56:1–22.

Grinberg, L. (1979). Countertransference and projective counteridentification. In *Countertransference,* ed. L. Epstein and A. H. Feiner, pp. 169–191. New York: Jason Aronson.

Heimann, P. (1950). On countertransference. *International Journal of Psycho-Analysis* 31:81–84.

Joseph, B. (1983). On understanding and not understanding: some technical issues. *International Journal of Psycho-Analysis* 64:291–298.

Kanzer, M. (1961). Verbal and non-verbal aspects of free association. *Psychoanalytic Quarterly* 30:327–350.

Khan, M. M. R. (1963). The concept of cumulative trauma. *The Psychoanalytic Study of the Child* 18:286–306. New York: International Universities Press.

Kinston, W., and Coen, J. (1986). Primal repression: clinical and theoretical aspects. *International Journal of Psycho-Analysis* 67:337–355.

Langs, R. (1975a). The therapeutic relationship and deviations in technique. *International Journal of Psychoanalytic Psychotherapy* 4:106–141.

——— (1975b). Therapeutic misalliances. *International Journal of Psychoanalytic Psychotherapy* 4:77–105.

——— (1975c). The patient's unconscious perception of the therapist's errors. In *Tactics and Techniques in Psychoanalytic Therapy,* ed. P. Giovacchini, pp. 239–251. New York: Jason Aronson.

Lichtenberg, J. D. (1981). The empathic mode of perception and alternative vantage points for psychoanalytic work. *Psychoanalytic Inquiry* 1:329–355.

Limentani, A. (1966). A re-evaluation of acting out in relation to working through. *International Journal of Psycho-Analysis* 47:274–282.

Lipin, T. (1963). The repetition compulsion and "maturational drive representatives." *International Journal of Psycho-Analysis* 44:389–406.

Little, M. (1981). *Transference Neurosis and Transference Psychosis.* New York: Jason Aronson.

Loewald, H. W. (1960). The therapeutic action of psychoanalysis. *International Journal of Psycho-Analysis* 41:16–33.

—— (1986). Transference–countertransference. *International Journal of Psycho-Analysis* 34:275–287.

Maenchen, A. (1970). On the technique of child analysis in relation to stages of develoment. *Psychoanalytic Study of the Child* 25:175–208. New York: International Universities Press.

McDougall, J. (1979). Primitive communication and the use of countertransference. In *Countertransference*, ed. L. Epstein and A. H. Feiner, pp. 267–304. New York: Jason Aronson.

Mendelsohn, R. (1987a). The eye of consciousness. In *The Synthesis of Self*, vol. I, pp. 25–43. New York: Plenum.

—— (1987b). The principles that guide the ideal therapist. In *The Synthesis of Self*, vol. IV, pp. 71–85. New York: Plenum.

Milner, M. (1952). Aspects of symbolism in comprehension of the not self. *International Journal of Psycho-Analysis* 33:181–195.

Modell, A. H. (1976). "The holding environment" and the therapeutic action of psychoanalysis. *Journal of the American Psychoanalytic Association* 24:285–308.

Nathanson, D. L. (1986). The empathic wall and the ecology of affect. *Psychoanalytic Study of the Child* 41:171–187. New Haven: Yale University Press.

Piontelli, A. (1987). Infant observation from before birth. *International Journal of Psycho-Analysis* 68:453–463.

Racker, H. (1957). The meaning and uses of countertransference. *Psychoanalytic Quarterly* 26:303–357.

Rexford, E. N. (1966). *A Developmental Approach to Problems of Acting Out.* New York: International Universities Press.

Rosenbaum, D. (1987). International Psychoanalytic Association, *Educational Monograph* no. 1, chap. 8.

Rosenfeld, H. (1971). Contribution to the psychopathology of psychotic states: the importance of projective identification in the ego structure and the object relations of the psychotic patient. In *Problems of Psychosis*, vol. 1, ed. P. Doucet and C. Laurin, pp. 115–128. Amsterdam: Excerpta Medica.

REFERENCES

Schwaber, E. (1983). Construction, reconstruction, and the mode of clinical attunement. In *The Future of Psychoanalysis*, ed. A. Goldberg, pp. 112-127. New York: International Universities Press.

Searles, H. F. (1975). The patient as therapist to his analyst. In *Tactics and Techniques in Psychoanalytic Therapy*, vol. II, *Countertransference*, ed. P. L. Giovacchini, pp. 95-151. New York: Jason Aronson.

Sechehaye, M. A. (1951). *Symbolic Realization*. New York: International Universities Press.

Segal, H. (1981a). Notes on symbol formation. *International Journal of Psycho-Analysis* 38:81-87.

────── (1981b). Countertransference. In *The Work of Hanna Segal*, pp. 81-87. New York: Jason Aronson.

Segel, N. (1969). Repetition compulsion, acting out, and identification with the doer. *Journal of the American Psychoanalytic Association* 17:474-488.

Stein, M. (1973). Acting out as a character trait. *Psychoanalytic Study of the Child* 28:347-364. New Haven: Yale University Press.

Stern, D. N. (1984). *The Interpersonal World of the Infant*. New York: Basic Books.

Stolorow, R. D., and Lachman, F. M. (1980). *Psychoanalysis of Developmental Arrests*. New York: International Universities Press.

Stone, L. (1961). *The Psychoanalytic Situation*. New York: International Universities Press.

Strachey, J. (1934). The nature of the therapeutic action of psychoanalysis. *International Journal of Psycho-Analysis* 15:127-129. Reprinted in *International Journal of Psycho-Analysis* (1969), 50:275-292.

Tolpin, M. (1971). On the beginnings of a cohesive self. An application of the concept of transmuting internalizations to the study of the transitional object and signal anxiety. *Psychoanalytic Study of the Child* 26:316-354. New York: Quadrangle Books.

Tustin, F. (1980). Autistic objects. *International Review of Psycho-Analysis* 7:27-39.

Viderman, M. (1976). The influence of the person of the analyst on structural change: a case report. *Psychoanalytic Quarterly* 45:231-249.

Weigert, E. (1954). The importance of flexibility in psychoanalytic technique. *Journal of the American Psychoanalytic Association* 2:702-710.

Weill, A. P. (1985). Thoughts about early pathology. *Journal of the American Psychoanalytic Association* 33:335-352.

Winnicott, D. W. (1954). Metapsychological and clinical aspects of regression within the psychoanalytic setup. *International Journal of Psycho-Analysis* 36:16-26.

―――― (1960a). Countertransference. In *The Maturational Processes and the Facilitating Environment*, pp. 158–165. London: Hogarth Press, 1965.

―――― (1960b). The theory of the parent–infant relationship. *International Journal of Psycho-Analysis* 41:585–595.

―――― (1960c). Ego distortion in terms of true and false self. In *The Maturational Processes and the Facilitating Environment*, pp. 140–152. London: Hogarth Press, 1965.

―――― (1963). Dependence in infant-care, in child-care, and in the psychoanalytic setting. In *The Maturational Processes and the Facilitating Environment*, pp. 83–92. London: Hogarth Press, 1965.

Wolf, E. S. (1983a). Concluding statement. In *The Future of Psychoanalysis*, ed. A. Goldberg, pp. 386–389. New York: International Universities Press.

―――― (1983b). Empathy and countertransference. In *The Future of Psychoanalysis*, ed. A. Goldberg, pp. 309–327. New York: International Universities Press.

Index

Abandonment, clinical example, 8
Abstinence
　criteria for analyzability, 61
　errors of omission, therapeutic framework, therapeutic alliance and, flexibility requirements, 239–243
Academic underachievement, acting out, encouragement of, leap introduction through, 168–170
Acting out, 153–177
　character trait/psychoanalytic contrasted, 167n8
　as communication, 153–154
　countertransference, regressive identification based on, leap emanating from, 141n8, 150
　dangerous, empathic lapse evoking requiring leap, 156–163
　destructive/constructive forms of, distinguishing between, 170–177
　encouragement of, leap introduction through, 167–170
　leaps and, 278
　participation in, leaps and, 163–167

pathological defense reenforcement, errors of commission, 221n1
primitively structured patients and, 154–156
therapeutic framework, decision-making in modifications, 69n4
transference/counter transference sphere and, 42
Action, therapeutic progress and, 19–25
Affective response. *See* Intuitive affective response
Age level
　acting out and, 153n1
　preverbal experience, 181–184. *See also* Preverbal trauma
Alexander, F., 102n2, 123n4
Allen, S., 68, 78n5, 267n3
Analyzability, criteria for, 61
Anonymity
　criteria for analyzability, 61
　errors of omission, therapeutic framework, therapeutic alliance and, flexibility requirements, 239–243

INDEX

Anxiety
  leap introduction and, 43
  malignant regression and, 27
  participation of therapist and, 4
  symbiosis and, countertransference, regressive identification based on, leap emanating from, 145
  therapeutic boundary establishment and, 30
Arlow, J. A., 96n1, 136n7
Arvanitakis, K., 141n8
Authoritarian style, therapeutic framework formation and, 34
Authority. See Power
Autism
  clinical example, 5-10
  countertransference, conflicted reactions, unconscious empathic response leading to leap and, 124, 126, 129
  empathic responsiveness, leap engagement on basis of nonverbal communication, 99-100
  intervention characteristics, 65
  preverbal trauma, communication, leaps for achieving, 193-197
Autonomy
  therapeutic alliance and, 26
  therapeutic framework formation and, 34

Balint, M., 27n5, 68, 103n2, 187n4, 198n9
Basch, M. F., 109n4, 116n5
Behavior, therapeutic progress and, 19-25
Benign regression
  therapeutic alliance and, 27
  therapeutic framework formation and, 32
Beres, D., 96n1
Berger, D., 109n4, 124n5
Bettelheim, B., 96n1, 104n3
Bion, W. R., 65n2, 141n8, 240n1, 281
Bird, B., 221n1
Bleger, J., 68, 90n6, 122n3, 182n1, 250n6
Blum, H. P., 193n6, 233n4

Body ego
  acting out, encouragement of, leap introduction through, 170
  countertransference, unconscious empathic response leading to leap and, 132
  preverbal trauma
    communication, leaps for achieving, 193-197
    regression, leap requirement, 187-193
Body image
  distortions in, 6
  errors of omission, unrecognized, destructive impact of, 250n6
Body sensation, acting out, encouragement of, leap introduction through, 168-169
Boesky, D., 160n5
Bott-Spillius, E., 68, 121, 155n3
Brain damage, countertransference, conflicted reactions, unconscious empathic response leading to leap and, 126

Cannibalistic fantasy, 6
Coen, J., 67n3, 69n4, 141n8, 155n3
Cohesive personality, leap contraindication, preverbal experience, 184-187
Cold-pack, therapeutic framework and, 50-51
Commission errors. See Errors of commission
Commitment, therapeutic boundary establishment and, 29
Communication
  acting out and, 153-154
    as avoidance, 168
    participation in, leaps and, 163
  leaps for achieving, preverbal trauma and, 193-197
  psychoanalytic principles and, 265
Contraindications, for leaps
  cohesive personality, 184-187
  psychoanalytic principles, 80-88
  schizophrenia, 80-88
  transference, 83-84

INDEX

Control
  hypnosis and, 13
  malignant regression and, 27
  therapeutic framework formation and, 34
Countertransference
  acting out and, 42
  conflicted reactions, unconscious empathic response leading to leap and, 124–135
  empathic response lapse, evoking dangerous acting out and requiring leap, 162
  empathic responsiveness contrasted, 115–116
  empathy admixed with, resulting in silent leap, 135–140
  empathy and, generally, 9–10
  empathy interrelations and distinctions, 119–124
  errors of commission, effects of avoiding, by application of rules in place of psychoanalytic principles, 231
  inappropriate leap risks, errors of commission, 214
  infantile trauma
    leap requirement, empathic responsiveness, 109–114
  intuitive affective response and, 6–7, 8
  preverbal trauma, pathological defense reinforcement, to reach strivings for growth, 199
  re-creation of, by leap, errors of commission, 222–223
  regressive identification based on, leap emanating from, 140–150
  therapeutic boundary establishment and, 29
Culture, psychoanalytic framework and, 243n3

Defenses. *See also* Resistance
  acting out and, 153
    destructive/constructive forms of, distinguishing between, 171
  countertransference, conflicted reactions, unconscious empathic response leading to leap and, 130
  empathic responsiveness, therapist's subjective responses and, 98
  errors of omission, unrecognized, destructive impact of, 249–253
  inappropriate leap risks, errors of commission, 215
  infantile trauma, re-creation of, by leap, errors of commission, 222–230
  leaps introduction, unconscious empathic responsiveness and, 104
  pathological defense reenforcement, errors of commission, 216–222
  patient sensitivity to defensiveness in others, 243n3
  preverbal trauma, pathological defense reenforcement, to reach strivings for growth, 197–209
  unwillingness to introduce leap, as serious error, 253–257
Depression
  clinical example, 12
  therapeutic framework formation and, 34
Destructive impulses. *See* Self-destructive impulses; Suicide
Developmental factors, preverbal experience, 181–184
Dickes, R., 68
Dorpat, T. L., 68
Dream analysis, drugs and, 16, 17
Drugs
  experimentation with, 14, 15, 34
  therapeutic relationship and, 15–19

Ego strength, parameters concept and, 63
Ego weakness, preverbal experience, 181
Eissler, K., 62, 233n5, 250n5
Ekstein, R., 150n9, 153n1, 153n2
Emde, R. N., 184n3, 234n6

Emergency situations, therapeutic framework and, 46–47
Empathic responsiveness, 93–116
  countertransference, regressive identification based on, leap emanating from, 145
  countertransference admixed with, resulting in silent leap, 135–140
  countertransference and, 9–10
  countertransference contrasted, 115–116
  countertransference interrelations and distinctions, 119–124
  errors of commission, effects of avoiding, by application of rules in place of psychoanalytic principles, 234n6
  identification and, 104n3
  inappropriate leap risks, errors of commission, 213
  infantile trauma, leap requirement, 109–114
  lapse in, evoking dangerous acting out and requiring leap, 156–163
  leap engagement on basis of nonverbal communication, 98–103
  patient needs and, 20
  power imbalance and, 93–94
  preverbal experience, 182
  primitively organized patients and, 271–272
  projection and, 109n4
  therapist's subjective responses and, 95–98
  unconscious
    leading to leap, conflicted countertransference reactions preventing second leap, 124–135
    and leap introduction, 103–109
Errors of commission, 213–236
  effects of avoiding, by application of rules in place of psychoanalytic principles, 230–236
  inappropriate leap risks, 213–216
  infantile trauma re-creation, by leap, 222–230
  pathological defense reenforcement, 216–222
Errors of omission, 239–259
  correction of, by leap, 243–249
  therapeutic framework
    therapeutic alliance and, flexibility requirements, 239–243
    therapist responsibility for innovation, 258–259
  unrecognized, destructive impact of, 249–253
  unwillingness to introduce leap, as serious error, 253–257
Etchegoyen, H. R., 66n2, 121n2

Fairbairn, W., 28n6, 232n4, 266n2
False self, errors of omission, unrecognized, destructive impact of, 249–253
Family dynamics, therapeutic referral and, 24
Fantasy
  acting out
    destructive/constructive forms of, distinguishing between, 170–171
    participation in, leaps and, 164
  acting out and, 153
  clinical example, 5, 49
  countertransference/empathy interrelations and distinctions, 122–123
  empathic response lapse, evoking dangerous acting out and requiring leap, 160
  empathic responsiveness, therapist's subjective responses and, 95n1
  errors of omission, unrecognized, destructive impact of, 249–253
  preverbal experience, 181
  rigidity/flexibility issues in decision-making, 72
  silence and, 136n7
Fantasy play, psychic reality and, 4

INDEX

Fee payment, acting out,
    participation in, leaps and,
    164, 166
Flexibility, errors of omission,
    therapeutic framework,
    therapeutic alliance and,
    requirements for, 239–243
Free association
    acting out and, 153
    errors of omission, therapeutic
        framework, therapeutic
        alliance and, flexibility
        requirements, 239–243
    intervention characteristics, criteria
        for analyzability, 61
Freedman, D. A., 193n7
Freud, A., 156n4, 231n3, 233n5, 281
Freud, S., 193n6
Frosch, J., 191n5

Gaddini, E., 69n4, 198n8, 231n3, 281
Games, psychic reality and, 4
Gedo, J., 68, 78n5, 123n4, 155n3,
    234n5, 268n5, 279n8
Giovacchini, P. L., 26n4, 58n8, 243n3
Green, A., 233n5
Greenson, R., 280
Grinberg, L., 254n7
Group, psychoanalytic framework
    and, 243n3

Hallucination, rigidity/flexibility
    issues in decision-making, 72
Hartmann, H., 281
Heimann, P., 266n2
Holding concept, therapeutic alliance,
    prerequisite for leaps, 90n6
Home visits, therapeutic relationship
    and, 23–24
Homosexuality
    rigidity/flexibility issues in
        decision-making, 76–77
    therapeutic framework formation
        and, 37
Honesty, therapeutic boundary
    establishment and, 29
Hospital environment
    regression and, 13, 44–45
    relationships within, 48–49

Hypnosis
    control and, 13
    regression and, 14–15
    submission and, 13–14

Identification
    countertransference/empathy
        interrelations and distinctions,
        122–123
    empathic responsiveness, therapist's
        subjective responses and,
        95n1
    empathy and, 104n3
    errors of commission, effects of
        avoiding, by application of
        rules in place of
        psychoanalytic principles, 230–
        236
    regressive, countertransference-
        based, leap emanating from,
        140–150
Immediacy. *See* Urgency
Inappropriate leap, risks of, errors of
    commission, 213–216
Inappropriate silence, empathic
    response lapse, evoking
    dangerous acting out and
    requiring leap, 156–163
Individual, psychoanalytic framework
    and, 243n3
Individual differences
    preverbal experience, 184n3
    psychoanalytic principles and, 264–
        265
    therapeutic framework, decision-
        making in modifications, 66–
        70
    therapeutic framework and, 263
Infanticide, 37
Infantile trauma. *See also* Preverbal
    trauma
    acting out, participation in, leaps
        and, 163
    acting out and, 155
    countertransference, regressive
        identification based on, leap
        emanating from, 140
    leap requirement, empathic
        responsiveness, 109–114

Infantile trauma (*continued*)
  psychoanalytic principles and, 264–265
  re-creation of, by leap, errors of commission, 222–230
  therapeutic framework, decision-making in modifications, 67n3
  therapeutic framework formation and, 36, 37–38, 40
Instinct, expression of, 4
Insurance companies, therapeutic framework formation and, 36–37
Interpersonal boundaries, therapist self-disclosure and, 19
Interpretation
  of game fantasies, 4
  inappropriate leap risks, errors of commission, 213
  incorrect, empathic response lapse, evoking dangerous acting out and requiring leap, 156–163
  intervention characteristics, 62
  therapeutic boundary establishment and, 28
  therapeutic framework, decision-making in modifications, 68
Introjective mode, empathic responsiveness, leap engagement on basis of nonverbal communication, 101–102
Intuitive affective response
  countertransference and, 6–7, 8
  therapeutic boundary establishment and, 29
  therapist self-disclosure and, 20

Joseph, B., 103n2

Kanzer, M., 102n2
Khan, M. M. R., 199n10
Kinston, W., 67n3, 69n4, 141n8, 155n3
Kleinian analysis, 120–121, 155n3, 281
Kohut, H., 280, 281

Lachman, F. M., 18n1, 58n8, 66n2, 68
Langs, R., 18n2, 47n7, 68, 121n2, 241n2

Leaps
  acting out and, 153–177, 278. *See also* Acting out
  contraindications for
    cohesive personality, 184–187
    psychoanalytic principles, 80–88
  countertransference and, 119–150. *See also* Countertransference
  dangers in, 10–19
  definitions, 3–10
  empathic responsiveness and, 93–116. *See also* Empathic responsiveness
  engagement of, on basis of nonverbal communication, empathic responsiveness, 98–103
  errors of commission and, 213–236. *See also* Errors of commission
  errors of omission and, 239–259. *See also* Errors of omission
  errors of omission correction by, 243–249
  introduction of
    in therapeutic setting, 41–56
    unconcious empathic responsiveness and, 103–109
  management of, 272–273
  metaphor and, 270
  need for, 281–283
  prerequisite for, therapeutic alliance, 88–90
  preverbal trauma and, 181–209. *See also* Preverbal trauma
  psychoanalytic principle flexibility and, 56–58
  rigidity/flexibility issues in decision-making, 70–80
  silent leap, countertransference, empathy admixed with, resulting in, 135–140
  therapeutic framework and, 32–41, 266
  therapeutic progress and, 19–25
  therapist self-examination and, 276
  treatment boundary and, 25–32
  unwillingness to introduce leap, as serious error, 253–257

Lichtenberg, J. D., 282*n*9
Limentani, A., 150*n*9, 154*n*2, 156*n*4
Lipin, T., 199*n*10
Little, M., 19*n*3, 68, 103*n*2, 141*n*8
Loewald, H. W., 68, 131*n*6

Maenchen, A., 47*n*7
Mahler, M., 281
Malignant regression, therapeutic alliance and, 27-28
Masturbation
  acting out, encouragement of, leap introduction through, 169-170
  infantile trauma, leap requirement, empathic responsiveness, 110
McDougall, J., 18*n*1, 68, 150*n*9, 281
Memory, acting out, destructive/constructive forms of, distinguishing between, 176-177
Mendelsohn, R., 63, 65
Mental retardation, countertransference, conflicted reactions, unconscious empathic response leading to leap and, 126
Milner, M., 26*n*4, 63*n*1, 160*n*5
Mirroring, countertransference, regressive identification based on, leap emanating from, 141*n*8
Misalliances concept, 18
Modell, A. H., 66*n*2, 68, 267*n*2, 281
Mourning, leaps introduction, unconscious empathic responsiveness and, 106

Narcissistic transference, regression, preverbal trauma, leap requirement, 187-193
Nathanson, D. L., 116*n*5
Neutrality
  criteria for analyzability, 61
  errors of omission, therapeutic framework, therapeutic alliance and, flexibility requirements, 239-243
Non-ego, defined, 122*n*3

Nonverbal communication
  countertransference, conflicted reactions, unconscious empathic response leading to leap and, 126-127
  leap engagement on basis of, empathic responsiveness, 98-103

Omission errors. *See* Errors of omission
Optimal gratification/frustration, intervention characteristics, 61-62

Parameters concept, intervention characteristics, 62-63
Personality
  cohesive personality, leap contraindication, 184-187
  errors of omission, therapeutic framework, therapeutic alliance and, flexibility requirements, 239-243
  preverbal experience, 181-184
  treatment framework and, 45-46
Physical contact, rigidity/flexibility issues in decision-making, 76-77
Play therapy, conflict and, 4
Power
  empathic responsiveness and, 93-94
  therapeutic alliance and, 25-27
Preverbal trauma, 181-209. *See also* Infantile trauma
  cohesive personality, leap contraindication, 184-187
  communication, leaps for achieving, 193-197
  developmental factors, 181-184
  errors of commission, effects of avoiding, by application of rules in place of psychoanalytic principles, 234
  pathological defense reenforcement, to reach strivings for growth, 197-209
  regressive reenactment of, leap requirement, 187-193

Primitively organized patients
  acting out and, 154–156
  contraindication for leaps, 80–88
  countertransference, regressive identification based on, leap emanating from, 141
  countertransference/empathy interrelations and distinctions, 122–123
  empathic responsiveness, therapist's subjective responses and, 95–98
  empathy and, 271–272
  preverbal experience, 182
  psychoanalytic intervention characteristics, 63–65
  therapeutic framework, decision-making in modifications, 66–70
  therapeutic framework and, 267
Projection
  empathic responsiveness, therapist's subjective responses and, 96n1, 97
  empathy and, 109n4
Psychic reality, games and, 4
Psychoanalytic principles, 61–90
  contraindication for leaps, 80–88
  criteria for analyzability, 61
  culture and, 243n3
  curative elements, 263
  errors of commission, effects of avoiding, by application of rules in place of, 230–236
  errors of omission, therapeutic framework, therapeutic alliance and, flexibility requirements, 239–243
  flexibility in application of, 56–58
  flexibility/inflexibility in, 267–268
  inappropriate leap risks, errors of commission, 214
  individual differences and, 264–265
  intervention characteristics, 61–70
    decision-making in modifications, 66–70
    expanded conditions for, 62–63
  primitively organized patients and, 63–65
  therapeutic framework, 61–62
  leap introduction and, 41–42
  rigidity/flexibility issues in decision-making, 70–80
  therapeutic alliance, leap prerequisite, 88–90
  therapeutic framework and, 46
  therapeutic framework formation and, 35
Psychosis. *See also* Schizophrenia
  countertransference, regressive identification based on, leap emanating from, 141n8
  leap introduction and, 43

Racker, H., 120n1, 124n5, 162n7
Referral
  family dynamics and, 24
  therapeutic framework formation and, 33
  violence and, 21
Regression
  acting out and, 153
  countertransference/empathy interrelations and distinctions, 122–123
  empathic response lapse, evoking dangerous acting out and requiring leap, 161–162
  errors of commission, effects of avoiding, by application of rules in place of psychoanalytic principles, 231
  hospital environment and, 13, 44–45
  hypnosis and, 14–15
  infantile trauma, leap requirement, empathic responsiveness, 114
  leap introduction and, 43–44
  leap introduction, unconscious empathic responsiveness and, 104
  preverbal trauma,
    leap requirement, 187–193
    pathological defense reenforcement, to reach strivings for growth, 199

INDEX

rigidity/flexibility issues in decision-making, 76
therapeutic alliance and, 27
therapeutic boundary establishment and, 30
therapeutic framework and, 36, 50, 51
unwillingness to introduce leap, as serious error, 253–257
Regressive identification, countertransference-based, leap emanating from, 140–150
Repression, normal/pathological differences, 263n1
Resistance. *See also* Defenses
hypnosis and, 14
intervention characteristics, 62
leaps and, 57
malignant regression and, 27
participation of therapist and, 4
silence and, 136n7
therapeutic boundary establishment and, 30
Responsibility, therapeutic boundary establishment and, 29, 30
Rexford, E. N., 160n5
Risk, therapeutic relationship and, 21, 23
Rosenbaum, D., 123n3
Rosenfeld, H., 123n3

Schafer, R., 280
Schizophrenia. *See also* Psychosis
contraindication for leaps, 80–88
countertransference, regressive identification based on, leap emanating from, 142–150
leap introduction and, 43
rigidity/flexibility issues in decision-making, 71
Schwaber, E., 120n1
Searles, H. F., 68, 121n2
Sechehaye, M. A., 68
Seduction, acting out, participation in, leaps and, 163–165
Segal, H., 68, 123n3, 263n1, 274n7
Segel, N., 229n2
Self boundary, therapeutic boundary establishment and, 30

Self-destructive impulses
acting out, destructive/constructive forms of, distinguishing between, 170–177
acting out and, 156
leap introduction and, 42, 43, 44
preverbal trauma, pathological defense reenforcement, to reach strivings for growth, 201
Self-disclosure. *See* Therapist self-disclosure
Self-object relations, errors of omission, therapeutic framework, therapeutic alliance and, flexibility requirements, 241n1
Silence
countertransference, empathy admixed with, resulting in silent leap, 135–140
inappropriate, empathic response lapse, evoking dangerous acting out and requiring leap, 156–163
therapeutic boundary establishment and, 28
Spitz, R., 281
Splitting, therapeutic framework, decision-making in modifications, 66–70
Stein, M., 167n8
Stern, D. N., 184n3, 278n8
Stolorow, R. D., 18n1, 58n8, 66n2, 68
Stone, L., 26n4, 58n8, 104n3, 123n4, 267n4
Strachey, J., 46n7
Submission, hypnosis and, 13–14
Suicide
errors of omission, unrecognized, destructive impact of, 251
leap introduction and, 42, 44
preverbal trauma, pathological defense reenforcement, to reach strivings for growth, 200
rigidity/flexibility issues in decision-making, 71–72, 75

Symbiosis, anxiety and
    countertransference, regressive
    identification based on, leap
    emanating from, 145
Symbolization
  acting out and, 153
  countertransference and, 131n6
  empathic response lapse, evoking
    dangerous acting out and
    requiring leap, 160
  functions of, 63-64
  leaps and, 10
  preverbal experience, 181, 185
  therapeutic framework, decision-
    making in modifications, 66-
    70

Telephone calls, leap introduction
    and, 43, 44
Therapeutic alliance
  errors of omission, therapeutic
    framework and, flexibility
    requirements, 239-243
  inappropriate leap risks, errors of
    commission, 214
  prerequisite for leaps, 88-90
  therapeutic framework formation
    and, 36
  treatment boundary construction
    and, 25-32
  unwillingness to introduce leap, as
    serious error, 253-257
Therapeutic boundary. *See* Treatment
    boundary
Therapeutic framework
  acting out and, 154-155
  cold-pack and, 50-51
  culture and, 243n3
  dangers of deviating from, 269-270
  decision-making in modifications,
    66-70
  description of optimal, 61-62
  emergency situations and, 46-47
  empathic responsiveness, therapist's
    subjective responses and, 95
  errors of commission, effects of
    avoiding, by application of
    rules in place of
    psychoanalytic principles, 232

errors of omission, therapeutic
    alliance and, flexibility
    requirements, 239-243
  errors of omission correction by,
    244
  flexibility/inflexibility in, 267
  formation of, 32-41
  inappropriate leap risks, errors of
    commission, 213, 215
  individual differences and, 263
  infantile trauma
    leap requirement, empathic
      responsiveness, 111-112
    re-creation of, by leap, errors of
      commission, 224-225
  leaps and, 266
  personality of patient and, 45-46
  therapeutic alliance, prerequisite
    for leaps, 88-90
  therapist responsibility for
    innovation, 258-259
  unconscious and, 263-264
Therapeutic relationship
  drugs and, 15-19
  trust and, 7-8
Therapist self-disclosure, therapeutic
    progress and, 19-20
Third-party payers. *See* Insurance
    companies
Tolpin, M., 183n2
Transference
  acting out and, 42
  contraindication for leaps, 83-84
  countertransference and, conflicted
    reactions, unconscious
    empathic response leading to
    leap and, 126
  countertransference/empathy
    interrelations and distinctions,
    120-121
  deepening of, 4
  empathic response lapse, evoking
    dangerous acting out and
    requiring leap, 160
  errors of commission, effects of
    avoiding, by application of
    rules in place of
    psychoanalytic principles, 230-
    236

errors of omission, unrecognized, destructive impact of, 249-253
narcissistic, regression, preverbal trauma, leap requirement, 187-193
preverbal trauma, pathological defense reenforcement, to reach strivings for growth, 197-209
therapeutic framework, decision-making in modifications, 68, 69
therapeutic framework and, 37, 38-39, 49-50
therapist's authority and, 94
Transitional object, intervention characteristics, 61-62
Trauma. *See* Infantile trauma; Preverbal trauma
Treatment boundary
construction of, 25-32
leap introduction and, 41-42, 44
therapeutic framework formation and, 32, 35
Treatment framework. *See* Therapeutic framework
Trust
leaps and, 10
therapeutic framework formation and, 40
therapeutic progress and, 19
therapeutic relationship and, 7-8, 24
Truth
errors of omission, therapeutic framework, therapeutic alliance and, flexibility requirements, 240
therapeutic boundary establishment and, 29
therapeutic framework formation and, 40
Tustin, F., 197n8, 233n4

Unconscious
acting out
destructive/constructive forms of, distinguishing between, 170-171
participation in, leaps and, 163, 165-166
acting out and, 153, 156
countertransference/empathy interrelations and distinctions, 119-124
criteria for analyzability, 61
empathic response, leading to leap, conflicted countertransference reactions preventing second leap, 124-135
empathic responsiveness
leap engagement on basis of nonverbal communication, 101
therapist's subjective responses and, 97
infantile trauma, re-creation of, by leap, errors of commission, 223
preverbal experience, 181
silence and, 136n7
therapeutic boundary establishment and, 29
therapeutic framework and, 33, 34-35, 263-264
therapist's authority and, 94
Urgency
therapeutic relationship and, 22
unwillingness to introduce leap, as serious error, 253-257

Viderman, M., 68
Violence
infantile trauma, 37-38
referral and, 21
rigidity/flexibility issues in decision-making, 76-77
Vulnerability, therapeutic alliance and, 25-27

Weigert, E., 46n7, 68, 266n2
Weill, A. P., 183n2
Winnicott, D. W., 58n8, 67n3, 68, 78n5, 90n6, 131n6, 154n3, 183n2, 231n3, 249n4, 269n6, 281
Wolf, E. S., 109n4, 116n5, 161n6, 241n1